Placenames of Portsmouth, is the most valuable and original and – dare I say – "entertaining" reference volume to come along in decades. ... This revolutionary reference book is manna for historians and mind candy for those who just love Portsmouth. ... I expect my brand new copy of *Placenames of Portsmouth* to become the most-used and dog-eared Portsmouth reference on my bookshelf. That is ultimately the highest complement a reader can pay.

Dennis Robinson, *SeacoastNH.com*

The Placenames of Portsmouth started as a labor of love and has blossomed into a potential nationwide franchise. Nancy has grown from an amateur historian and part-time writer into a one-woman writing/researching/promoting /publishing entrepreneurial whirlwind. ... The caring and love in this process shows in Nancy's finished product, which, by the way, really will never be finished. She is already working on corrections and updates for upcoming editions.

Emily Wiggins, *Portsmouth Herald*

Grossman's entertaining book should be tucked under one's arm while strolling the historic district of Portsmouth or kept among the dictionaries and thesauruses above one's desk and pulled out when a curious placename comes along that catches the eye. ... Rest assured, over the years, this book is likely to become quite dog-eared.

Darryl Cauchon, *Foster's Daily Democrat*

You book is wonderful. Connie and I will put it into our library as another resource for future family discussion on our beloved Portsmouth.

Bill Warren, author of *Portsmouth Then & Now*

You have done a wonderful job of fusing the past and the present together. I am particularly pleased with the time based approach to the development of the small areas and neighborhoods rather than the much more logical block by block approach. As I travel about the city, I see the story of development by the age of the houses; now I will be armed with a place name dating tool too.

David Adams, Adams & Roy, Preservation Contractors and Consultants

THE
PLACENAMES
OF
PORTSMOUTH

BEING AN ANECDOTAL STROLL THROUGH
THE CENTURIES & NEIGHBORHOODS OF
PORTSMOUTH, NEW HAMPSHIRE...

NANCY W. GROSSMAN

back channel press
portsmouth, new hampshire

BACK CHANNEL PRESS
170 Mechanic Street
Portsmouth, NH 03801
ngstudio@comcast.net

Second edition, published 2014. First edition published 2005.
Printed in the United States of America

Cover and book design by Nancy Grossman
www.nancygrossmanbooks.com

Library of Congress PCN 2010915571

The *PLACENAMES OF AMERICA Series* is a registered trademark.

For John
...my mentor, tutor, inspiration, and long-suffering in-house IT guy,
who turned our home into the McDowell Colony South
to help me see this undertaking through to completion.
You are truly missed.

❧ CONTENTS ❧

We shall not cease from exploration
And the end of all our exploring
Will be to arrive where we started
And know the place for the first time.

From the *4th Quartet* – T.S. Eliot

INTRODUCTION

A graveyard inhabited by the living...

~ Shakespeare

THIS BOOK BEGINS, as so many things do, with a chance conversation, in this case at a 1988 25th high school reunion, in Darien, Connecticut, where I grew up. As self consciousness gave way to comfortable curiosity, I found myself chatting with Judy Miller (today Judy Sabin), who I had known as Judy Geelhood, back in our student days. Names – and the changing of names – who can appreciate that subject more than women?

Judy Miller was flying for American Airlines in those days. Her hobby, though, was far more sedate. On her off days, she told me, she drove a carriage on the streets of her adopted home, Portsmouth, New Hampshire. She told me about this special place and about Ray Parker, a gent who sat

Ray Parker started the Portsmouth Livery Company in 1986 with one horse, one carriage and one top hat. Courtesy of Judy Sabin.

atop the box seat of a fine old Victoria in Market Square greeting the tourists who were just beginning to find their way back to a reborn town with a rich brew of history he loved to share. "Teach me to drive," she begged him. "I'll drive for you."

It took a lot of pestering to break down a loner with one horse and one carriage who saw no need for an extra driver. "Put on another carriage and I could do weddings for you, catered picnic suppers down the coast. Teach me the history and we can both do tours..." My old chum was persistent. The Portsmouth Livery Company was born.

Judy is a natural-born guide – when my husband and I came to Portsmouth as part of a two-week ramble up the coast of New England six months later, she gave us a tour that inspired us to move here.

THAT WAS IN 1991. We came to town, bought a fine old manse, opened a bed and breakfast and *really* started getting to know Portsmouth.

Having moved here from southern California, few of our possessions looked quite right in our fine old manse, so we dove headfirst into the wild world of auctions in search of more appropriate furnishings – six months of auctions, three or four a week, within a two-hour radius.

Built originally as the Portsmouth Academy, today's DISCOVER PORTSMOUTH CENTER *moved into space vacated by the Portsmouth Public Library when it left for Parrott Avenue in 2007. An undertaking of the Portsmouth Historical Society, the Center provides locals and visitors alike with Portsmouth-related gallery showings, lectures and information. It's also home to the Seacoast African American Cultural Center and the Star Island Corporation.*

We got the house furnished, but by then, we discovered, we had developed a fairly serious addiction, one of the few left for which there are no twelve-step programs, so we kept on going to auctions, just for fun. After all, a big manse can soak up whatever you cart in the door. Our purchases grew more whimsical, less pragmatic. Which explains how, in 1994, I found myself buying a little box of diaries. The writings, it turned out, were those of a Victorian-era woman from St. Louis who summered in Rye and whose sister ending up living in Rye. Those diaries eventually sent me to St. Louis in pursuit of more information about my diarist.

A week is a short time to try and get the hang of a city as big as St. Louis. My first stop was a bookstore. My first purchase was *The Streets of St. Louis,* a slim volume by William B. Magnan, a retired letter carrier whose interest in the streets he walked had grown into an avocation over the years. Neighborhood by neighborhood, he walked me through 237 years of St. Louis history. The book proved a palatable, easily digested little feast of facts, spiced with more than a few dashes of fable and fancy. And just like my friend Judy pestered Ray, the memory of the delight and downright usefulness of *The Streets of St. Louis* pestered me. Back home, I found myself wondering, then casually asking, then poking in earnest around the Portsmouth shelves in the library. I found myself interjecting into dinner conversation, quite often apropos of nothing, "Did you know that Daniel Street was called 'Daniels' Street – for forty years? And do you know *why?*" I didn't know it yet, but I had started writing my own *Streets of St. Louis* for my adopted home of Portsmouth.

*Built in 1803 for the New Hampshire Fire and Marine Insurance Company, in 1817 this Market Square landmark was purchased to house the **Portsmouth Athenaeum**. An important repository for large portions of Portsmouth's history, it has grown over the years by annexing floors of the buildings to either side. TG*

Portsmouth, being a historic town, is chockablock full of historians – you're apt to run into one on any street corner waiting for a light. And so I found myself at a party, in 2001, chatting with a historian. Something came up about Daniel Street and I trotted out my Daniels Street anecdote. The historian responded, as historians do, with related facts and anecdotes of his own. And suggestions. And encouragement. Which apparently was all I needed. I was now writing a book.

I BEGAN MY RESEARCH with the same sources that all Portsmouth historians rely on: Nathaniel Adams' 1824 *Annals of Portsmouth*, and Charles Brewsters' 1859 and

1869 *Rambles About Portsmouth.* Then I went to work on the more recent writings of Richard Candee, Russell Lawson, Ray Brighton, Bruce Ingmire, the prolific Dennis Robinson and many others. The Portsmouth Athenaeum's copious files on both our local families and streets provided numerous clues, as did the staff of this incomparable institution. In some cases, I was able to find clear statements as to the derivation of a particular street name. In most, I could only amass the facts and draw conclusions. I make no claim that I have the final word on any of the latter, and I trust that those who know and love this city will not hesitate to set me straight.

NOTE: The majority of the images in the book, those marked 'PA,' have been furnished by the Portsmouth Athenaeum. A great number came from the excellent postcard collection of Ted Gray; they are marked 'TG.' Those from the Portsmouth Historical Society are marked 'PHS.' Those from other sources are duly identified. Photos I have taken myself, and images in the public domain carry no credit information.

CHAPTER 1

WHAT'S IN A NAME?

If the fairest features of the landscape are to be named after men, let them be the noblest and worthiest men alone.
~ Henry David Thoreau

NEW HAMPSHIRE – Founder John Mason named the state after his home county, *Hampshire*, on the south coast of England.

ROCKINGHAM COUNTY – Royal Governor John Wentworth divided the state into five counties, naming them for his friends, the Dukes of Strafford, Grafton, Hillsboro, Cheshire and for Charles Watson-Wentworth, the second Marquis of *Rockingham,* America's friend in Court.

PORTSMOUTH – New Hampshire's *port* at the *mouth* of the Piscataqua; also the name of a city in southeastern Hampshire, England, on the English Channel 65 miles southwest of London, the chief home port of the Royal Navy. New Hampshire founder John Mason was named commander of the fort there in 1634.

*The second **Marquis of Rockingham, Charles Watson-Wentworth.** National Portrait Gallery, London.*

THERE ARE ACTUALLY NAMES for this naming of things. The broad field, the study of naming itself, is called ONOMASTICS. TOPONYMY is the name these onomasts have given to the naming of *places*, and they refer to the naming of *streets* as odonymy.

In the early history of American urban development, streets took their names from landmarks around them – in Portsmouth, it was MARKET, CHURCH and COURT;

topographic or hydrological elements they passed or crossed – WATER, SPRING, HILL; or geographic location – SOUTH, MIDDLE, NORTHWEST. As time went by, most early towns also acknowledged the powers that be – Portsmouth once had its KING and QUEEN streets – and nostalgia for the old country inspired countless street names of English origin. With the American Revolution, heroes provided names for the new streets of our ever-growing town.

IN THE EARLY DAYS, the word "street" following the name was merely a descriptor and therefore was not capitalized. A road leading out of town was generally named for the next town over, the town it would take you to – as are GREEN-LAND and NEW CASTLE AVENUES today.

And so it was until the 1850s. As the industrial revolution deepened the stark contrast between city and country, a nature-centric aesthetic – a romanticized vision of nature – came into its own. Namers of streets had to look no further than the botany books for inspiration. Lawrence Kestenbaum, in an essay on street naming, tells us that the leader in street name choices in the 1850s nationwide was OAK, followed closely by ELM, MAPLE, PINE and WALNUT. Portsmouth had one of each of them – until recently, two Pines, actually, one Pine Street and one Pine Avenue, but as of this edition, only Pine Street has stood the test of time.

THE PERIOD FROM 1890 to 1910 brought home the reality that the agrarian way of life in America was vanishing, that industrialization and urban life were now the norm. But the quickly decaying urban center, abandoned for the suburbs by those with money, gave rise to

The first survey of the streets of Portsmouth was conducted in 1778 by **Nathaniel Adams** and **John Parker, Jr.** Describing the young city's 37 streets and 53 lanes, Adams later wrote, "The streets are generally very narrow and irregular. They seem to have been laid out by the owners of the land for their own accommodation, without any regard to the public convenience or ornament."

squalor, fear, unrest and violence. The need to control such forces in turn gave rise to armories and reformers.

WHILE MILITIAS WERE FORMED to address violence, efforts to inspire the downtrodden to moral and civic virtue resulted in improvements in sanitary conditions, the opening of missions like Jane Addams' Hull House in Chicago, and reform of the landscape, the so-called "City Beautiful" movement, whose advocates believed that beauty itself could develop civic loyalty and foster social calm. In the realm of street naming, developers began to choose names with an eye to shaping the image of their subdivisions. In Portsmouth, such inspiration can be seen in a late 19th-century development whose streets were named for our regional poets and authors – THAXTER ROAD, ALDRICH ROAD, FIELDS ROAD and the later SEWELL ROAD.

AFTER WORLD WAR I, "streets" became "drives" as the automobile began to change both our lives and our maps. Names incongruously reminiscent of what had been lost came to the fore. "Builders name streets or entire subdivisions after the little furry critters that their bulldozer just displaced," reads one California newspaper article. The random use of suffixes like "wood" and "land" could turn almost any bucolic noun into a handy moniker. LEDGEWOOD, OAKWOOD and WOODLAWN – Portsmouth spawned plenty. A second wave of Anglophilia swept the country, resulting in subdivisions of faux Tudor homes on streets – or now often "terraces" – named for English universities, counties and foxhunts. A left on ESSEX, another left on MELBOURNE and a quick right on SHEFFIELD...

DAVID THOMPSON ESTABLISHED the first settlement in the area in 1623, at what is known today as Ordione's Point. Thompson named his outpost PANNAWAY; it is sometime more grandly referred to as PANNAWAY PLANTATION. In a paper on our region's founder, Genevieve

Cora Fraser suggests that Thompson, a well-educated gentleman, might have had Pan, the Greek god of nature, woods and music, in mind when he coined the name.

Portsmouth proper was settled in 1630, under the name of **STRAWBERY BANKE**, inspired by the welcoming sight of wild strawberries that grew down to the river's edge. In 1653, the people of Strawbery Banke petitioned the colonial government to change the town's name to **PORTSMOUTH**. Why? Did they consider the early namers' first choice too frivolous for a city that was fast growing in dignity and importance?

*The old **Pannaway Club** on Sagamore Creek, above, and **Pannaway Manor**, the neighborhood abutting Pease Air Force Base developed in the 1940s, two other incarnations of the name David Thompson gave his settlement in 1623. The Pannaway Club, once a popular gathering spot for Portsmouth's Italian community, today belongs to the the local chapter of the Benevolent and Protective Order of Elks. Courtesy of Esther Kennedy.*

JUST AS THERE IS NO RECORD of the reasons behind the town's name change, neither is there any record of the deliberations of a committee set up in 1778, just prior to the first official survey and mapping of Portsmouth. The commission was tasked with the codification and clarification of the names of the town's streets and, in due time, their report was handed in. The map was drawn up, numerous mentions of which come down to us – but not the map itself, which was said to have hung in the rooms in which the selectmen met, only to go missing sometime in the last century. The earliest street map of Portsmouth that we do have dates to 1813.

In 1838, another commission's efforts were expended prior to the town's issuing of the map of

1839. Not everyone saw this as a good thing. The Reverend Alfred Gooding, pastor of the Unitarian Church from 1884 to 1934, remarked in a speech on the opening of the Portsmouth Historical Society in 1917: "Nearly 100 years ago, Portsmouth began to destroy some of its most interesting historical landmarks... It was the same spirit of indifference to old things that caused the extensive renaming of streets in 1838." And again, no notes or details of the commission's report to the city fathers exist.

AND FROM WHENCE COMES the name of the swift and mighty **PISCATAQUA RIVER**, at whose mouth our port town sits? In 1878, the *Portsmouth Weekly* suggested that Piscataqua comes from the Latin, meaning river of fishes, "pisces" + "aqua." In fact, the *Christian Science Monitor* perpetuates this assumption to this day. Other early toponymists suggested that the name was taken from the Eastern Algonquin, meaning "dark river." Writing in 1929, Indian language expert Fannie Eckstorm cited the combination of "peske," meaning "branch" and "tegue," a river with a strong current, which certainly applies to one of the swiftest-flowing rivers in North America.

Another theory was put forth in a letter to the editor of the *Portsmouth Journal* from a writer by the name of J. Bell. Quoting one Judge Barr, whom Bell credited with being quite a student of Indian tongues, he suggested that the name was a composite of "pos," meaning great; "attuck," meaning deer; and "aquke," place – or "great place for deer." However, according to Bell, Indians never named rivers, lakes or

Charles H. Bell, in his 1888 History of the Town of Exeter, New Hampshire, suggested his reader picture the tributaries of the Great Bay, the Bay itself and the Piscataqua as the fingers, back and wrist of the left hand.

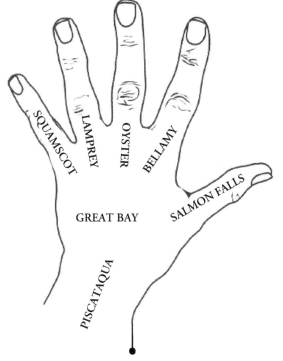

mountains, but rather places on or near them. The English, he went on, called the river Piscataqua, Piscatoway, Paskataway, Piscattaquak, among other equally inventive spellings, all intended to represent the same sound.

PORTSMOUTH HAS ITS pseudonyms. 19th-century humorist, newspaperman and poet Benjamin Penhallow Shillaber (1814-1892) dubbed it **RIVERTOWN** in his once famous novels about the young Ike Partington and his dotty Aunt Ruth. Shillaber's youth was spent in Portsmouth. And for Thomas Bailey Aldrich (1836-1907), this rich setting for his *Story of a Bad Boy*, published in 1869, became **RIVERMOUTH**.

THE CHANGING OF NAMES always brings the letter writers out of the woodwork. From a letter to the editor of the *Portsmouth Herald* in 1935: "Recently quite a lot of discussion has been caused by the sign "**SHAPLEIGH'S ISLAND**," placed near the west end of the island known for many years as "**MARVIN'S**." The habit of calling a place by its one-time owner may be all right for local people, but for our summer visitors who may have read some of our history, they look in vain for the old names and very few now living can give any information."

Even earlier, in the late 19th century, the local press lamented: "The frequent change of names of streets makes confusion in these times to preserve the old names for historical data, but modern boards of officials perhaps do not stop to consider this."

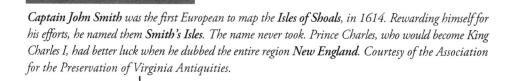

Captain John Smith was the first European to map the Isles of Shoals, in 1614. Rewarding himself for his efforts, he named them Smith's Isles. The name never took. Prince Charles, who would become King Charles I, had better luck when he dubbed the entire region New England. Courtesy of the Association for the Preservation of Virginia Antiquities.

NAME CHANGES CONTINUE TO be as controversial today as ever. As the first edition of this book went to press, a debate simmered on the proposed renaming of **PEARL STREET** in honor of slain civil rights leader Dr. Martin Luther King Jr. In 1952, King, then a young seminarian, addressed the congregation of the People's Baptist Church on the corner of Pearl and Hanover.

In 2005, proponents wanted to rename the block off Islington **MARTIN LUTHER KING JR. WAY.** Arguments against ran the gamut, from a concern that the little street wasn't worthy of carrying such a grand name, to the opinion that an old name is just as deserving of protection as an old building. As of 2012, Pearl Street is still Pearl Street.

> Another kind of name change: The 1715 **Alms House** became known as the **Work House**, which in time became the **City Farm**. The entire operation moved out and became the **County Farm**, at some point after 1883.
>
> **Alms House Field** became **Sladen Park**, briefly, c. 1904, named for one William Sladen, a civic-minded grocer, who at 84 years of age, fought for a park in this location.

CITIES AND TOWNS CHANGE street names frequently, usually for reasons of clarity and safety. The city of Raleigh has a form online just for the purpose of changing a street name, a process which takes five to eight weeks; however, "unless there is a public purpose to be served, requesting a name change is not encouraged."

The city of Annapolis reminds its staffers that "poorly chosen street names can cause inconvenience such as misdirected mail, lost visitors and delayed deliveries. More importantly, they can result in loss of life when emergency vehicles are sent to the wrong address."

The powers that be sometimes come up with some pretty convoluted reasoning behind the naming or renaming of streets. Quoting verbatim a 1998 article from *The Christian Science Monitor*: "In Fullerton, Calf., debate is in – um – full flower over how to discourage youth gangs. Some city councilors favor changing the name of one gang's turf from Baker Street to Pansy Circle in the hope it would send the toughs somewhere with a more macho-sounding name. But homosexual activists objected. Now under consideration: rhododendron and chrysanthemum – which, it's assumed, would be too hard for spray-painters to spell."

Creativity is alive and well in California. Another west coast developer uses street naming as a motivational tool. Each street in his latest development will be named for the first person to snap up a lot on that street.

AND PICKED UP OFF an Internet bulletin board, a posting from May 14, 2000:

> By the way, in figuring out what to name the road, let's use Avenue, Street or Road, but NOT 'Hemings Way.'

The Seal of the City, crafted by Portsmouth blacksmith Peter Happny in the 1980s and on display in the City Council Chambers. According to city ordinance, "The seal of the City shall be … encompassed with laurel; upon the border of the disk shall be the words: "**City of Portsmouth, New Hampshire, Incorporated 1849.**" *Upon the face of the disk shall be a shield with the following devices symbolic of commerce and manufacturing: a wharf and docks, two schooners, several factory buildings and an engine with transportation cars, and at the bottom of the shield shall be the words* "**Settled 1623.**"

CHAPTER 2

A BRIEF HISTORY OF PORTSMOUTH

> "Whereas the name of this plantation att present being **Strawbery Banke**, accidentally soe called by reason of a banke where strawberries were found in this place, now Your petitioners' Humble desire is to have it called **Portsmouth**, being a name most suitable for this place, it being the river's mouth and a good harbor as any in this land."
>
> ~ Petition to the General Court in Boston, 1653

PORTSMOUTH'S FIRST DOCUMENTED visitors arrived here some 12,500 years ago. Paleo-Indian hunters, North America's first pioneers, reached New England after the retreat of the last continental glacier. Hunter-gatherers, they roamed these shores until about 700 B.C. With a developing understanding of ceramics and horticulture, Native Americans began to cultivate corn, beans, squash and tobacco during what is known as the "Early Woodland" period, 700 B.C. to 1000 A.D. The so-called "Late Prehistoric" period, from 1000 A.D. to the arrival of European explorers in the early 1600s, saw an increase in population and settlements.

Coastal New England tribes spoke languages related to the Eastern Algonquin, and were known as the ABENAKI, from an Algonquin word meaning "living nearest to the morning sun" or "people of the dawn."

The largest village of the Piscataqua tribe of Abenakis was believed to have developed by the Great Bay, in present-day Greenland.

Early Europeans arriving in New England found and benefited by a vast network of long-established trails. The Abenaki trail led from Newburyport through Hampton, along the shore to the Piscataqua River and on to Oldtown, Maine.

UNLIKE THE PILGRIMS FLEEING religious persecution, this region's first European settlers were merchant adventurers. In 1603, privateersman Martin Pring made a brief foray up the Piscataqua, it is said, in search of sassafras (then thought to cure syphilis, among other maladies). Captain John Smith, as mentioned, mapped what we call today the Isles of Shoals in 1614.

> Laconia is the southernmost of the seven prefectures of Greece; ancient Sparta is its primary city. Why Mason and Gorges chose the name for their grant holding is a mystery, as is the Cunard Lines' choice of name for its ill-fated passenger ship. The sinking of RMS *Laconia* by a German U-boat in 1917 finally brought the United States into World War I.

But it was 28-year-old Scotsman David Thomson, in the employ of English businessmen Ferdinando Gorges and John Mason, grant holders for the province they named LACONIA, who established the first settlement of the area, in 1623. PANNAWAY MANOR took its name from that used by the indigenous population for what we call today Odiorne Point, where it was located. Also often referred to as PANNAWAY PLANTATION, it served as a trading post for a fur and fishing colony.

In 1629, John Mason was granted land between the Merrimack and the Piscataqua Rivers; in 1630, his Laconia Company sent a complement of planters, stewards, servants and a surgeon, aboard the *Pied Cow* and led by Captain Walter Neale, to settle at the mouth of the Piscataqua. Naming their new home STRAWBERY BANKE, they built what they called a "GREAT HOUSE" at the corner of today's Court and Marcy Streets, to serve as their thousand-acre plantation's trading post, living quarters and storehouse. Within ten years, Strawbery Banke's population numbered 140. The Great House would go on to become home to Puritan merchant John

Cutt, who at his death in 1681 was among New Hampshire's wealthiest men.

WITH JOHN MASON'S DEATH in 1635 leaving the young colony with no clear external government, the settlers agreed to simply govern themselves, and in 1643, the embryonic towns of Strawbery Banke, Hampton, Exeter and Dover decided to throw in their lot with the state of Massachusetts. This voluntary union would last until New Hampshire became a separate royal province in 1679 and, except for the brief period of 1690-92, would remain so until the Revolution.

In 1640, the town fathers deeded 50 acres of land for a parsonage or "GLEBE," as it was called, a standard practice derived from English custom. This included 12 acres in the central part of town adjacent to the North Church. By the beginning of the following century, the 12-acre parcel was subdivided, with the agreement of the current minister, into building lots "for the peopling of the town."

IN 1652, THOSE IN POWER took a most unusual step: they destroyed the records of Strawbery Banke's first 23 years. As reported by Nathaniel Adams, almost 175 years after the fact, "this year [1652] the selectmen examined the old town books; and what was not approved was crossed out, and what was approved, was left to be recorded in a new book." Why, one can only wonder.

Some theorize that growing Puritan influence in New England – and Portsmouth's entrepreneurial rather than religious roots – inspired this exercise in retroactive political correctness. Others suggest that information was intentionally expunged that might help further claims of heirs of the original grant holder, John Mason. The following year, the town petitioned the Massachusetts general court for permission to rename itself.

In 1645 the first African slave was purchased by a local citizen, a practice that would continue well into the 18th century. In 1707, seventy slaves were known to be held in New Hampshire. By the time of the Revolution, over 650 individuals were being held in slavery in the state.

PORTSMOUTH WAS GROWING. Its economy, based at first on fishing and the export of lumber via its deep-water port, was secured by the richness of the region's natural resources. The British tested the feasibility of shipbuilding with local materials and English craftsmen. With the building of H.M.S. *FALKLAND* in 1690, a century and a half of New Hampshire shipbuilding was underway. In 1693, Portsmouth became the seat of colonial government and the first provincial post office was established here, though it would be another sixty years until a State House would be built.

For more about the **HMS Falkland***, see page 159.*

THE DAWN OF THE 18th century found Portsmouth, with its ice-free, deep-water port, the center of commerce for the region. Trade with foreign ports was the basis of a flourishing economy in a town of mixed neighborhoods, where the wealthy lived side-by-side with artisans and common laborers. A succession of Portsmouth's powerful WENTWORTHS ruled the province on behalf of the Crown. From 1689 to 1763, New Hampshire men fought in the French and Indian Wars on behalf of their British rulers. But the independence that the early colonists had nurtured and advanced produced fertile soil for unrest. With the Stamp Act in 1765, England's domination became openly questioned. In 1774, citizens of Portsmouth took the first overt step towards war against England. The last royal governor, John Wentworth, dissolved the provincial government, hoping to prevent

New Hampshire from sending delegates to the Continental Congress. The Assembly was moved to Exeter.

In 1775, Wentworth fled to Nova Scotia. In early 1776, 497 citizens of Portsmouth signed the Association Test (New Hampshire's version of the Articles of Association being signed throughout the colonies in support of independence). Thirty-one did not. The colonies went to war and emerged an infant nation. Many of Portsmouth's sons played important roles in the formation of the new nation's government.

ALREADY THE BIRTHPLACE OF three American warships, Portsmouth was chosen as the location of the first of thirteen naval shipyards established by the fledgling federal government in 1800. The PORTSMOUTH NAVAL SHIPYARD would take the Navy from sail to submarine over the next two hundred years.

War is disruptive to trade, and Portsmouth's maritime economy had suffered through much of the remainder of the 18th century. Riding high again as the new century arrived – Portsmouth was the 12th largest town in America in terms of population in 1800 – shipping was dealt another blow with the embargos of the War of 1812. Privateering became the order of the day and new fortunes were amassed. Shipbuilding flourished through the clipper ship era, serving the needs of both the China trade and the California gold rush, from the 1830s into the 1860s. The arrival of steam, in the form of steam ships, steam-powered

The USS **Portsmouth**, *a 24-gun sloop built at the Portsmouth Naval Shipyard in 1844. PA*

machinery and the railroad, brought the industrial revolution to Portsmouth.

As industry took hold, the need for worker housing fueled development to the west of downtown. New neighborhoods sprang up along with the factories whose employees would fill them. The Portsmouth Steam Factory, steam-powered foundries, the still evident Morley Button Company, factories turning out stockings and knit goods, shoes, organs and pianos, and the liquid gold produced by three breweries, changed the face of Portsmouth. **FRANK JONES** – brewer, industrialist, politician and entrepreneurial visionary – came to town and systematically built a fortune, leaving his mark from one end of Portsmouth to the other.

*The **Franklin Block**, ca. 1986. PA*

A CALAMITOUS TRIO OF FIRES, in 1802, 1806 and 1813, also left their mark on the city. In response, the state passed "**BRICK LAWS**" in 1814, ordinances enforced until 1824 banning construction of wooden buildings in excess of twelve feet in height in the central business district. The result: a downtown of handsome edifices that stand to this day, including Merchants Row along Market Street and Bankers Row along the north side of Market Square. "Blocks," the skyscrapers of their day, still bear the name of their builders. All were built on the ashes of prior structures, after the brick laws took effect.

THE **RETURN OF THE SONS**, first celebrated in 1853, then again in 1873, brought a diaspora of Portsmouth natives back home to the city of their birth. They were feted with parades, festivities and commemorations – and, in the wings, developers were waiting to sell them homes in the newly opened Victorian neighborhood surrounding Lincoln Hill. Through the 19th and early 20th centuries, civic pride exhibited itself in elaborate parades and spectacles. No less than 1200 citizens took part in "The Pageant of Portsmouth," an epic recreation of the town's history for its tercentennial in 1923.

The new century saw a move to clean up the seedier sections of town, particularly the stagnant decay of Water Street and **PUDDLE DOCK**. Once a prosperous inlet of busy wharves and chandleries, the area had fallen on hard times as shipping gave way to the railroads. Its waterway was rapidly becoming a city dump; by 1907, Puddle Dock had been completely filled in. A neighborhood of immigrants, Water Street was also home to a thriving red light district. In 1912, Water Street became Marcy Street, the red light district was shut down and a new esthetic took hold.

The **COLONIAL REVIVAL** period, a direct response to the brutishness and displacement of industrialization, spoke to a yearning for simpler, gentler times, a return to the country's roots. A new appreciation for

Just one of many celebrations held during the first of the **Returns of the Sons of Portsmouth***. PA*

the old evidenced itself in the opening of the Thomas Bailey Aldrich house to the public in 1908.

THE CITY STEPPED INTO the international limelight in 1905 as it played host to delegations from Russia and Japan, brought together in Portsmouth by President Theodore Roosevelt for the purpose of working out an end to war between the two powers. Primarily a naval conflict, the Russo-Japanese War required a month of hard negotiation before both sides were willing to sign the **TREATY OF PORTSMOUTH**.

AMERICA'S ENTRY INTO **WORLD WAR I** fueled a boom at the Portsmouth Naval Shipyard. While developers hurried to build housing for a burgeoning workforce, the Navy began turning out an entirely new class of vessel, ushering in the age of the submarine. The shipyard quickly became the largest employer in the area.

Support for preservation of the 17th-century Puddle Dock area gained momentum through the 1930s, but had to be deferred as the country prepared itself for a second World War. Women left their kitchens to take up the jobs of men who went off to fight. Between 1939 and 1945, the shipyard built and launched 75 submarines, 33 in 1944 alone. The country's first nuclear sub, USS *Swordfish,* came off the shipyard's ways in 1958.

The city's municipal airport was leased by the Navy during **WORLD WAR II**; its use was transferred to the Air Force in 1946 and in 1956 it formally opened as Portsmouth Air Force Base. It was renamed a year later as **PEASE AIR FORCE BASE** in honor of New Hampshire native and Medal of Honor recipient Captain Harl Pease, Jr., an Army Air Corps pilot killed during World War II.

BY THE 1950s, MUCH OF Portsmouth had decayed into a shabby reminder of its former glory. Federal "urban renewal" programs were addressing blighted areas of aging cities nationwide, and Portsmouth came in for its share of those dollars. The entire north end of the downtown was leveled. Puddle Dock was facing the same fate when preservationists petitioned Washington to permit instead the creation of an historic neighborhood museum. Through their efforts, **STRAWBERY BANKE MUSEUM** was born. Located across Marcy Street from the emerging beauty of the new Prescott Park, reclaimed from the wharves and coal pockets of earlier times, Strawbery Banke Museum inspired others to take even bolder steps in developing a latent tourist trade.

Artists, actors, musicians and restaurateurs began moving into town and the process of gentrification gathered steam. Market Square received a much-needed face-lift in 1977. Portsmouth, steeped in history and tradition, demonstrated once again her ability to grow and develop as an appealing place to both visit and live.

AS THE MILLENNIUM DREW to a close, Portsmouth's boom and bust history caught up with her once again. The Seacoast became an epicenter of technological know-how in the 1990s, earning the area the new nickname, E-COAST. Likewise, the closure of Pease Air Force Base in 1991 paved the way for the development of the new PEASE INTERNATIONAL TRADEPORT. As has been the case practically from its inception, the Portsmouth Naval Shipyard constantly faces imminent threat of closure. History is always nipping at our heels.

NOTE: As we journey through Portsmouth's neighborhoods, in roughly chronological order, you will see asterisks after certain street names.

A SINGLE ASTERISK (*) indicates a name that appears on the Inventory of the Polls and Estates – the taxpayers of the Town of Portsmouth in 1727.

TWO ASTERISKS (**) denote the names of Portsmouth's earliest settlers, those adventurous souls whom Adams lists in his Annals of Portsmouth as grantees, stewards or servants of the Laconia Company in the year 1631.

Whether streets were actually named for these individuals or for later luminaries of the same name, it seems fitting for us to remember those who came first, regardless.

CHAPTER 3

THE SOUTH END
THE ORIGINAL SETTLEMENT OF STRAWBERY BANKE

A contemporary photo of the South End as seen from New Castle Avenue.

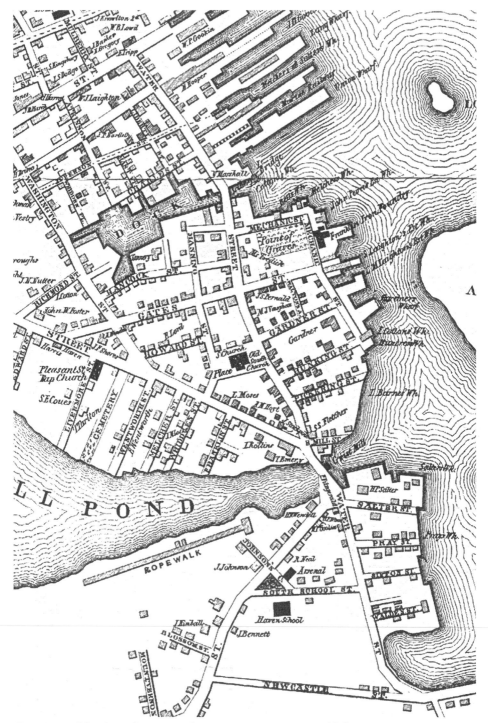

From Map of the City of Portsmouth, N.H. *C.W. Brewster, Publisher, 1850.*

MARCY STREET
THE 'MAIN STREET' OF OLD PORTSMOUTH

**Oracle House – Prescott Park – Hovey Fountain – Sawtelle Pier
Strawbery Banke Museum – Puddle Dock – The Liberty Pole
Children's Museum – Washington Street – Atkinson Street**

WHEN THE TOWN'S FIRST inhabitants erected a public meeting house in 1659, "two or three rods to the southward of the Mill Dam," the rude track that led to it was referred to as the **GREAT STREET**. In those days, all roads ran to Pickering's mill and dam.

BY THE TIME THE 1813 map was drawn up, the Great Street had taken the name of **PARTRIDGE STREET**, named most likely for shipwright William Partridge (1671-1718), who served as lieutenant governor from 1697 to 1703. He and Nememiah Partridge (1663-1709) share a tombstone in Point of Graves cemetery.

But by 1839, Partridge had been renamed **WATER STREET**, in keeping with Portsmouth's developing commercial waterfront. Wharves and busy warehouses lined the swift-flowing Piscataqua's gentler backwater channels. Along with burgeoning commerce, Water Street also developed other flourishing, if less welcome, industries: houses of ill repute stood cheek to

*Nememiah Partridge, who owned property at today's 200 New Castle Avenue, may well be the artist responsible for the grand mural portraits of Native Americans discovered in 1850 under numerous layers of wallpaper in the **Macpheadris-Warner House**.*

George D. Marcy, the last of the Marcy line. From a painting hanging in the City Council Chambers.

jowl with taverns and saloons that prospered amidst the chandleries, brick yards and tanneries, oil and gas tanks, mast works and boat yards. As the years went by, the neighborhood descended into squalor and neglect.

In 1912, the bordellos were shuttered. The town fathers in their wisdom – and in an effort to salvage the area's reputation – renamed the disreputable section of the thoroughfare from the Liberty Bridge to Newcastle Avenue **MARCY STREET**. Perhaps they were honoring their recent mayor, George D. Marcy, who had held office ten years earlier. Or perhaps they were hoping that some of the honor and respect once commanded by sea captain, shipbuilder, businessman and politician Daniel Marcy (1809-1893) might just rub off on the blighted neighborhood.

Daniel Marcy went to sea at the age of thirteen. By twenty-one, he was the master of a ship. In 1848, he was at the helm of the clipper *Peter Marcy*, a ship he and his brother Peter of New Orleans commissioned famed Portsmouth shipbuilders Fernald & Pettigrew to build for them. Peter Marcy built the first drydock in New Orleans.

Daniel Marcy, who lived at 57 Pleasant Street, was a leader on land as well on the seas. In 1854, he was elected to the New Hampshire State House of Representatives, then served as a State Senator from 1856 to 1858, and again in 1871-72. Marcy was elected to the U.S. House of Representative in 1863, serving in Washington through the darkest days of the Civil War. By 1926, all of what we know today as Marcy bore the name, from the corner of State Street to the New Castle Avenue intersection.

*According to journalist Ray Brighton, sea captain **Daniel Marcy** "probably took more new ships, clippers and work-horse freighters out of Portsmouth than any other skipper." PA*

A STROLL DOWN Marcy Street takes us past the peripatetic **ORACLE HOUSE,** which started life in 1702 just off Market Square, was relocated once circa 1800 to Haymarket Square, and then again in the 1930s, coming to rest once again atop the site of the original 1634 Great House which sheltered John Mason's first colony of settlers.

One-time home to the *Oracle of the Day,* New Hampshire's oldest daily newspaper, the Oracle House has also seen incarnations as a restaurant and as a bed and breakfast inn.

*The **Oracle House,** as it made its way from Haymarket Square down Court St. to the corner of Marcy, on August 12, 1937. PA*

ACROSS THE STREET lies Portsmouth's jewel, **PRESCOTT PARK,** a gift given to the city by sisters Josie (1858-1949) and Mary (1855-1939) Prescott, two spinster school teachers who grew up amidst the shambles of early 20th-century Marcy Street. Their father, Charles Smith Prescott, was a Puddle Dock dealer in provisions.

A brother, Charles W. Prescott (1853-1932), left Portsmouth at 24 to make his way in the world of commerce, and did, most successfully. The two sisters were equally successful in contesting a specious will upon his death, finally inheriting their brother's considerable fortune in 1933, upon which this two-woman urban renewal team set about buying up, tearing down and beautifying the benighted neighborhood of their childhood. The park, in total just a bit more than six acres, is dedicated to the memory of their father, while the bridge

*Sisters **Josie** and **Mary Prescott.** Mary (below) taught at Haven School. Josie (above) taught first at the Franklin School, then in Boston. PA*

at the end of the park that leads over to Peirce Island, the **PRESCOTT MEMORIAL BRIDGE**, is dedicated to the memory of the sisters themselves.

Portsmouth has seen more than its share of fortunes, but the sisters Prescott are its only citizens of wealth to have ever left such a magnanimous gift of beauty to the city of their birth.

THE **HOVEY MEMORIAL FOUNTAIN** within the park remembers Portsmouth native Charles Emerson Hovey (1885-1911), who died an ensign in the U.S. Navy, killed in action in the Philippines. Among others things, Hovey wrote the first edition of the *Watch Officer's Guide* for the Navy before his death in 1911, according to Windy Burns, a Hovey family descendent. The guide details every aspect of a watch-stander's duties, both at sea and in port. The 15th edition of the guide continues as the essential reference for naval officers today.

Like the Oracle House across the street, the statue of Neptune that graces the **HOVEY MEMORIAL FOUNTAIN** also began life elsewhere – it was taken from a palace in Sienna, Italy. When Hovey's mother gave the fountain to the city in 1912, the renaissance sculpture graced an elegant basin and pedestal of Carrara marble. For 62 years, it anchored the corner of State and Pleasant Streets in front of what was Portsmouth's second post office and customs building. In 1974, with traffic on the increase, a Hovey relative opted to move the fountain to a safer location.

The Navy launched the USS *Hovey* in 1919, a destroyer which had a distinguished 26-year career. It

*Above, **Charles Emerson Hovey** and his father, the Rev. Henry Hovey, rector of St. John's Church from 1883 to 1909. PA Below, damaged in the move to Prescott Park, the marble basin of the original **Hovey Memorial Fountain** was replaced by today's circular brick basin. TG*

sank off the Philippines in January of 1945 after sustaining direct hits by both a kamikazi and a torpedo in the invasion of Luzon. The Veterans of Foreign Wars Post No. 168 also carries Hovey's name.

THE JOE SAWTELLE PIER occupies the site of the oldest pier along the park's shoreline, dating back to the 1700s. It received its latest restoration in 2001, when it was renamed in memory of local developer and visionary Joseph Sawtelle (1929-2000). Sawtelle gave much back to the community: just a few of his lasting contributions include the purchase and donation of much-needed space for the Portsmouth Athenaeum, and the creation of such important seacoast institutions as the Greater Piscataqua Charitable Foundation, Cross Roads House, the FUTURES college scholarship program, the Portsmouth Marine Society and the USS *Albacore* Park.

Developer, philanthropist, visionary – all apt descriptors for **Joe Sawtelle**, *above. Sawtelle was working with the Navy to breathe new life into the old Naval Prison at the time of his death. From* USS Albacore: Forerunner of the Future, *by Robert Largee and Hames Mandelblatt, with permission of Peter E. Randall Publisher.*

USS Albacore, *whose active life spanned the years between 1953 and 1972, was the prototype for nuclear submarines. Brought ashore as the focal point of Joe Sawtelle's* **Albacore Museum**, *she was opened to the public in 1985. Official U.S. Navy photograph, now in the collections of the National Archives.*

LOCATED ACROSS THE STREET from Prescott Park, the ten-acre **STRAWBERY BANKE MUSEUM** chronicles 350 years of Portsmouth's history. The typography of the area once included a wharf-lined inlet, a body of water large enough to accommodate small ocean-going vessels, known since at least the 1780s as **PUDDLE DOCK**.

The *Portsmouth Journal* once wrote, "Puddle Dock was, indeed, when the tide was out, a mere puddle." But don't be fooled by the "puddle" part of the name – on flood tides, its waters crossed Washington Street onto Langdon House property. Puddle Dock took its name from a similar area of wharves and warehouses in the ancient Blackfriars section of London.

By the end of the 19th century, Puddle Dock had fallen into decay and disuse. The silt-filled inlet's final insult: use as a city dump. By 1907, the inlet was completely filled in. The 1920 Sanborn Fire Insurance map shows a crowded neighborhood abounding in junk yards and scrap heaps.

By the 1950s, the neighborhood was slated for the most invasive form of federal urban renewal. Led by city librarian Dorothy M. Vaughan, a determined cohort of local historians and preservationists acted to save the legacy of Portsmouth's earliest settlement. Residents were relocated and any buildings more recent than the 18th century were removed or demolished. What remained formed the core of a museum that today attracts thousands of visitors annually.

Many Jewish families lived in Puddle Dock and swam frequently in the Piscataqua in an area that came to be known in the tight-knit neighborhood as **Palestine Beach**.

*Portsmouth's waterfront and **South End**, before the days of Prescott Park and Strawbery Banke Museum. Today the piers in the foreground are the site of the New Hampshire end of the Memorial Bridge. PA*

A number of Puddle Dock's streets – and street names – were lost to the Stawbery Banke development. No longer on today's map: JEFFERSON STREET, PUDDLE LANE, MAST LANE, HORSE LANE, NEWTON AVENUE, LIBERTY STREET, CHARLES STREET, WHIDDEN PLACE, MANNING PLACE and SCRUTTON STREET. The intersection of Mast and Puddle Lanes was once known as LIBERTY SQUARE.

*Streets and street names weren't all that that Portsmouth lost to 20th-century **urban renewal**. In a first-of-its-kind compromise worked out by preservationists and agreed to by the federal agencies overseeing these programs, 1815 was chosen as the cut-off date for houses that would be permitted to remain and form the core of the embryonic Strawbery Banke Museum. The **Marconi family** fought in vain to save their recently purchased two-family home, built in 1930 on Marcy Street directly across from the Liberty Pole. Courtesy of Evelyn Marconi.*

PORTSMOUTH'S **LIBERTY POLE** MARKS the site of the former Liberty Bridge (referred to as Canoe Bridge in the mid 1800s) that spanned the Puddle Dock inlet. Liberty poles or liberty trees were to be found in many cities in colonial times, gathering spots for Sons of Liberty to meet. Boston's was a tree perfectly suited for the hanging in effigy of offending representatives of the crown.

Portsmouth's Liberty Pole was erected in 1766 to fly a No Tax flag that read: "Liberty, Property and No Stamp," and is one of the few liberty poles still standing – but today's is certainly not the original. The initial pole was actually a ship's mast, and stood in this spot for fifty-eight years. It was replaced with much Fourth of July fanfare in 1824 by a pole 58 feet in height.

*This earlier incarnation of the **Liberty Pole's eagle** soars proudly above the circular staircase of the new Portsmouth Public Library. PA*

In 1899, today's 110-foot shaft of Oregon pine was installed. The current eagle atop the pole, carved by Strawbery Banke cooper Ron Raiselis and installed in 2002, functions as a working weathervane.

The Liberty Pole's shield, restored in 1984, reads: *"Erected July 4, 1824, in commemoration of July 4, 1776, that declared our emancipation from tyranny and gave us the privileges of free men."*

*The **Liberty Pole**, c. 1930. PA*

CONTINUING DOWN MARCY, the road rises to MEETING HOUSE HILL and the SOUTH MEETING HOUSE. In 1731, the original meeting house south of the mill pond was replaced by a new building in this location. The open area in front of the meeting house was known as the SOUTH PARADE; the Milldam Rangers mustered here.

In 1731, the congregation left the South Meeting House and moved to a fine granite building on State Street. Thirty-seven years later, the city purchased the abandoned structure and took it down. In its place rose a combination schoolroom, auditorium and ward hall, with a clock tower whose chimes help South Enders mark the hour – give or take a minute or two, most of the time.

*Long a South End fixture, the **Children's Museum** has moved to Dover. The South Meeting House continues, however, to serve as a great example of the creative reuse of a sound old structure. It's next tenant will be **Portsmouth Public Media**.*

RUNNING PARALLEL TO MARCY STREET, WASHINGTON STREET most certainly must have been named for the nation's first president. Six months after his inauguration in 1789, George Washington paid a four-day visit to New Hampshire's first capital city as part of a tour of his fledgling country's thirteen states. Under autumn skies, cheering crowds, tolling church bells and thirteen-gun salutes welcomed him to town. During his stay, he attended church services, toured and praised the harbor, took tea with prominent patriot John Langdon as well as with his secretary Tobias Lear's mother and her family, sat for his portrait by Dutch-born artist Christian Gullager, was feted in grand style by the town's gentry – and still found time to fish.

*1789 portrait of **George Washington** by Christian Gullager. Courtesy of the Massachusetts Historical Society.*

TUCKED IN BETWEEN Washington and Marcy Streets is today's one block of **ATKINSON STREET**. Cross over Court Street and enter one of Strawbery Banke's back gates and you can follow colonial Atkinson another few blocks into the old Puddle Dock neighborhood museum.

Theodore Atkinson (1697-1779) was born in New Castle, the son of a provincial official. He graduated from Harvard in 1718, then returned to serve as a lieutenant at Fort William and Mary for two years. In 1720, he was appointed Clerk of the Court of Common Pleas. Four years later, he was sent to Canada as a commissioner from the Governor of New Hampshire to deal with boundary and Indian concerns.

In the mid-1730s, Atkinson took both a seat on the Council and the hand of Hannah Wentworth in marriage. Hannah's brother Benning was appointed royal governor in 1741; perhaps it is no coincidence that Atkinson took on the duties of provincial secretary and was appointed a colonel in the New Hampshire militia the same year.

In 1754, the colonies took their first tentative steps towards the forging of a union. Theodore Atkinson served as the New Hampshire delegate to the Albany conclave that tried to not only redefine the colonies' relationship with England but relations between themselves as well. Their well-intentioned deliberations proved futile at the midpoint of the century. Twenty-five years later, the same issues would ignite the Revolutionary War.

Following the Albany meetings, Atkinson was appointed chief justice of New Hampshire, while continuing in his position as provincial secretary. His son, Theodore Atkinson, Jr. (1736-1769), took over the duties of provincial secretary from 1761 until his death, at which time his father resumed the post until the Revolution in 1775.

Atkinson became Major General of the New Hampshire militia in 1769. But as a loyalist, he refused to sign the Association Test in 1776 and lost all his positions at the outbreak of the war.

At his death, Atkinson left £200 sterling to the Episcopal Church of Portsmouth, the income from which was to be used to provide bread for the poor. He also gave "a lot of land" for the building of "tombs, vaults and monuments" on Church Hill.

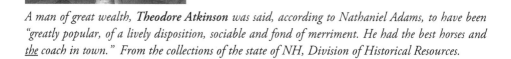

*A man of great wealth, **Theodore Atkinson** was said, according to Nathaniel Adams, to have been "greatly popular, of a lively disposition, sociable and fond of merriment. He had the best horses and the coach in town." From the collections of the state of NH, Division of Historical Resources.*

PLEASANT STREET TO THE MILL POND
Pleasant Street – Edward Street – Livermore Street
Haven Park
Wentworth Street – Melcher Street – Whidden Street
Webster Way – Franklin Street

B UILT ON LAND DEEDED to the town by the Picker-ing family in 1673, PLEASANT STREET is the other main artery that converges with Marcy at the mouth of the South Mill Pond. Originally named DIVINITY STREET, it was home to both Reverends Dr. Samuel Langdon of the North Church and Dr. Samuel Haven of the South Church. It received its present name at the time of the 1778 mapping of the town, but it began then at the corner of the present State Street. As late as 1813, the section from Market Square to State Street was called COURT STREET, a new court house occupying the corner on Market Square in those days. By 1850, that building had been replaced by a court house on today's Court Street, taking the name along with it.

A list of the builders and residents of the homes long gone or still standing along Pleasant Street reads like a *Who's Who* of colonial Portsmouth – Governor John Langdon, Captain Thomas Thompson, Charles Treadwell, merchant Jacob Wendell, and the Reverends Nathan Parker, Samuel Langdon and Samuel Haven, to name just a few.

The Universalist Church, founded in 1777, once stood at the corner of today's Pleasant and Junkins. Previously home to the Sandemanian Meeting House,

In 1859, Brewster commented: "Although not always the case, streets sometimes have significant names. In going south from Market Square, we proceed for half a mile through what once was regarded as the most attractive street in Portsmouth, on which governors, lawyers, clergymen and merchants had residences, and pass over a neck of land with water not very far distant on either side – hence *Pleasant* Street was very appropriately named."

the corner had long been called **BRIMSTONE HILL**. Some would suggest a connection between the name and the strict tenets of the fundamentalist Sandemanian Church; Charles Brewster could only scratch his head over the hill's nickname.

RUNNING FROM PLEASANT STREET down to the shores of the South Mill Pond are half a dozen pocket-sized streets: Edward, Livermore, Wentworth, Melcher, Whidden and Franklin.

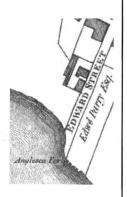

THE STORY BEHIND THE naming of **EDWARD STREET** has eluded us. One particularly colorful character, Edward Parry (1766?-1834), occupied a house on Edward Street, however. Perhaps he lent his Christian name to the street itself?

This is the same Edward Parry who circa 1800 built little **FORT ANGLESEA** (named for his birthplace in Wales) at the end of Edward Street on the South Mill Pond – in response to being suspected of having Loyalist leanings when not one but *two* consignments of British tea arrived addressed to him. Elsewhere, this structure is referred to as Parry's "fort-summerhouse." Parry's fort came complete with one cannon.

THE GENESIS OF **LIVERMORE STREET** is far clearer. The Hon. Matthew Livermore (1703-1776), a school master, came to Portsmouth at the age of twenty-one and ran the grammar school for seven years. In 1731, he changed careers and became an attorney. Livermore must have found his calling. Soon after, he was appointed attorney general of the Province and advocate for the King in the Courts of Admiralty. By the end of the 1730s, he'd built a mansion on the north side of what would become Livermore Street. Matthew did not live long enough to see the outcome of the Revolutionary War.

Samuel Livermore (1732-1803), one of the outstanding attorneys of *his* day, came to Portsmouth in
1758 and took up residence with Matthew, to whom he
was related. Samuel was appointed King's Attorney
for New Hampshire and became an advisor to Royal
Governor John Wentworth. After the Revolution,
Samuel served as a delegate to and moderator of the
convention that produced New Hampshire's constitution, and was both a representative and senator in
Congress, as well as a chief justice of the state.

*The Hon. **Samuel Livermore**. Courtesy of the U.S. Senate Historical Office.*

BOUNDED BY THE South Mill Pond, Edward, Pleasant
and Livermore Streets, the 2.2-acre **HAVEN PARK** was
named for the Rev. Dr. Samuel Haven (1727-1806),
pastor of the South Church for fifty-four years. Haven
graduated from Harvard in 1749, also holding doctorates
from the University of Edinburgh and Dartmouth. According to Brewster, Dr. Haven was "a
genuine 'son of liberty,' giving the whole
weight of his character, influence and
exertion to the American cause."

Haven Park was created after the death of the last member of the Haven family in 1898. TG

Haven's house, which stood at the
intersection of Pleasant and Gates
Streets, no longer remains. Haven's will
provided that when the last member of
the Haven family died (and a large family it was; the Reverend fathered seven-
teen), the home was to be taken down and the grounds,
along with the Parry and Hatch estates on either side,
were to be purchased for the city for a park. Samuel
Haven's son, Nathaniel Appleton Haven (1762-1831),
served in Congress from 1809 to 1811.

SERVING AS A FOCAL POINT of Haven Park is the heroic equestrian statue of GENERAL FITZ JOHN PORTER. We will come to Porter's controversial story when we reach the street bearing his name.

The statue of Civil War hero Fitz John Porter, sculpted by James Edward Kelly (1855-1933), that created such a big "not in my front yard" controversy when first proposed. Porter was born in the house once the home of Matthew Livermore, now situated across the park at 32/34 Livermore Street.

The statue itself became mired in a controversy all its own when it was first suggested that it should grace the center of Haymarket Square, at the intersection of today's Court and Middle Streets. Haymarket Square by the end of the 19th century was a prestigious address, and no one living in any of its fine residences wanted to step out his front door to be greeted by the sight of the rear end of General Porter's noble steed. Haven Park provided a happy solution to the problem. The statue, his tail to the South Mill Pond and the complex of buildings that would one day house City Hall, was dedicated in 1906.

RUNNING DOWN TO THE Mill Pond, is WENTWORTH STREET. Never has so short a street born the weight of so illustrious a family! Ray Brighton has compared New Hampshire's Wentworths to Massachusett's Kennedys, but when it comes to generations of influence at the highest levels, even the Kennedys can't hold a candle to our Wentworths.

Wentworth Street could be said to be named for Governor John Wentworth, the most prominent Wentworth to inhabit the mansion at the corner of Pleasant and Wentworth Street that today anchors the rambling Mark H. Wentworth Home. But to fully appreciate the Wentworths, one needs to shinny back down the family tree several branches and take a look at the famous family as it flourished in Portsmouth over many generations.

Our first, Samuel Wentworth, was the son of Elder William Wentworth of Dover. Samuel was licensed to "entertain strangers and to sell and brew beare." The first Wentworth house built in the area stood at the corner of Manning and Marcy Streets until 1926.

Whether the Marcy Street structure served Samuel, who died in 1690, as a tavern or was built by his son John (1671-1730) at the time of his marriage in 1693 or 1694 to Sarah Hunking, are facts lost to history. By some accounts, thirteen children were born to John and Sarah in this house; other sources enumerate either fourteen or sixteen children born to the couple. John, a sea captain and justice of the Court of Common Pleas, was appointed lieutenant governor of Massachusetts in 1717, with responsibility for the Province of New Hampshire. He served in this capacity until his death in 1730.

*Lt. Governor **John Wentworth**. Both paintings on this page from the State of New Hampshire Division of Historical Resources.*

Then we have Benning Wentworth (1696-1770), the oldest of the above-mentioned thirteen, fourteen or sixteen siblings, who was appointed, first, surveyor of the King's Woods in North America, and, later, the first royal governor of New Hampshire, a post he held for 26 years, from 1741 to 1767. Early in his tenure, Benning leased a fine home in town from his sister, Sarah MacPheadris. When unable to persuade the government to purchase it for him, he packed up and removed his offices to the family's far less conveniently situated Little Harbor property. Benning is long remembered for marrying,

*New Hampshire's first Royal Governor, **Benning Wentworth**. The white pines in this 19th-century copy of a 1760 portrait represent Wentworth's earlier role as Surveyor of the King's Woods in North America. Under his administration, Wentworth increased the state's size, wealth and stature by laying claim to lands west of the Connecticut River, granting townships in these areas to companies of so-called "proprietors." The first of 129 such land grants he named **Bennington**.*

*New Hampshire's last royal governor, **John Wentworth**. From the collections of the State of NH, Division of Historical Resources.*

at the age of sixty, his servant, the twenty-year-old Martha Hilton.

Benning was succeeded in office by a nephew, yet another John Wentworth (1737-1820), who at 29 became the last royal governor of New Hampshire. Popular and well-respected, he did much to improve roads and advance agriculture in the state; he was also active in the establishment of Dartmouth College. He detested the Stamp Act, but continued to carry out his duties as the appointed representative of the Crown. As acts of open rebellion became more and more numerous, he dissolved the New Hampshire Assembly on June 8, 1774, finally fleeing in 1775 to Nova Scotia to live out the American Revolution in exile.

Not all of the Wentworths sided with the Crown. Hunking Wentworth (1697-1784), one of Benning's brothers, was a staunch patriot. As chairman of the local Committee of Safety, he took an active role in the December 14, 1774, attack on Fort William and Mary – at 78 years of age. Hunking Wentworth lived on the corner of Church and Congress Streets.

THE GENESIS OF **MELCHER STREET** is difficult to

*The home last occupied by **Mark Hunking Wentworth**, son of New Hampshire's last royal governor, became, first, the Mark H. Wentworth Home for Chronic Invalids, today more charitably referred to as simply the **Mark H. Wentworth Home**. TG*

pin down. References can be found to Edward Melcher, a baker active in Portsmouth in 1685; to a John Melcher, apprentice to printer and journalist Daniel Fowle, who afterward took over publication of the *New Hampshire Gazette*; to another John Melcher, merchant, whose handsome sideboard today resides in the Strawbery Banke collection; to two Nathaniel Melchers, one listed simply as a merchant; the other as a supplier of construction materials to the John Paul Jones sloop-of-war *Ranger* in 1777; to a George Melcher, who in 1812 co-commissioned *Nancy,* a schooner of forty-six tons, carrying five carriage guns and four swivels for use as a privateer under Captain Richard O. Smart; and, in 1821, to possibly the same Melcher, packet master, whose dwelling was listed as the corner of Pleasant and Melcher Streets. Nobody said this name business was going to be easy!

WHIDDEN STREET started out life as LOCK STREET. Named WHIDDONS STREET on the 1813 Hales map, by 1850, the spelling had settled into the singular Whidden we know it as today.

Elisha Whidden and his wife Sarah were living on Pleasant Street at the corner of today's Whidden Street. Portsmouth was home to several other Whiddens of note as well. Housewright and joiner Michael Jr. is credited with a 1720s Deer Street house relocated to a part of Portsmouth known as The Hill, as well as with the Assembly House which once stood on Vaughan Street, site of the gala event attended by George Washington during his visit in 1789. Michael III's hand can be seen in the Governor Langdon mansion's interior finish joinery, just a few blocks down Pleasant Street. And perhaps Daniel E. Whidden walked from the street that bears his family's name down to board a ship that would take him around the Horn, bound for California and gold in 1849.

LITTLE WEBSTER WAY, off Whidden Street, rarely makes it onto Portsmouth maps. It may just be one of our shortest streets, with one of the South End's newest street names. Some folks by the name of Webster reside in the only house on Webster Way. When  they moved in, it was called FRANKLIN WAY. This little stub of a street once went by the even grander appellation of FRANKLIN AVENUE.

The city's planning department finally decided it was time to address the problem of emergency response. A Franklin Drive, Franklin Street and Franklin Way were considered just one too many Franklins for emergency services to have to cope with. Consulting with the owners of the only house on the street, changing its name to Webster Way was agreed to be a convenient solution for this particular street.

Webster Way reminds us of an earlier Webster of local – and national – significance, orator and statesman Daniel Webster (1782-1852), who made Portsmouth his home from 1807 to 1816. A native of Salisbury, NH, and graduate of Dartmouth College, the young Webster opened his first law practice here. He resided first on Vaughan Street, then later on Pleasant Street. When the disastrous fire of 1813 claimed that house, Webster moved into rooms on High Street.

Five years after his arrival here, as the War of 1812 was breaking out, New Hampshire sent the eloquent lawyer to Washington, where he quickly came to prominence, vociferously opposing the war's supporters. In 1961, Webster's High Street house escaped demolition and was moved to Strawbery Banke for safe keeping, where it stands today at the corner of Washington and Hancock Streets. His Vaughan Street residence was not so fortunate.

*On his arrival in Portsmouth, **Daniel Webster** moved into what was then known as the Meserve House on Vaughan Street, right, part of the historic North End that, like much of Puddle Dock, fell to the bulldozers of urban renewal in the 1950s. PA*

THE LAST OF THESE short streets, FRANKLIN STREET was known as COTTARS LANE in 1813. Cottars, in feudal parlance a corruption of the term "cottager," were landless tenants, and so were many of the residents of the street in Portsmouth developed between 1800 and 1815. The little street was home to a population of craftsmen – joiners, a mason, a carpenter, a shoemaker, a blockmaker, a boatbuilder – as well as a merchant and a ship master. Half of the residents of Cottars Lane were renters.

*Perhaps Benjamin is the **Franklin** who inspired the renaming of Franklin Street?*

However, by 1850 the name of the street had changed to Franklin. I am going to go out on a limb and suggest that Benjamin Franklin was the inspiration for the change, though as to why this street at this time took his name, I can offer no conjecture.

Benjamin Franklin (1706-1790) – printer, publisher, inventor, statesman, one of the signers of the Declaration of Independence, member of the Constitutional Convention, postmaster general for North America – is said to have installed or overseen the installation of the first lightning rod in New Hampshire, on the west end of the Warner House on Daniel Street. Some accounts say this work was done as early as 1762, others in 1767. Whatever the date, on this particular visit, he is said to have "pulled," or printed, some copies of Daniel Fowle's *New Hampshire Gazette* as well.

The fact that Dr. Franklin held a pew at St. John's Church (in his day it would have been called Queen's Chapel) and was a benefactor thereof suggests that he may well have come to Portsmouth on a regular basis. Any one of these specifics are reason enough to upgrade the name of a street.

Portsmouth Yacht Club's first home once stood at the foot of the bridge across to Peirce Island. The club relocated to New Castle in 1937 in search of deeper waters. PA

FROM MARCY TO THE MILL POND DAM
Gates Street – Mechanic Street – Gardner** Street – Walton Alley
Hunking* Street – Pickering* Street – South Mill Street

An early marker for
Gates Street, courtesy
of Peter Bresciano.

Horatio Gates

JIM GARVIN, the State Architectural Historian with the New Hampshire Division of Historical Resources suggests, I'm told, that the name of **GATES STREET** could refer to actual gates in a stockade that most likely encompassed Strawbery Banke's original thousand-acre Great House plantation. No maps survive of the 1631 settlement, unfortunately.

Another theory: Horatio Gates (1727-1806), the hero of the Revolution, might be the inspiration behind the name. An Englishman, Gates came to this country to fight in the French and Indian War, returned to America in 1772 and settled in what would become West Virginia. At the beginning of the Revolution, he joined the American cause as a general, first training troops near Boston and later as commander in the north. His overwhelming defeat of the British at Saratoga Springs late in 1777 was a turning point in the war.

Gates was considered a serious challenger to General George Washington; some would have preferred seeing him commander-in-chief. However, he was ordered south in 1780 and his poor performance in that region and a rout at Camden, South Carolina, led to his downfall. His commitment to the cause was undiminished, though; in a letter printed in a 1777 issue of the *New Hampshire Gazette,* General Gates assured a friend that "it seems now if we can secure the New England States, that America, Peace, Freedom, and Independency are our own." Gates Street was named the same year.

DOWN MARCY STREET at the end of Prescott Park we find **MECHANIC STREET**, an oddly configured thoroughfare that heads first towards the Peirce Island

*Just so there's no confusion, **Chandler's Loft** is not owned by someone named Chandler. Originally a nautical term, **chandlers** primarily deal in supplies and equipment for ships and boats, and the crews who sail and fish from them.*

bridge. Then it veers off to the right before it can go onto the bridge and parallels the river's "Back Channel" until it comes to the seasonal Chandler's Loft at the bottom of Pickering Street.

Industrialization came early to this part of town, if on a small scale. Small factories and foundries serviced the needs of ship builders along this quiet body of water that let out into the otherwise fast-flowing Piscataqua. A Mechanics' Society was founded in 1803. The name of the street predates the 1813 map. Perhaps this is where you came to find a good mechanic?

The section from Marcy Street to the bridge was still called GRAVES END STREET on the 1813 map of Portsmouth. Little wonder, leading as it does to the town's (and the state's) oldest cemetery, POINT OF GRAVES.

In 1671, Captain John Pickering agreed "that the towne shall have full libertie without any molestation to inclose about half an acre on the neck of land on which he now liveth, where the people have been wont to be buried, which land shall be impropriated forever for the use of a burying place, only the said Pickering and his heirs forever shall have libertie to feed the same with neat [meaning domestic] cattle." The earliest readable gravestone dates back to 1684.

*The **Point of Graves Cemetery**, from the 1913 Vignettes of Portsmouth, illustrated with engravings by Helen Pearson. Courtesy of the Portsmouth Public Library.*

The bit of road that leads onto the Peirce Island bridge and continues across the island to the sewage treatment plant at its far end appears on current maps as PEIRCE ISLAND ROAD. There will be more about Peirce Island at the end of this chapter.

Major William Gardner. PA

THE STORY OF **GARDNER STREET** (still known as **ANN STREET** as of 1813) goes hand in hand with the story of the **WENTWORTH-GARDNER HOUSE**, built by mast merchant Mark Hunking Wentworth in 1760 as a wedding gift for his son Thomas, brother of the last royal governor. Thomas dying within eight years, his widow remarried and returned to England and the house left the family. The house was purchased in 1793 by Major William Gardner (1751-1833) who made extensive renovations to the property, adding among other things, a wharf, barn and store, and an "arch-house" which spanned the top of the street at the corner of Marcy and which still stood in the 1850s. Above this arch, Gardner had his office.

The son of a tailor, Gardner had been brought up to mercantile pursuits. An acting commissary in the Revolution, it was his commission to furnish the army with supplies. Funds were scarce; at one point he paid for blankets from his own purse, for which he never received compensation from the bankrupt government. His service did not go unnoticed, however; after the war, Washington appointed him commissioner of loans for this section. The office in the arch was known as the United States Loan Office. A political appointment, he lost the job when John Adams became president in 1797, but was reappointed by Thomas Jefferson in 1802 and remained in this position almost until his death in 1833. Known as both a patriotic and generous man, Gardner eventually lost his sight but not his interest in public affairs. Encouraging the young in various ways, he was patron to a juvenile military company known as the "Gardner Whites."

*The fine **Wentworth-Gardner House** as it appeared early in the 20th century, not long after Mechanic Street was extended to pass in front of it. TG*

DIMINUTIVE **WALTON ALLEY** forms a shortcut between Gardner and Gates Streets. It hasn't always a mere alley. In It has been known as **LAIGHTON'S**, **PEIRCE'S** and **GATES LANE** and, quite grandly, **WILSON'S AVENUE**. It may be named for Col. Shadrich Walton (1741-1783), or for the Reverend Joseph Walton, who is listed in the 1821 city directory, but my nomination goes to George Walton, just for sheer interest. (This may be the same George Walton appointed a Portsmouth constable in 1654.)

Brewster recounts this tale of suspected witchcraft in the words of no less an authority on the supernatural than Cotton Mather. Mather's source was a first-person account written by one Richard Chamberlain, secretary of the colony of New Hampshire and agent of the Mason family, who was boarding at the Walton tavern and witnessed much of the attack. Chamberlain titled his tale "LITHOBOLIA OR THE STONE-THROWING DEVIL."

On June 11, 1682, showers of stones were thrown by an invisible hand upon the house of George Walton at Portsmouth. Whereupon the people going out found the gate wrung off the hinges, and stones flying and falling thick about them, and striking of them seemingly with a great force, but really affecting 'em no more than if a soft touch were given them. The glass windows were broken by stones that came not from without, but from within; and other instruments were in a like manner hurled about. Nine of the stones they took up, whereof some were as hot as if they came out of the fire; and marking them they laid them on the table; but in a little while they found some of them again flying about. The spit was carried up the chimney, and coming down with the point forward, stuck in the back log, from whence one of the company removing it, it was by an invisible hand thrown out at the window. This disturbance continued from day to day; and some times a dismal hollow whistling would be heard, and sometimes the trotting and snorting of a horse, but nothing to be seen. The man went up the Great Bay in a boat on to a farm which he had there; but there the stones found him out, and carrying from the house to the boat a stirrup iron, the iron came jingling after him through the woods as far as his house; and at last went away and was heard no more. The anchor leaped overboard several times and stopt the boat. A cheese was taken out of the press, and crumbled all over the floor; a piece of iron stuck into the wall, and a kettle hung thereon. Several cocks of hay, mow'd near the house, were taken up and hung upon the trees, and others made into small whisps, and scattered about the house. A man was much hurt by some of the stones. He was a Quaker, and suspected that a woman, who charged him with injustice in detaining some land from her, did, by witchcraft, occasion these preternatural occurrences. However, at last they came to an end.

HUNKING STREET was originally known as HUNT'S LANE, possibly because HUNTRESS WHARF once sat at its terminus.

Hunking Street owes its name to the Hunking family, and the Wentworth dynasty owes a goodly portion of its genetic material and its Little Harbor estate to Mark Hunking, who bought some buildings and eleven acres on Little Harbor from a fisherman named Christopher Souten in 1663. His will, dated 1667, cites three children, including Mark, Jr., who inherited the Little Harbor property. Mark Jr. started his career as a shipmaster, then settled into a life ashore as a merchant and public official, serving as a provincial councilor from 1710 to 1712 and a justice of the Superior Court from 1712 to 1727, just two of the many positions he held. His only surviving child, Sarah, married Massachusetts Lieutenant Governor John Wentworth; it was through Sarah that the Little Harbor property came into the Wentworth family.

Tobias Lear (1762-1816), George Washington's personal secretary and tutor to Washington's adopted children, grew up in the 1740 house on Hunking Street that bears his name. Lear and his wife Polly were a part of the presidential household; Washington served as their son Benjamin Lincoln Lear's godfather.

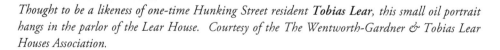

*Thought to be a likeness of one-time Hunking Street resident **Tobias Lear**, this small oil portrait hangs in the parlor of the Lear House. Courtesy of the The Wentworth-Gardner & Tobias Lear Houses Association.*

RUNNING PARALLEL TO Hunking Street is PICKERING STREET. As early as 1633, John Pickering (1590-1669) arrived here from Massachusetts. In 1655, the town granted him a 500-acre landholding on the Great Bay (a PICKERING'S BROOK runs from the Great Bay in Greenland into the Great Bog), and in 1658, the town further granted him mill privileges on the South Mill Pond. On his death, he was buried in the aforementioned Point of Graves Cemetery. A succession of Pickerings continued to manage the mill through to the fifth John Pickering.

The original John Pickering (many sources refer to him as John Pickerin) had two sons and four daughters. The second John Pickering (?-1719) inherited Pickering's Neck, his father's "small and pleasantly situated farm," a landholding in town that was described as running from Point of Graves and the Puddle Dock inlet to the mill bridge and dam, taking in the whole shore, probably around to near the original site of the Universalist church on Pleasant Street near the corner of Junkins Avenue – basically all of the South End that lay to the north of the South Mill Pond. His brother Thomas (1644-1719) inherited the Great Bay farm.

The last Pickering to inherit the mill, according to Brewster, was the fifth – and last – John. This Pickering had two sons, neither of whom had sons. Capt. Thomas Pickering, his only brother, never married. On his death, this particular line of Pickerings died out.

John II wore many hats: he was a military man, lawyer, miller, carpenter and "kept a house of publique entertainment." Captain Pickering commanded a company of Portsmouth militia, and was one of Portsmouth's representatives to the first New Hampshire assembly in 1680. In 1673, two years after he inherited his property, Pickering gave the town the right-of-way for the construction of a highway two rods wide through his land to the dam – this was the opening of Pleasant Street. He also bequeathed the lot on which the parishioners of the old South Church built their house of worship in 1729. And this is the John Pickering who gave the town the half acre for the Point of Graves cemetery.

But we cannot leave the Pickerings without hearing a bit more about the Captain Thomas Pickering (c. 1745-1779) mentioned in the sidebar above, and his role in the War for Independence.

On December 13, 1774, Paul Revere rode into Portsmouth with the information that the British were placing an embargo on arms to the colonies, and that the munitions at Portsmouth's FORT WILLIAM AND MARY were soon to be removed. The Committee of Safety – John Langdon, John and Thomas Pickering, John Sherburne and others – quickly convened to consider the ominous development. John Langdon and Thomas Pickering were ready to take the fort that night, by themselves if necessary; a mere six soldiers of the Crown garrisoned the fort. Cooler heads prevailed. For such an offense, the two could be hung. A mob would be much harder to punish. And so a mob was assembled.

Fort William and Mary, renamed Fort Constitution in 1808, scene of the first overt action against England in 1774. PA

Some three to four hundred patriots rowed out to the fort the next day, wading ashore through freezing waters. According to Brewster (who had the story from a participant, albeit many, many years after the fact), Pickering led the charge, scaling the ramparts of the fort, seizing the sentinel and threatening death if he let out a sound.

Pickering then proceeded to the quarters of Captain Cochran, the officer in charge, who surrendered the fort and handed over his sword. Pickering is said to have handed it back to the officer, observing the rules of gentlemanly behavior – at which point he was attacked, parried, then knocked his ill-mannered enemy senseless.

Before the night was over, some 97 barrels of gunpowder were on their way first to Durham for safekeeping, and thence to Cambridge in time to be used against the British at the Battle of Lexington four months later.

This attack was the first amphibious invasion in American military history, the first armed act of rebellion against the British and the only action of the Revolution taken on New Hampshire soil. Thomas Pickering helped set the wheels of American history into motion, and the the fort was rechristened FORT CONSTITUTION in 1808.

OF COURSE, SOUTH MILL STREET takes its name from John Pickering's mill, which existed until 1881 and was most probably a gristmill, grinding grain into flour for the sustenance of Strawbery Banke's early settlers.

Today's Old Mill Fish Market rests on the site of the original Pickering mill. Mills have been with us at least since Roman times. Windmills, watermills, animal-powered mills; saw mills, textile mills, paper mills, mills to provide a water supply, mills to drain water away, mills that create electricity. Watermills were (and are) fed by either vertical (waterfalls, either manmade or naturally occurring), horizontal (river-current driven) or tidal sources of water. Pickering's was tidal.

THE OLD MILL Fish Market sits where four streets converge: Marcy crosses in front of it, South Mill takes off from it, and Pleasant Street and SOUTH STREET terminate there. South Street appears on the 1813 map as SOUTH ROAD. By 1850, it's been promoted to street status.

*The Hollywood Walk of Fame centers on the corner of Hollywood and Vine. Anyone looking for the corner of South Street and Vine in Portsmouth is on a wild goose chase – tiny Vine Street takes off from Islington. But a trip to **South Street and Vine**, on the corner of Marcy and South Mill Street, will net you a celebrity-worthy selection of fine wines and cheeses.*

THE OTHER STREETS OF MEETING HOUSE HILL
Richmond Street – Hancock Street – Howard Street – Manning Street

IN 1838, THE TOWN fathers changed the name of COLD LANE to RICHMOND STREET. Why I do not know.

CHARLES BREWSTER IN HIS *Rambles* often waxed poetic in his imaginative flights of fancy describing times past, as in this example: "Who is this alighting from his coach, dressed with so much taste and attended by his servants – to take up his quarters here? It is one whose name stands out on the Declaration of Independence, like the pencilings of a thunderbolt on a clear sky – JOHN HANCOCK truly." This man, most certainly, must be the inspiration for the naming of HANCOCK STREET. Known as DOCK LANE until some point between the mappings of 1813 and 1850, an attempt was made to revive the earlier name in the 1970s, when Strawbery Banke Museum opened, but as is often the case, the renaming never took.

Ray Brighton tells us Hancock, a resident of Boston, came to Portsmouth often, having business in the area and frequently stopping to visit a former clerk, Richard Billings, a modest merchant of groceries and pewterware with his dwelling and place of business on Congress Street.

Hancock was born in 1737. At 27, he inherited his uncle's mercantile interests and control of what some refer to as the largest fortune ever amassed in New England. His wealth and his strongly held position opposing the Stamp Act and England's insistence on taxing the

> A short, narrow passageway known most odoriferously as **Pig Turd Alley** once made its miasmic way between Gates and Hancock Streets. In polite society, it was more discreetly referred to as 'PT Alley.'

colonies propelled him to the forefront of the rebellion. He was both a member and president of the Continental Congress. He was also governor of Massachusetts from 1780 to 1785, and again from 1787 to 1793.

PARALLELING GATES STREET IS **HOWARD STREET**, which was still known as **MAUDLIN LANE** as late as 1813. I have yet to find an explanation for either name.

ONCE CALLED **WENTWORTH STREET** (from Puddle Dock to the corner of Gates) and **PEIRCES LANE** (from Gates to Meeting House Hill), **MANNING STREET** was named for Captain Thomas Manning (1747-1819), the man who inspired the famous renaming of another thoroughfare: the dropping of King Street in favor of Congress Street.

A fervent patriot, Manning often joined in or led public protests against the colonial government. Charles Brewster described him as a "leading spirit of the day," adding that "where he led, there was ever a host to follow, when he spoke, his words were with effect." Standing on the steps of the State House on the Parade as Sheriff John Parker read the 1776 Declaration of Independence to an eager throng, Thomas Manning "led the cheering and

Captain Thomas Manning's "mansion fronts Liberty bridge on the south side," Brewster recounts. Characterized by Brighton as always ready to take an active role as goad or gadfly, his epitaph simply reads: "An honest man." PA

roared out the suggestion that the name be changed, an informal motion that was swept into adoption," according to Ray Brighton. Brewster tells us that Manning's exact words were, "Huzza for Congress Street!"

Manning rented space for a store on the Portsmouth Pier at the foot of State Street, and owned, invested in and/or commanded privateers during the Revolution and the War of 1812. Visiting Portsmouth in 1856, President Franklin Pierce remembered Captain Thomas Manning and two others of his ilk as "true patriots and noble men."

FROM THE MILL POND DAM TO THE NEW CASTLE BRIDGE
Salter Street – Pray* Street – Partridge* Street Holmes* Court – Walden Street – South School Street Humphreys Court – Johnson Court – Blossom Street Mount Vernon Street – New Castle Avenue – South Street

SEA CAPTAIN TITUS SALTER (c. 1722-1798) lived in the handsome, gambrel-roofed home on the corner of Partridge Street (today's Marcy Street) at the inlet to the South Mill Pond, and lent his name to the street it anchored, then called SALTER'S LANE, today called SALTER STREET.

Born at the Isles of Shoals, Titus settled at some point in Portsmouth, marrying Elizabeth Bickford in 1745. Fifteen years later, Henry Bickford, Elizabeth's father, deeded waterfront property over to Salter for the sum of 200 pounds. On this property and in the same year, Salter built the large gambrel-roofed house on the corner of Marcy. The small gambrel house opposite on Salter Street was built for his servants, who were most probably slaves.

Titus Salter is credited with being the first commissioned privateersman to sail from this port. From 1776 to 1778, he commanded the New

*One of many Captain Salters, **Captain Charles H. Salter** was master of the clipper ship* Typhoon, *the fastest clipper ship of her day.* Typhoon *was built in 1851 by the famed Portsmouth firm of Fernald & Pettigrew. PHS*

Hampshire militiamen who defended the Fort Washington fortifications on today's Peirce Island.

Titus must have been a civic-minded individual; his name appears on many committees, including one petitioning the government to provide local mariners with a light to find their way into Portsmouth harbor after dark. A beacon was duly established at Fort William and Mary in 1771, at the mouth of the harbor. By 1784, the beacon was replaced by a wooden structure, and Salter himself was hired as the Portsmouth harbor light's first keeper. Story has it that during his 1789 visit to Portsmouth, George Washington came and spent four days with Salter for the purpose of evaluating his performance – an amazing piece of micro-management in what had to be a very busy year for this country's first president. An uncomplimentary report from Secretary of the Treasury Alexander Hamilton attests to the fact that Salter's work did not pass muster – though he did manage to hold on to the position until 1793.

The Salter family supplied three generations of sea captains to play roles in Portsmouth's naval history. In 1823, Henry, John and Joseph Salter were listed in the city directory as ships' masters. Charles Salter would one day command *Typhoon*. On her maiden voyage to Liverpool over the cold seas of March, *Typhoon* set a record for a trans-Atlantic crossing of only 13 days 10 hours, earning her the nickname "*Portsmouth Flyer*."

At one time, SALTER'S WHARF sat at the end of Salter Street.

*The second **Portsmouth Harbor Light**, circa 1863. This 85-foot octagonal tower replaced the 1771 structure in 1803. It in turn was replaced in 1878 and automated in 1960. PA*

PARALLELING SALTER STREET is **PRAY STREET**, named for the Pray family who owned a wharf at its terminus on the Back Channel. A John Pray was not only listed on the town's tax rolls in 1727, he helped compile them.

Portsmouth's town records in the book of 1720 attest to the citizenship of one "Nememiah Partrg."

THE NEXT OF THE short streets south of Pray is **PARTRIDGE STREET**, most probably taking that name when the original Partridge Street became known as Water Street. On the 1850 map, it appears as **STETON STREET**. It can be found elsewhere as **SIFTON STREET**.

NEXT TO THE SOUTH is today's **HOLMES COURT**, one of the narrowest streets in town. We have numerous candidates for the honor of this name. A Joseph Holmes, age twenty, was listed among the fourteen killed in the Indian raid on the outpost community at the Portsmouth Plains in 1696. A Captain Holmes commanded both *Neutrality* and the *Charming Sally*, a ship taken by the British in 1777. And a Benjamin Holmes, master joiner or house carpenter and one of the founders of the local Mechanic's Society in 1803, built himself a home circa 1795 at 395 Pleasant Street, at the corner of Manning Street.

THE LAST OF THE DENSELY settled side streets running down to the Back Channel is **WALDEN STREET**. Brewster lists a Colonel Walden as holding two slaves in 1727. A Jacob Walden was on the committee charged with planning Washington's visit to Portsmouth in 1789. The 1821 directory shows a William Walden, shipmaster; a Nathan Walden, ship master; a Jacob and a Jacob Jr., "gentlemen."

TODAY REFITTED WITH condos, the old Haven School sits on the site of the first school built in Portsmouth, for the education of "righters, reeders and Latiners," and thus we have SOUTH SCHOOL STREET. Predating the school house was an early arsenal or armory, referred to as the "Gun House" on the 1813 map.

The half-acre park across the street from the old school is known officially as the HAVEN SCHOOL PLAYGROUND.

*The **Gun House** once sat adjacent to the Haven School site. From C.S. Gurney's 1902* Portsmouth, Historic and Picturesque.

IN 1802, THE ESTATE of Captain William Trefethen was broken up amongst his heirs and a new thoroughfare was proposed to give them access to their respective parcels of land. Running from Partridge Street (today's Marcy Street) straight through to South Road (today's South Street), it paralleled South School Street and most probably would have been called TREFETHEN STREET, had it been opened. It wasn't until late in the 19th century when carpenter/developer William Humphrey was able to buy up several of these properties and build a number of the houses that still stand on the two legs of HUMPHREY'S COURT. Humphrey himself lived just around the corner on Newcastle Avenue.

JEREMIAH JOHNSON(1799-1864) operated a ropewalk and lived on JOHNSON'S COURT, according to both the 1850 map of the city and the city directory for the same period. Jeremiah's apostrophe disappeared over the years.

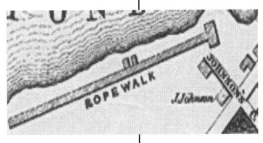

Detail from the 1850 map. PA

A STREET OF MODEST homes on equally modest lots, Portsmouth's **MOUNT VERNON STREET** was most probably inspired by George and Martha Washington's magnificent home and 8,000-acre Virginia plantation of the same name.

ONE WORD OR TWO? The village of New Castle, originally called Great Island, was a part of Portsmouth until 1693, when it separated and became a town in its own right. **NEW CASTLE** (or **NEWCASTLE**) **AVENUE**, which shows up in contemporary map books under both spellings, leads to the series of bridges and causeways that have carried traffic over to the island town since 1822.

Merely a continuation of Partridge Street in the early days, this stretch became known as **NEW CASTLE STREET** when the bridges, and a toll controlling passage over, came into existence. In 1886, it was decided that this gateway thoroughfare should be dubbed an avenue.

> A reader of the day grumbled in a letter to the editor of *The Penny Post* that the byway leading to **New Castle** resembled more of a country lane than any avenue he'd ever seen.

SILK DYER WILLIAM DAVIS'S black mare was stolen from Peter Ball's pasture in 1764, but if that field lay in proximity to today's **BALL STREET** is unknown. True M. Ball, merchant, lived in the Islington Street vicinity in 1782 and later on Court Street. John Ball incorporated with Ichabod Goodwin and Thomas B. Laighton to form the Portsmouth Whaling Company in 1824.

What is known for sure is that Samuel and Mary Ball lived on **BALL'S LANE** in 1827. Samuel was a joiner (carpenter) by trade, and residents of the lane today say that he built at least a few of the houses there. The house that stands today on the corner of Ball Lane at 180 Newcastle Avenue is said to have been built by Daniel Ball.

THE ISLANDS OF THE PISCATAQUA'S BACK CHANNEL
Peirce Island – Four Tree Island – Shapleigh Island
Round Island – Goat Island – Pest Island – Belle Isle

THE ISLANDS OF THE Piscataqua, like most islands everywhere, began their toponomical life with apostrophes, proclaiming the names of their owners. The majority of them have lost their apostrophes over the years, leading one youngster I know to think there is a flourishing colony of badgers living just over the Memorial Bridge. He was disappointed when I burst his bubble, informing him that it took its name from the Badger family, but perked up after a description of shipwright William Badger (1752-1830) and the nearly one hundred sailing vessels that slid down Badger's ways.

IF THERE WERE A naming derby, **PEIRCE ISLAND** would win hands down. For one thing, no one seems to be able to agree if the spelling is Peirce or Pierce, or whether perhaps it should be called Peirce's or Pierce's Island. A map I picked up at the library spells it Pierces, no apostrophe. And that's just today. Historically, we're not the only ones to have a problem with the spelling of this slippery name. The town clerk wrestled with it in 1720, recording one resident as a "George Peairs."

Go to the Internet. A Google search for "Pierce Island" generates in excess of 34,500,000 hits as of this edition, including citations on City of Portsmouth pages. A 2002 dredging feasibility study was done for the waters around Pierce's Island. "Peirce Island" nets a mere 1,140,000 hits, but the Chamber of Commerce prefers

City signs that can be found within twenty yards of one another on the island today .

this spelling, as does the Mayor's Blue Ribbon Committee. It was Peirce's Island in the days of Brewster and Thomas Bailey Aldrich. Enough confusion! For the sake of clarity, if not sanity, let's agree to spell it "Peirce" for these purposes.

The twenty-seven acre island that sits just to the east of Point of Graves began its colonial history as the property of Dr. Renald Fernald, who arrived in the area, as surgeon to John Mason's company in 1631, and from this it took its first name: DOCTOR'S ISLAND.

Records show Fernald dying in 1656. A 1688 deed conveys the island property from a Thomas Fernald, "eldest lawful begotten" son of the doctor (here named Reginald), to Thomas's sister, Sarah Fernald Waterhouse; at that time, the island was being called WATERHOUSE ISLAND. However, at some point a half sister, Mary Fernald Partridge, gained title to the eastern or far end of the island. Her husband, John Partridge, was in the ferry business in New Castle. The eastern end came to be referred to separately as PARTRIDGE ISLAND.

Joshua Peirce came to Portsmouth in 1694. (He wasn't the only Peirce in town – seven Peirces appear on the tax rolls for 1727.) He served as town clerk in 1700 and again from 1714 to his death in 1743. He was a selectman nine times between 1703 and 1732, a representative from 1718 to 1721, registrar of deeds and a justice of the peace. Taking a mortgage on the Partridge end of the island, he eventually came to own that portion.

As time went by, with the marriage of a great granddaughter of Sarah Fernald Waterhouse to Nathaniel Mendum, the western or near end became MENDUM'S ISLAND. By 1776, that end was known as JANVRIN'S ISLAND after the marriage of Elizabeth Mendum and George Janvrin.

Dr. Benjamin Waterhouse (1754-1846), introduced the kine (cow) pox vaccine in this country in 1800.

In 1775, the entire island was taken over by the Committee of Safety. General John Sullivan threw a pontoon-style bridge of gundalows, moored head to stern, across to the island and fortified the eastern end. FORT WASHINGTON was manned through 1778 by 180 New Hampshire militia under the command of Captain Titus Salter, and the island was renamed the ISLE OF WASHINGTON. The island was refortified during the War of 1812.

*The **Fort Washington** fortifications on the far end of **Peirce's Island**. Some of the earthen bulwarks, detailed on this 1850 map of Portsmouth, are still visible today. PA*

Eventually the entire island came to be owned by the Peirce family, and the name, or at least its many permutations, stuck. The island remained in the family until 1923. The one end was leveled for a sewage treatment plant and in 1926 part of the island was designated as the Boynton Park, in honor of the late city coucilman Harry E. Boynton.The WPA built a pool there in the 1930s, and the island was used for rest and recreation by the troops before World War II.

Today, the bulk of Peirce Island is enjoyed by the public as the 25.8 acre PEIRCE ISLAND PARK.

❧ Proposed Uses for Peirce Island ❧ Over the Years

1866 ~ a park for a Civil War monument
1889 ~ a site for a soldiers' and sailors' home
1894 ~ a site under consideration for what would become the Bath Iron Works, Bath, ME
1895 ~ a park, plus building lots to fund the city's purchase of the island
1899 ~ development of building lots by an out-of-town group
1903 ~ actually used as horse pasturage
1908 ~ the idea of a shipbuilding plant revisited
1977 ~ a public marina
1998 ~ a new home for the Children's Museum

WOULD YOU BE SURPRISED if I told you that **FOUR TREE ISLAND** once had four pretty sizeable trees? Two of them were destroyed by fire in 1906; the other two were felled by lightning in 1920.

> In the past 375 years, **Four Tree Island** has passed thru the hands of John Nelson, Jonathan Warner, George Long, Capt. John C. Long, Leonard Cotton, Theresa (Cotton) and Frederick A. Marston, the City of Portsmouth, John Henry Bartlett, Charlie Gray, "Cappy" Stewart, Charles M. Dale, Josie Prescott – and back to the City of Portsmouth in 1954.

We've given Four Tree Island a raft of names over the years: it's been known as **FIVE TREE, THREE TREE** and **ONE-TREE ISLAND, LONG'S ISLAND, OUTER ISLAND** and/or **OYSTER ISLAND,** and **CHARLIE GRAY'S ISLAND.** People say it was Charlie who really put Four Tree on the map.

Charles E. Gray purchased the island for $40 in 1877 and proceeded to build himself quite a little compound out there, complete with its own Main Street – something Portsmouth proper has never had, come to think of it!

Charlie, who had a total of five wives over the years, was best remembered for the dance hall, the frequent cockfights and the house of ill repute he maintained, but that was only part of the "entertainments" offered. He also managed a menagerie and a museum of curios from all over the world, some suggest most probably taken in trade. The dance hall came complete with a "wire-enclosed orchestra section at the end of the room," recounted Puddle Docker Harriet Munz in the early 1980s, remembering her father's nostalgic tales of the

Four Tree Island, as it appeared in 1895. PA

exotic goings-on over there. Charlie's little empire burned to the ground in 1906.

But Four Tree Island wasn't always a place of "entertainment." During the Revolution, it sheltered a small armada of fire ships, boats of every description loaded with all manner of flammable materials, ready to be set aflame to drift with the tide against an assault force should the town be attacked from sea.

In time for the bicentennial festivities of 1976, the Trustees of Prescott Park, with matching funds from the Federal Bureau of Outdoor Recreation (an arcane bit of bureaucracy that no longer exists), took it upon themselves to develop Four Tree Island into the handsome park and picnic area it now is, exorcising once and for all the ghosts of depravities past.

My Mother the Wind, by artist Cabot Lyford, was sculpted from a block of granite hauled clear around the world to the Granite State – from Australia. She carries the inscription, "For those who sailed here to find a new life."

*None of that granite was wasted. **Fisherman's Luck**, below, a favorite climbing apparatus for young patrons of shows staged by the Prescott Park Arts Festival, is said to have been carved from some of the leftover granite. Lyford retired to Maine after teaching art at Phillips Exeter Academy for 23 years.*

NO CONVOLUTED explanation is required for the name of ROUND IS-LAND, which has also been called LITTLE ISLAND. The current owner wishes it to go by both entirely accurate descriptors, but was disappointed to discover at the closing that a brothel for which LITTLE ROUND ISLAND was rumored to have been known was no longer in operation. He claims to have been compensated with a modest reduction in price.

PEST ISLAND takes its name from the early practice of isolating those with contagious diseases, smallpox in particular, which raged through the area with alarming frequency. In 1718, Pierce Island (called Partridge's Island at the time) was used for such quarantining. Dr. Hall Jackson (1739-1797), whom Brighton refers to as

"one of the really great physicians of the century," introduced a form of smallpox inoculation, exposing the patient to the pox, hoping that a light case would bring with it immunity to further attacks of the virus. Brewster tells us that "all who wished to be secure from taking the small pox in the natural way were vaccinated for it, and withdrew for three or four weeks from intercourse with the world." He described gatherings of such intrepid souls as almost festive social events, getaways that participants often looked back on with nostalgia.

Dr. Hall Jackson apprenticed with his father, Dr. Clement Jackson, furthered his studies in London and became a highly respected physician and surgeon in Portsmouth. His practice of surgery extended to the battlefields of Bunker Hill. Credited with groundbreaking discoveries in the care of dropsy (congestive heart failure), he brought the foxglove and its derivative, digitalis, to North America. He was also the first physician to perform a cataract operation in the New World. PA

By 1754, the town had acquired the island, building on it a "pest asylum" or rudimentary hospital which served the town's needs for almost 150 years. In 1896, a new pest house opened on Jones Avenue, and not a bit too soon. The following year, the old asylum blew down in a gale.

ACCORDING TO BREWSTER, nine-acre SHAPLEIGH ISLAND and three-acre GOAT ISLAND were purchased by Reuben Shapley (?-1825) in 1787 for the princely sum of two hogsheads (think a bit more than two 55-gallon drums) of Tobago rum. Captain Shapley became a successful merchant after quitting the sea, owning large brick store houses and a wharf on Water Street. From 1773 to 1797, Shapleigh Island also served as a pest island.

The island passed through many hands before coming into the Captain's possession. The first owner was Dr. Renold Fernald, who passed it along to his son Samuel. John Clark purchased it in 1674, at which point it was known as **CLARK'S ISLAND**. Clark's heirs sold it to a brother-in-law, one William Knoaler, sometimes referred to as Nolar or Knowles; it was called **KNOWLES ISLAND** until 1759. Nathaniel Adams purchased it in 1764. It passed into the hands of Reuben Shapley, as mentioned, in 1787.

Shapley, one of the incorporators of the New Castle Bridge Company, sold a right-of-way across it in 1821.

Eagle-eyed reader Jim Cernys points out that J. Worth Estes and David M. Goodman, in their 1983 *Changing Humors of Portsmouth,* tell us that actually three islands were used as pest asylums: Pest, Shapleigh and a **Henzell's Island**, which does not appear on any early maps. Adams, in his 1824 *Annals of Portsmouth,* also mentions a Henzell's Island, reporting that Hall Jackson and three fellow physicians were given permission by the town to open a quarantine hospital there in 1782, "under such rules and regulations as shall secure the town from danger, provided said hospital shall be no expense to the town." Adams also refers, in 1778, to Pest, Henzell's and Salter's Islands being used for such purposes. By inference, this would make Henzell's an early name for **Shapleigh Island**.

The ill-fated Louis XVI brought France's might to aid the colonists in June of 1778, making enormous contributions and sacrifices in support of the American cause – only to see the ideals he championed come home to roost, with a vengeance.

As mentioned earlier, in 1935 a letter to the editor noted that the island, long referred to as **MARVIN'S ISLAND**, had reverted back to today's name of Shapleigh.

In 1782, five ships of the tremendous French fleet then anchored in Boston sailed into Portsmouth harbor. During their three-month stay, lightning struck the largest of the ships, killing four sailors. A fifth Frenchman met his fate ashore (see Frenchman's Lane, page 106-7). The bodies of these French sailors were buried on the south side of Shapleigh Island, on what came to be known as **FRENCHMAN'S POINT**. "As the bank washes away," writes Charles Brewster in the 1850s, "their remains are from time to time disclosed."

CURRENTLY SHOWN ON Delorme maps as **LADY ISLE**, the fifteen acre island that anchors Little Harbor was home for 49 years to the Catholic **LADY ISLE SCHOOL**, its sprawling convent house, school buildings, caretaker's house and barn. On the 1972 city map, it was called **BELLE ISLE**; the road that joins it to the mainland is still known as Belle Isle Road.

Lady Isle once went by the name of **SALTER'S ISLAND** – Captain John Salter (1744-1814) built his home on the side of the island facing the New Castle bridge (see Salter Street, page 50-51).

A number of Marstons lived on Salter's Island – fish merchants George H., and John W., and farmer Alphonso were listed in the city directory as late as 1881. Soon after, bridge contractor William H. Keeper was inhabiting what was by then listed as **MARSTON'S ISLAND**; in 1899 the map finally caught up with current ownership, calling it **KEEPER'S ISLAND**, if only for a few years. By 1901, though Keeper still lived there, the island had taken on half of its present name – **BELLE ISLAND**.

CHAPTER 4

THE OLD DOWNTOWN
THE "COMPACT PART OF THE TOWN"

The circus comes to town. PA

From Map of the City of Portsmouth, N.H. *C.W. Brewster, Publisher, 1850.*

MARKET SQUARE
The Old Parade

MARKET SQUARE functions as the very heart of Portsmouth. Once referred to as the PARADE, military companies drilled under the shade of spreading elms. It was also the site of the austere New Hampshire State House, built between 1758 and 1760, back when Portsmouth was the seat of government in New Hampshire, before that honor shifted, first to Exeter in 1774, then over to Concord in 1808.

Market Square served as a marketplace long before it took the name. From 1800 on, when the city erected a new Brick Market (on the site of the present Bank of America), the Parade became an open-air market, where everything from wood, charcoal, hay and poultry to herds of cattle and oxen were brought for trade.

*New Hampshire's first **State House** once occupied this space at the head of Congress Street. TG*

In 1904, the *Portsmouth Herald's* 'Idle Observer' mused:
> *"I have often wondered why the old name of the Parade was discarded for that of Market Square. The ancient cognomen had the merit of being distinctive and euphonious. In my humble opinion, the change should never have been made. There are thousands of Market Squares, while 'the Parade' is a name with a historical significance and around it cluster the memories of the past. If I could have my way, the old name would be re-adopted, even at this late day."*

MARKET STREET AND ENVIRONS
Market Street – Ladd Street – Haven Court – Commercial Alley
Daniel* Street – Portsmouth Naval Shipyard
Congress Street – State Street – Court Street/Place
Middle Street – Haymarket Square – Rogers* Street – Mark Street

SOME TIME AROUND 1767, the first street in town to receive a surfacing upgrade was known as PAVED STREET. The "paving" was wheel-jarring cobblestone. In 1761, a formal brick market building had been established on SPRING HILL, the spot at the corner of Bow and Market Streets where a spring of fresh water flowed, and by 1813, Paved Street had taken the name we know it by today, MARKET STREET, though its cobbles wouldn't disappear under macadam until 1883. The market was moved down to the river's edge in 1830 for the convenience of those bringing their goods in by water, and was used from then on exclusively as a fish market.   Much of what we know today as MARKET STREET EXTENSION was then named FORE STREET, a

The elegant Merchant's Row replaced a street of early wooden structures in the wake of the disastrous fire of 1802. PA

name that had crossed the ocean from England, where many waterfront thoroughfares are called just that.

On the day after Christmas, 1802, the first of downtown Portsmouth's three devastating fires destroyed 120 structures, including every building on both sides of Market Street from Market Square down as far as the Moffatt-Ladd House. When the area was rebuilt, the street was widened to its present width – fully twice as wide as the street it replaced – graced by a matching pair of sidewalks.

And what could you buy along Market Street, two hundred years ago? Melcher's Printing Office was offering copies of the Constitution in 1787. You could buy books, pictures, scales, slates and stationery. Bushels of rye and corn. Butter, teas, coffee, chocolate, molasses and groceries in general. Rum, gin, brandy and wine. Mules. Gunpowder, flints, common and patent shot and infantry muskets with bayonets, complete. Patent medicines, oil, spices, soaps and powders. Fabrics of every description from all over the world, lace and net, feathers, thread, ribbons, buttons and button "moulds." Shawls, mitts and gloves, bonnets, hose and hats, umbrellas and walking sticks, fans and muffs, combs and looking glasses. Shoes, slippers and boots, watches and watch chains, snuff boxes and smelling bottles, suspenders. Carpets and buf- falo robes. In short, just about anything a prosperous Colonial might want or need.

> You could also buy an education on Market Street, where Thomas Jackson ran a school "for both sexes." An ad in 1805 reminded parents:
>
> *'Tis Education forms*
> *the common mind.*
> *Just as the twig is bent,*
> *the tree's inclined.*

FEW EVER CITED little **LADD STREET** when giving directions to the old Peavey's hardware, the landmark emporium that handled Portsmouth's hardware needs for 218 years, from 1887 until 2005.

Exeter-born Eliphalet Ladd (1744-1806) moved to Portsmouth in 1792. Merchant, shipbuilder, developer and speculator, he soon set about opening Ladd Street

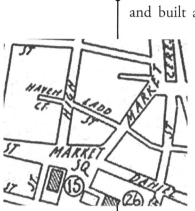

From the 1925 map of Portsmouth. PA

and built a block of buildings on it. When the block burned in 1802, he immediately rebuilt it.

Far more noteworthy, however, was Ladd's venture of bringing water to downtown. Incorporating as the Portsmouth Aqueduct Company, he purchased a spring two and a half miles from Market Square, constructed a viaduct of hollow logs and delivered water to two hundred families. Raise your glass and toast the entrepreneurial Eliphalet Ladd whenever you treat yourself to a drink of Portsmouth tap water.

Eliphalet fathered ten children. Many Ladds have left their mark on the region. Serving at two different times, descendant Samuel T. Ladd was mayor of Portsmouth as recently as 1923. Eliphalet Ladd's grandson Alexander (1815-1900) left his mark on the gardens of the MOFFATT-LADD HOUSE.

APPEARING ON THE MAP for the first time in 1895, HAVEN COURT's listing in the city directory indicated that it was tenanted for only thirty years. Though it may have functioned as more of an alley since then, it still carries the same resonant family name as Haven Park, Haven Road and Haven School.

AT THE CORNER OF COMMERCIAL ALLEY once stood the home of the Hon. John Pickering (1738-1805), one of the framers of the state's constitution and chief justice of the New Hampshire Supreme Court from 1790 to 1795. Graduating from Harvard in 1761, he first pursued a career in the church, then decided instead on the law, but he continued to teach religion while simultaneously maintaining his legal practice.

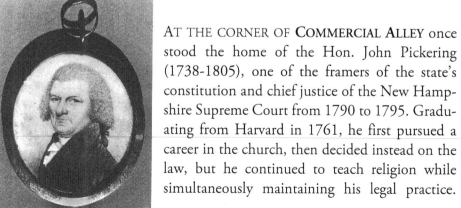

*Some suggest that **Judge John Pickering**'s Federalist leanings, not senility, were the basis for his removal from office. PA*

Dartmouth conferred on him a doctorate in law. Senility, it is said, eventually forced him from the bench.

IN 1700, BRIDGET DANIEL GRAFFORT gave the town land for a "highway" that would lead from Market Square east to the river. The new road was named GRAFFORT'S LANE, in her honor. The daughter of the wealthy Richard Cutts and widow of both Captain Thomas Daniel and Thomas Graffort, she also gave the town a piece of property at the corner of Daniel and Chapel Streets for the building of a high school. By 1813, for reasons unknown, the town decided to rename the street for her first husband and Graffort's Lane became DANIEL STREET.

Interestingly, in modern times Daniel Street was officially changed to DANIELS STREET, a move intended to please Josephus Daniels, then Secretary of the Navy under Woodrow Wilson. Early in the 20th century, the Portsmouth Naval Shipyard was perceived to be on the brink of closure – some things never change. Daniels was thought to be a "real friend of the yard," and the idea of adding one little s to a street name seemed like a good investment in the shipyard's precarious future. Daniels only held his post for seven years, but the street kept its s for the better part of fifty.

Josephus Daniels held the future of the Portsmouth Naval Shipyard in his hands at the end of the First World War. As Secretary of the Navy from 1913 to 1921, he banned the consumption of alcohol aboard his ships – at which time sailors began referring to coffee as a "cup of Joe" in his "honor." From www.firstworld war.com.

THE FUNCTIONS OF the 1967 THOMAS J. MCINTYRE FEDERAL BUILDING are slated to move to Pease International Tradeport in the near future. U.S. Senator Thomas J. McIntyre (1915-1992) served New Hampshire in Washington from 1962 to 1979. On hearing that he'd been rated the worst senator by the John Birch Society one year, McIntyre responded, "I must be doing something right."

*Laconia, N.H., native **Thomas J. McIntyre**. From the collections of the State of NH Division of Historical Resources.*

The old High School on Daniel Street.

BOYS AND GIRLS Attended the same high school for the first time when the 1858 HIGH SCHOOL opened its doors, though they did remain segregated by sex within the building until 1878.

In 1908, the structure took on the title of CITY HALL, and remained as such for the next eighty years.

The Connie Bean Center, before the addition of a gymnasium. TG

BUILT IN 1917 as the ARMY & NAVY BUILD-ING, the one-time recreation hall for soldiers and sailors was renamed in 1992 to honor longtime head of Parks and Recreation Connie Bean. Today only its first floor provides a home for the city's recreational programming; its future is currently under review.

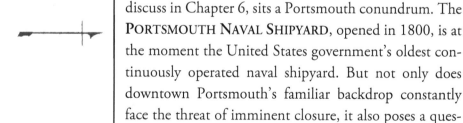

AT THE FAR END of the Memorial Bridge, which we shall discuss in Chapter 6, sits a Portsmouth conundrum. The PORTSMOUTH NAVAL SHIPYARD, opened in 1800, is at the moment the United States government's oldest continuously operated naval shipyard. But not only does downtown Portsmouth's familiar backdrop constantly face the threat of imminent closure, it also poses a question that is as old as the yard itself: is the Portsmouth Naval Shipyard located in New Hampshire or in Maine? Each state in 1800 was granted a shipyard. Maine didn't exist as a state until 1820.

In 2001 the U.S. Supreme Court pointed out that New Hampshire cannot argue, and win, a mid-river state boundary case in 1977, then arbitrarily push that boundary to the shores of Maine 25 years later. The case was dismissed.

*Only four public shipyards still exist today. Over the years, the **Portsmouth Naval Shipyard** launched a total of forty wooden vessels and, beginning in 1917 with the L-8, 138 submarines have left Portsmouth to prowl the high seas. Currently, the shipyard specializes in the refurbishing and refueling of Los Angeles class nuclear-powered subs.*

THOMAS BAILEY ALDRICH, writing in 1893, maintained that "CONGRESS STREET, a more elegant thoroughfare than Market, is the Nevski Prospekt of Portsmouth," and indeed it was a street of grand architecture at end of the nineteenth century.

Congress was first known by the humble name of CREEK STREET. By the time of the Revolution it was known by the far grander name of KING STREET. The dramatic reading of the Declaration of Independence from the State House balcony on July 18th, 1776, prompted patriot Thomas Manning to call for a change, and changed it was, by public acclamation.

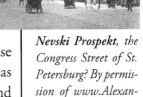

Nevski Prospekt, the Congress Street of St. Petersburg? By permission of www.AlexanderPalace.org.

In those days, Congress Street continued past its current end, around the bend to the left and on to Haymarket Square. Today that

*The **State House balcony**, site of the first reading of the Declaration of Independence in 1776. PA*

section is considered part of Middle Street. By 1838, Congress became Islington at the junction where Middle Street became Maplewood, just as we know it today, but the selectmen, in their wisdom, decreed that it was time to extend the name Islington all the way up to Market Square. The name change, like so many others, never took.

ANOTHER THOROUGHFARE of many names is STATE STREET. First trod as early as 1758 as the NEW STREET, it later was called QUEEN STREET, then changed again to carry two names: from Water to Pleasant Street, it is shown as BUCK STREET (perhaps named after a William Buck, who married Mary Rymes, a Wentworth grandchild, in 1755), and from Pleasant to Middle Street as BROAD STREET – though that incarnation of the street has been described as being very narrow. The fire of 1813 burned every house and place of business along its entirety to Water Street, 192 wood-framed buildings in all. By 1850, it carried its present name of State Street from one end to the other.

IN 2001, JAY SMITH (1939-2002) created a tiny park on State Street. City council member and one-time chairman of the Historic District Commission, Smith was Portsmouth's contemporary music scene impresario, angel of The Music Hall and a passionate preservationist, both of the built environment and of the land. JAY SMITH POCKET PARK now serves as a most appropriately unassuming memorial to its creator.

*Jay Smith, behind the bar at **The Pressroom**, where many of today's local musicians got their starts. A journalist who also worked in public television, Smith was also the moving force behind many important public initiatives during his lifetime. Photo by Peter Randall, used with his permission.*

THE LANDMARK **ROCKINGHAM HOUSE** on State Street began its illustrious life as a private home of the same name, built by Judge Woodbury Langdon in 1793. The stately home was adapted as a hotel for the traveling public in 1833. Frank Jones bought and expanded the hotel in 1870, and then, after a disastrous fire in 1884, the **ROCKINGHAM HOTEL** was transformed and updated it into the handsome structure we know today. In 1983, it was converted into elegantly appointed condominium apartments.

*A pair of terra cotta likenesses, the above of **Frank Jones**, the one below of **Woodbury Langdon**, grace the façade of the building today.*

*The **Rockingham House**, before Frank Jones took over. PA*

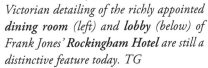

*Victorian detailing of the richly appointed **dining room** (left) and **lobby** (below) of Frank Jones' **Rockingham Hotel** are still a distinctive feature today. TG*

PORTSMOUTH BECAME HOME to its first Jewish immigrants, Abraham and Rachel Isaac, in 1780. More followed, settling primarily in the Puddle Dock area, though it would be another 125 years until thirty families joined forces to found the TEMPLE OF ISRAEL. In 1911, the fledgling congregation was able to purchase the Methodist Church building on State Street for use as its new synagogue; in the 1920s, the name was shortened to simply TEMPLE ISRAEL.

There was no state of Israel in 1905 when the congregation chose their name, so what did this "of Israel" actually mean, I found myself wondering. "Israel," it turns out was the name given to Jacob, after he had wrestled an angel, the name translating as "you have struggled with God." This Jacob fathered twelve sons; his sons' people became the twelve tribes *of Israel.*

*The **Court House** that gave Court Street its name. PA*

KNOWN AS COURT STREET since the building of a court house in 1836 on the site of today's central fire station, the street that runs from Haymarket Square to Prescott Park has sported as many names as any.

Court Street once ran from Market Square to today's junction of Pleasant and Court. Presumably, a court house sat along that stretch at the time. However, that wasn't the Court Street we know today. Today's Court Street, opening west of Pleasant Street running towards Haymarket Square, was called NEW HIGHWAY. Eventually, the street aged, the name was needed for a newer highway yet, and New Highway became LOW STREET. George Jaffrey (1682-1749), who distinguished himself through the years as a councilor, judge, treasurer and chief justice of the state – though not as a signer of the Association Test – bought the land along Low Street, which then came to be called JAFFREY STREET. (The town of Jaffrey, NH, is named for the same George Jaffrey, as was a street that once doglegged its way from the intersection of Bow and Market streets through to Daniel Street, called JAFFREY'S COURT.)

Crossing Pleasant, the road changed its name to PITT STREET, after the William Pitt Tavern, which sat at that corner. Formerly operating as the Earl of Halifax Tavern, proprietor John Stavers wisely decided to change the name of his establishment in 1777 to honor the English statesman who had defended the American cause in Parliament – after his signpost was hacked down by patriots and his own commitment to independence was questioned. For a long time, gardens belonging to Theodore Atkinson brought the street to a halt, but by 1839, the street was extended to meet Water Street and was called Court in its entirety.

*The **Rockingham County Court House** stood on State Street until the 1960s. Its site today is bank parking. TG*

THE FIRST HOUSE MUSEUM to be opened to the public in Portsmouth sits at the intersection of Court and Atkinson Streets. The NUTTER HOUSE, home of the grandfather of noted author THOMAS BAILEY ALDRICH (1836-1907), was home to the young Aldrich from 1849 to 1852, following the death of his father. An urbane wit, Aldrich counted among his friends writers Harriet Beecher Stow and Bret Harte, poet Henry Wadsworth Longfellow, actor Edwin Booth, author and painter James McNeil Whistler, even Samuel Longhorn Clemens, aka Mark Twain, who frequently acknowledged that Aldrich's *Story of a Bad Boy* was the inspiration for a lad named Tom Sawyer.

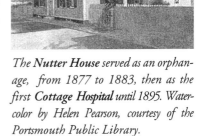

*The **Nutter House** served as an orphanage, from 1877 to 1883, then as the first **Cottage Hospital** until 1895. Watercolor by Helen Pearson, courtesy of the Portsmouth Public Library.*

The house passed out of the Aldrich family. Upon Aldrich's death in 1907, it was reacquired by his widow and faithfully restored to the period of his youthful stay there; Mark Twain returned to Portsmouth to participate in its dedication ceremony in honor of his old friend.

Cottage Hospital moved up to Hospital Hill, above the South Mill Pond, in 1895 and slowly grew into the complex that now houses City Hall. Reopened in 2004 as senior housing, the old Cottage Hospital now goes by the name of Connors Cottage, honoring Timothy J. (Ted) Connors, who headed up the Portsmouth Housing Authority for 35 years. PA.

THE INTERSECTION OF Court and Middle Streets known as **HAYMARKET SQUARE** developed at the end of the 18th century into a neighborhood of fine homes. But before it became an upscale address, its scales served the farmers who brought their hay for weighing and sale. Presumably, this included salt hay harvested from the coastal marshlands of Portsmouth and Rye. Salt hay (actually a salt-tolerant grass) was used from Colonial days well into the 19th century for both fodder and bedding, as well as a readily available material for insulation. Salt hay required little cultivation and offered the bonus of being harvestable twice each season.

Shortly after the Return of the Sons in 1873, a proposal surfaced to change the name of Haymarket Square to **MANHATTAN SQUARE,** in honor of the sons from New York City. The idea was met with immediate protest. The New York City sons voted to provide a flag staff and flag for "their" square, and continued to press their

*Built in 1799 for **John Peirce**, the Federal style **Peirce Mansion** with its handsome belvedere originally sat directly on Haymarket Square. In 1955, it was moved back and annexed to the Middle Street Baptist Church. TG*

cause for some time, but the neighborhood stood its ground and eventually prevailed.

THE ORIGINAL **ROGERS STREET**, as shown on the 1813 map, was much longer than today's, taking a left hand jog and continuing straight out to Pleasant Street, where the Universalist Meeting House then stood. Today's Parrott Street has taken over that end of Rogers Street's duties.

Most likely the early town fathers named this street to honor their second minister, the Reverend Nathaniel Rogers (1669/71-1723). Son of a president of Harvard, Rogers graduated from that institution in 1687, was ordained and moved into Portsmouth's only pulpit in 1699, replacing the Reverend Joshua Moody. In 1712, with the center of population moving north, a separate parish was established and a North Parish Meeting House was erected on the site of today's North Church. A fire in 1704 destroyed Reverend Roger's home on Pleasant Street, killing his mother, daughter and a slave.

*One notable out-of-towner with clear-cut local connections for whom Rogers Street could also have been named is **Major Robert Rogers** (1721-1795). Some put Rogers' place of birth in Londonderry, others in Dunbarton, NH. During the French and Indian Wars, this farmer's son raised his own company of like-minded woodsmen, dubbed them **Rogers' Rangers**, and made quite a name for himself. Locally, he's remembered for his lightning courtship of Elizabeth Browne, the daughter of the pastor of Queen's Chapel, the Reverend Arthur Browne.*

Many slaves were given the last names of their owners. Perhaps the slave who perished in the Rogers fire was the Pharaoh Rogers who is referenced in Portsmouth's Black History Trail materials. Whether he was or was not, he certainly would have wanted to shake the hand of yet another local Rogers, Frederick C. Rogers, a 19th-century anti-slavery worker active in the Underground Railroad in the decades leading up to the Civil War.

THE NORTH END
Hanover Street – High Street – Deer Street – Russell* Street
Vaughan** Street/Mall – Raynes Avenue

STARTING ITS LIFE OUT as **CROSS STREET**, by 1839 Cross Street had changed to its modern name and form as **HANOVER STREET**, though it did at one time bear the name of **MARLBOROUGH STREET** west of Bridge Street. Its name most likely derives from the House of Hanover, the Protestant dynasty of kings ruling 18th-century England that included George III, monarch during the Revolution. However, if that is the case, it is surprising that its name remained unchanged post-1776.

JUST AS EVERY SEASIDE TOWN in England had its Fore Street, most every town in the old country had its **HIGH STREET**, usually denoting the town's major business thoroughfare. Little wonder that the custom was continued in the American colonies.

On the 1813 map, early Portsmouth's High Street runs from Deer Street all the way through to Congress. Urban redevelopment and construction of the High/Hannover parking structure have left us with only the tail ends of our High Street, the block that runs between Deer and Hanover past The Hill, and its terminus, the stunted block off Congress that accesses the parking structure's back entrance.

ON THE NORTH SIDE of **DEER STREET**, near the corner of Market, was once a public house that operated under the sign of a deer. The street took its name from the sign, and appears on the earliest maps as such.

TWO MORE STREETS ONCE paralleled Deer Street. The first was **RUSSELL STREET**, which today skirts the back side of the Sheraton Hotel, but in the old days ran "from the old ferry ways to the rope walks." Either version of Russell takes its name from Eleazer Russell, the state's first postmaster, who received his appointment in 1762. He also served as Customs Collector in the early days after the Revolution, in spite of the fact that he had refused to sign the Association Test. His residence, located on the south side of the ferry landing, doubled as the Custom House.

Russell's mother, Margaret Waldron, was a granddaughter of President John Cutt, and the property around the ferry ways and up Russell Street came to him by inheritance. The land between Russell Street and **BACHELOR'S LANE** was Russell's orchard. (It's probably no coincidence that Russell was a bachelor.)

> Bachelor's Lane's name was changed to **Green Street**, by order of the selectmen in 1838.

TODAY'S ONE-BLOCK **VAUGHAN MALL** was once the terminus of the original **VAUGHAN STREET**, another downtown thoroughfare that was lost to urban redevelopment in the 1970s. The history of Portsmouth is well supplied with Vaughans of note.

William Vaughan (?-1719), a wealthy merchant of Welsh extraction, emigrated from England about 1660. He was appointed a member of the Royal Council of New Hampshire established by King Charles II in 1679, serving 35 years, from 1680 to 1715. He was also a justice in the Court of Common Pleas, from 1680 to 1686, and chief justice of the superior court from 1708 to 1815. A major commandant of Provincial forces, he was the son-in-law of the powerful Richard Cutt. William Vaughan lies buried at the Point of Graves.

George Vaughan (1676-1724), the second son of Major Vaughan, served as lieutenant governor of New

Hampshire during 1715 and 1716, under the governorship of the Irish Earl of Bellomont. One of Governor Vaughan's sons, frontiersman William Vaughan (1703-1746), settled the Damariscotta area, and served as a lieutenant colonel in the siege of Louisbourg in 1745. He appointed himself emissary to England to report the victory, only to arrive and find that the officially appointed envoy had already spread the news – and there he died of smallpox.

When I stroll down today's Vaughan Mall, however, I find myself thinking of historic Portsmouth's greatest champion: **Dorothy M. Vaughan** (1905-2004). Born in Concord, she graduated from Portsmouth High in 1920 and took a job at the Public Library the following year. In 1974, fifty-three years later, Portsmouth's head librarian retired.

Dr. Dorothy Vaughan, historic Portsmouth's veritable pit bull of a watchdog. PA

But that's only half of the story. In 1956, after watching a fine old historic building being torn down across the street from the library and seeing urban renewal's handwriting on the wall, Dr. Vaughan took herself to the Rotary Club and raised a hue and cry: "Do you want to wake up some day and find that you live on Main Street USA, and that you have nothing but bowling alleys and honkytonks and bars?" she asked the assembled Rotarians. She challenged them to consider "what Portsmouth was throwing away each time a house was torn down or a piece of furniture was sold out of town." Ray Brighton dubbed her the "Joan of Arc of colonial restoration." She and a group of like-minded citizens succeeded in changing a state law to permit restoration as an option for urban renewal. Nine years later, thanks to the vision and leadership of Dorothy Vaughan, among others, Strawbery Banke opened its front gate to the public.

DOWN AT THE OPPOSITE END of what's left of Vaughan Street, connecting with Maplewood, is the diminutive **RAYNES AVENUE**, which must certainly be named after George Raynes Sr. (1799-1855). Listed as a "boat builder" in the 1821 Portsmouth Directory, Raynes acquired a shipyard on the North Mill Pond in 1832 and proceeded to build many of the finest – and fastest – and biggest – clipper ships to carry Portsmouth's fame to the four corners of the world. By this time, Raynes was no boat builder; he was the acknowledged master ship builder of such legendary clippers as *Sea Serpent, Witch of the Wave* and *Coeur de Lion,* vessels that rushed to San Francisco, many of their their passengers delirious with gold fever, then raced on to the Orient for tea. Raynes Avenue was established in 1882, effectively cutting the famed old shipyard in two.

*Launched in 1854 from the **Raynes boatyard** for George W. Tucker, the majestic clipper ship **Coeur de Lion** sailed the seas for more than fifty years. PA*

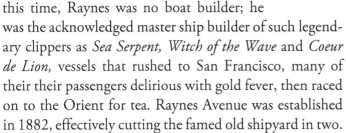

OFF CONGRESS
Church Street – Porter Street – Fleet Street – Chestnut Street

THE LITTLE STREET ON the west side of the North Church, the site of the old North Meeting House, has always been called **CHURCH STREET**.

Portsmouth may have originally been founded as a place of commerce, but it wasn't long until religious concerns became as much a focus of the inhabitants as those of the colonies settled for purely religious reasons. Much of the early recorded history of Portsmouth, as related in Adams' *Annals of Portsmouth*, revolved around the often thorny problem of attracting, hiring and keeping pastors to tend to the well-being of the town's congregations.

*The original clapboard-sided **North Church** was built in 1713. The brick structure we know today was constructed in 1854. PA*

ESTABLISHED IN 1757 as the NEW WAY, today's PORTER STREET is named for Portsmouth native General Fitz John Porter (1822-1901). In 1862, at age 39 and already a hero of the Mexican War, Major General Porter led the Fifth Corps at the Second Battle of Bull Run under General John Pope – to a crushing defeat. Relieved of his command, Pope in turn laid the blame for his defeat on his subordinates, particularly Porter, who he claimed disobeyed orders. Porter, summarily court-martialed and sacked, spent the next 24 years clearing his name.

*Through the administrations of seven presidents, **Fitz John Porter** fought to have his name cleared. He was reinstated in the United States Army in 1886, and buried in 1901 with full military honors. PA*

BRUCE INGMIRE SUGGESTED that FLEET STREET serves as a good example of homage to Old England in early Portsmouth – "Anglicization," he called it. Combining the currying of favor with the powers that be back in old England and a form of pretentious elitism here in the colonies, aspects of Anglicization ranged from the application of London placenames to local streets to the organization of an Anglican church in New England in the early 1730s.

Fleet Street began life as MASON STREET, surely named for Captain John Mason (see Mason Avenue, page 174). At some point, Mason Street came to be known as QUEEN STREET, and by 1778, its name was changed again, this time to Fleet Street. Ingmire proposed a couple of theories as to how this name was chosen, which is a couple of theories more than I have.

(1) London's Fleet Street was home to its printers. Ingmire suggested that the presence of the offices of Robert Gerrish's weekly *New Hampshire Mercury* at the

Bruce Ingmire, doing what he did best – bringing history to life. PA

PORTSMOUTH NEWSPAPERS DOWN THROUGH THE YEARS

The New Hampshire Gazette, 1756-present. *The Freeman's Journal*, 1776-78. *The Portsmouth Mercury*, 1765-66. *The New Hampshire Mercury*, 1784-88. *The New Hampshire Spy*, 1786-93. *The Oracle of the Day*, 1793-1799. *The United States Observer of the Day*, 1793-1821, which became *The Portsmouth Journal of Literature and Politics*, 1821-1903. *The Federal Observer*, 1798-1800. *The Republican Ledger*, 1799-1801, which became *The Rockingham Ledger and Portsmouth Price Current*, 1801-03. *The United States Oracle of the Day*, 1800-1801. *The United State Oracle and Portsmouth Advertiser*, 1801-1803. *The Portsmouth Oracle*, 1803-1822. *The Political Star*, June-November, 1804. *The Intelligencer*, 1806-17. *The Literary Mirror*, February-May, 1808. *The Herald of Gospel Liberty*, 1808-10 and 1814-16. *The War Journal*, March-December, 1813. *The Peoples' Advocate*, 1816-17. *The Oracle of New Hampshire*, 1817. *The Christian Herald*, 1818-31. *The Paraclete and Tickler*, 1822-23, which became *The Novator and Independent Expositor*, March-April 1823, which became simply *The Novator*, 1823-24. *The Evening Visitant*, January-June, 1823. *The Portsmouth Chronicle*, July-December, 1823. *The Portsmouth Weekly Magazine*, 1824-25. *The Commercial Advertiser*, 1825-29. *Signs of the Times*, 1827-28, which became *The Times*, January-November, 1828. *The New Hampshire Repository and Observer*, July-October, 1827, which became *The New Hampshire Observer*, 1827-38. *The State Herald, the Factory People's Advocate*, 1830-31, which became *The State Herald, The Manufacturer's & Mechanic's Advocate*, 1831-33. *The Evening Courier*, 1832-33. *The Hornet*, March-August, 1837. *The News and Courier*, 1837-38. *The Portsmouth Washingtonian*, 1841-43, which became *The Washingtonian and Philanthropist*, 1843-44, which became *The Olive Leaf*, 1844-45. *The Portsmouth Mercury*, 1843-46, which became *The Republican Union*, 1846-47. *The Mercantile Transcript*, 1846-47. *The Rockingham Messenger*, 1847-55. *The Morning Chronicle*, 1852-1918. *The American Ballot*, 1854-65. *The States & Union*, 1863-1918. *The Daily Evening Times*, 1868-1923. *Miller's New Hampshire Portsmouth Weekly*, 1877-81. *The Commercial Advertiser*, November, 1879. *The Rockingham Standard*, July-October, 1884. *The Penny Post*, 1884-90, which became *The Portsmouth Herald*, 1898 – present. *The Republican Daily News*, October-November, 1892, which became *The Portsmouth Republican*, 1898-99. *The Portsmouth Citizen*, 1928-29. *The Portsmouth Press*, 1987-92. *The Wire*, 2003 – present.

corner of Chestnut and Congress might have engendered the name. However, as the *Mercury* did not come into being until 1784, this cannot be the case.

(2) A comparison could be made between Portsmouth's Fleet Street and London's river Fleet. In the early days of the town, Fleet Street served as an overflow between the North and South mill ponds, just as London's river Fleet once made its way between two reservoirs. After the Great Fire of London in 1666, the lower reaches of the Fleet were given a facelift by Christopher Wren. A project worthy of the Army Corps of Engineers, the Fleet was transformed into a "New Canal" meant to rival the Grand Canal of Venice.

The banner of a 1785 edition of The New Hampshire Mercury, published on Congress Street by Robert Gerrish. PA

Unfortunately, pollution pouring down from further up the river doomed the project to failure; by 1732 the paving over of the Fleet was underway. But the Fleet's hoped-for days of glory would have been fresh in the minds of newcomers to Portsmouth and the comparison at flood tides would have been an apt one.

ON THE OLD Glebe map, today's CHESTNUT STREET appears as PRISON LANE; the town's jail stood at its intersection with Porter Street. The jail burned down in 1784, but the name persisted until it was changed, first in 1828 to ELM STREET, and then later to Chestnut (the early spelling was actually CHESNUT STREET).

Aside from the jail, the corner of Porter and Chestnut has been home to two other town institutions of note. The workhouse stood here from 1715 to 1756. Brewster, in his *Rambles About*

*The first alms house was replaced by a **Town Farm** located on the outskirts of downtown, on the old 170-acre Sheafe farm. (Today's **New Franklin School** is sited on land that was once Town Farm fields.) Its dormitories accommodated 250 persons, serving both the mentally ill and the debtor population. Amenities included a school for children of the indigent. From C.S. Gurney's* Portsmouth, Historic and Picturesque.

Portsmouth, suggests that Portsmouth had "the dubious distinction of being the first town, either here or in Europe, to erect a workhouse for paupers." However, the Oxford Dictionary's first record of the word dates back to 1652 in Exeter, England, and describes an institution that functioned along the same lines, though the concept was not codified into English law until 1834. Portsmouth's workhouse was replaced by a town farm the same year.

THE OTHER CHESTNUT STREET institution of note, a much happier one, is THE MUSIC HALL, which started life as the CHESTNUT STREET MEETING HOUSE in 1806. The building was renamed THE TEMPLE when it was enlarged in 1844 to seat a thousand. Twenty years later there was talk of replacing the structure with a new, more elaborate hall on the same site, intended to accommodate an audience of two thousand. However, when it came time for demolition to start, the owners backed off and rehabbed the "rickety old fire-trap" one more time, "a building so enfeebled in all its parts as to vibrate from foundation to ridgepole at the ringing of its own bell," according to a newspaper of the day.

> An 1867 letter to the editor simply signed "A SHIVERER" suggests one reason a recent concert had been so poorly attended was that the hall was so cold. "Applause [was] bestowed on a public spirited citizen who ventured to make up a fire during the interlude."

Mrs. Siddons, a leading actress of her day, performed in Shakespeare's *A Midsummer Night's Dream* in 1870. Tickets in the gallery went for thirty-five cents, "parquette" fifty cents, with reserved seats commanding a top price of sixty cents. In the same year, a bowling alley was installed in the basement, "with private rooms for such as wish to provide themselves with refreshments," and in 1871, T.P. Moses painted a handsome new drop curtain depicting Turks on the Bosporus celebrating the 1833 Treaty with Russia. In 1876, The Temple received its first fresh coat of paint in sixteen years, and then burned to the ground, drawing "one of its largest audiences at its grand conflagration."

The building we know today as The Music Hall was built the following year. Frank Jones purchased and renovated it in 1901, adding the theatre's fine proscenium arch flanked by grand opera boxes – purportedly to provide a suitable venue for a mistress with operatic aspirations. John Philips Sousa, George M. Cohan, Al Jolson and Harry Houdini were just a few of the performers to grace its stage during its youth.

*The Music Hall, 1984, during its 24-year incarnation as **The Civic Theatre**. On the marquee:* Deathtrap, *starring Christopher Reeve. PA*

*The Music Hall has recently expanded across Congress Street to a second facility, this with the lofty name of **The Music Hall Loft: The Center for Performing Arts, Literature and Education**.*

Through the decade preceding World War I, The Music Hall's focus shifted from large theatrical productions to vaudeville and silent movies. After a complete facelift in 1947, it reopened as THE CIVIC THEATRE, surviving again until 1971 when it was purchased by the Loew's theatre chain. In the early '80s it was closed to take it out of competition with another of their theatres in town. The Friends of The Music Hall saved the fine old structure from the wrecking ball in 1986. The hall has operated continuously as a venue for the presentation of both live events and film since 1988. In 2003, The Music Hall was designated an "American Treasure" by the National Trust for Historic Preservation.

BOW STREET AND BEYOND
Bow Street – Chapel Street – Ceres Street – Penhallow* Street
Custom House Court – Sheafe* Street

CERTAINLY, BOW STREET takes its name from its archer's bow shape. The streetscape we see today curving up and around the river's edge has changed little since the conflagration that redefined much of what would be built there from that day forward. Originally, it was known as COW LANE.

*The old **Rockingham Light and Power Company** on the corner of Bow and Daniel Streets became the cornerstone of the **Harbor Place** development. Just up the hill was the **Portsmouth Brewing Company**; the earliest parts of its building date to 1894. Today's **Seacoast Repertory Theatre**, housed in the old brewery, has precedent in the area. The 400-seat **Bow Street Theatre** was built in 1778 and flourished until its destruction in the 1806 fire. TG*

BEFORE THERE WAS was a ST. JOHN'S CHURCH, there was a QUEEN'S CHAPEL and thus we have a CHAPEL STREET, or CHAPPEL STREET as it was presented to the town council in 1778, but this street, too, had an earlier, darker name, TOMBS STREET. Originally Chapel Street terminated at Daniel Street, resuming on the other side of that thoroughfare as ROSEMARY LANE, which continued on down to today's State Street. The short stretch from the top of Church Hill down to Bow Street went by the name of CHAPPEL ALLEY. By 1838, all three sections were known simply as Chapel Street.

A church has stood atop the prominence known as CHURCH HILL from 1732 when Queen's Chapel was built and named in honor of England's Queen Caroline, consort to George II. The queen presented the church with a magnificent set of communion silver, which is still used today at Christmas and Easter. The chapel's belfry housed a bell brought back from the siege of Louisburg after its capture in 1745. With its sweeping view of the harbor, Church Hill was fortified in 1776 in response to the British threat.

Queen's Chapel was lost in the Christmas Eve fire of 1806. Maine builder/architect Alexander Parris designed its replacement. Construction on St. John's Church began in 1807, while the Louisburg bell was sent down to Boston to be recast by Paul Revere.

*Sarah Haven Foster's watercolor rendition of **Queen's Chapel**. Courtesy of the Portsmouth Public Library.*

St. John's Church, c. 1938. PA

Within the church today can be seen items saved from the 1806 fire: a porphyry font taken in 1758 by Colonel John Tufton Mason at the capture of Senegal from the French and presented to Queen's Chapel by his daughters in 1761; a pair of mahogany chairs, one of which President Washington may have sat in when he worshipped here in 1789 (one is original, the other a nineteenth century copy); and a particularly rare 1717 "Vinegar" bible, whose name derives from a famous misprint.

THERE MUST HAVE BEEN a poet in the Planning Department the year the alley that served the wharves, warehouses and market area along the Piscataqua finally received a name. Among the warehouses was a grainery. It is probably safe to assume that Ceres, the Roman name for the goddess of agriculture and the bounty of the harvest, was the inspiration for the naming of **CERES STREET**.

Six stories tall on the water side, the warehouses of **Merchant's Row** on Ceres Street were an architectural wonder of their day. Built in 1803, they were the tallest structures then standing in New England.

Ceres Street was the site of Portsmouth's original marketplace. It was not unusual to see forty or fifty rowboats tied up to the docks as folks from up-river brought their produce and wares to market. A permanent brick building, built in 1761, formalized what began as an open-air gathering of fishwives and housewives. However, not all the fishwives took advantage of the warm, dry – and costly – stalls available to them in the new market. Many continued to set up and hawk their wares on the street outside.

As the center of commerce moved up towards Market Square, the old market fell into disuse. In 1895, it became a ferry landing; the building itself was used as a waiting station. The ferry landing, in turn, inspired the name of the seasonal seafood restaurant in the same location, the **OLD FERRY LANDING**.

A NATURAL SPRING once flowed at the corner of Ceres and Bow Streets, so the corner became known as SPRING HILL. During construction of the DOLPHIN STRIKER RESTAURANT in 1974, the Spring Hill well was discovered in the basement of the building, conveniently providing its owners with a name for their new cellar tavern. (Incidentally, the Dolphin Striker's website offers the following explanation for the derivation of the restaurant's name itself: "Dolphin strikers were used back in the schooner era, to protect the bowsprits from damage by the playful dolphins as they jumped high alongside the ships while under sail." A dolphin striker was actually a small spar under the bowsprit; the bowsprit was the spar that carried a sail forward of the body of the ship.)

ANOTHER BYWAY WITH a name that resonates down the centuries in the history of the region is PENHALLOW STREET. Samuel Penhallow (1665-1726) arrived in Massachusetts in 1686. The second son of a Cornwall aristocrat came to this country fully intending to learn the language of the Narragansetts, then to live as a missionary among them. If he had seen his plan through, Penhallow Street would carry a different name today. Instead, he moved to Portsmouth, married the daughter of the president of the colony – Mary Cutt, daughter of John Cutt – and made a fortune trading with the Indians. This Samuel Penhallow's name was spelled "Samuel Penholo Esqr" in the 1720 town book.

With the death of his father-in-law, Penhallow became the largest landowner in the colony. In the course of his lifetime, he held

*Three generations of **Penhallows**, circa 1897. In the center, Charles Sherburne Penhallow (1852-1921), his wife Mary, and their children Charles, Helen and Evelyn; Charles' mother, Elizabeth Penhallow (1823-1909), to the right, and Elizabeth's mother, Eveline Blunt Sherburne (1801-1889), to the left. Courtesy of the Warner House.*

offices in government ranging from justice of the peace to judge to chief justice of the Superior Court, from treasurer and recorder of the province to speaker of the General Assembly. Before his death, he published a modest *History of the Wars of New England with the Eastern Indians*. The father of fourteen founded a line of prominent politicians, public servants and sea captains whose contributions to New Hampshire were legion. In 1807, John Penhallow *et al* deeded land to the city to be used as "a publick highway forever."

The section of Penhallow Street between Daniel and State Streets was known as **ARK LANE** until 1838, when the name was discontinued in favor of

Penhallow. At the time of the Revolution, one Noah Parker dwelled here in a sizeable, eccentric and, some have said, pretentious house that came to be known as Noah's Ark, from which the street took its original name. Noah Parker was another of the few who declined to sign of the Association Test.

*The old **Customs House**, above, has gone through many incarnations since its sale by the federal government in 1867, from providing space for numerous organizations to its current usage as home to two shops, six condominiums and a fine dining establishment in the basement. Below, the second **Customs House and Post Office**, built in 1860 at the corner of Pleasant and State Street. One of twenty-five designed by Ammi B. Young as Supervising Architect of the U.S. Treasury Department, it has easily recognizable cousins in Waldoboro, Belfast, Bath and Ellsworth, Maine.*

EASY TO OVERLOOK, dead-end **CUSTOM HOUSE COURT** takes its name from the federal-style building that sits to the north of it at the corner of today's Daniel and Penhallow Streets. Built after the fire of 1813 by locals Jonathan Folsom and his partner Langley Boardman, it served as the federal Customs House from 1816 to 1850. As was usual with customs houses, the first floor served as a post office; the Customs Office was housed on the second floor. The third floor housed the fledgling Athenaeum library until it moved to its present Market Square location in 1817.

THE SHEAFES WHO LENT their names to **SHEAFE STREET** (and to the **SHEAFE WAREHOUSE** located today along the shores of Prescott Park) could trace their ancestry back to 12th-century England, though the first Sheafe didn't settle in Portsmouth proper until 1742. Boston merchant Sampson Sheafe (?-c. 1772) came to New Castle, owned a fishing fleet, carried on as a merchant and also served as the Collector of Customs. In 1698, he was appointed a member of His Majesty's Council and secretary for the province.

Senator James Sheafe. Courtesy of the United States Senate Historical Office.

Jacob Sheafe (1715-1791), merchant, was appointed commissary to the New Hampshire forces at Louisburg in 1745 and served as representative from Portsmouth from 1767 to 1774. As a ship captain, he chose to run the British blockade as the Revolutionary War loomed. Included in the National Archives is a document dated April 9, 1800, certifying the payment of $2570.81 to Jacob Sheafe, Agent of Fortifications at Portsmouth, New Hampshire, balance due on account of expenditures.

In 1798, Thomas Sheafe's ship *Mentor* came into port, returning from a voyage to Martinique, its holds laden with sugar, molasses, coffee – and yellow fever. Eight weeks later, fifty-five of Portsmouth's six thousand residents, including three Sheafe children, were dead.

James Sheafe (1755-1829) served as a state representative, a state senator, sat on the Governor's Council, went to Washington as a representative and a senator from New Hampshire, and was a candidate for governor – apparently forgiven for having never signed the Association Test.

CHRISTIAN SHORE
Jackson* Hill Street – The Jackson House
Freeman's Point – Northwest Street

IN ORDER TO FULLY APPRECIATE the derivation of the name CHRISTIAN SHORE, it is necessary to imagine a sparsely populated area across the North Mill Pond bridge, comprised of both a smattering of strictly religious settlers and a handful of their less doctrinaire neighbors. Now, picture a few of the latter, who tended to spend their 17th-century evenings carousing in town into the wee hours. Imagine, at final call, one of these irreverent lads hauling himself out of his chair, squaring his hat upon his head, catching up the elbow of a like-minded neighbor and quipping, "Well, we must be leaving for Christian Shore." That's how Brewster tells us the name came to be. One 19th-century journalist referred to the area as "holy ground." Presumably his readers got the reference.

However, as with any good moniker, alternate theories abound. Some characterized the area as "a stronghold of militant Bible readers." Benjamin Shillaber, writing in 1879, said the area got its name "from the fact that there were many cases of baptism on the shore of the millpond."

KNOWN AS **FRESH CREEK** in the 17th century, the **NORTH MILL POND** was the site of one of the town's first mills, a grist mill established by John Cutt in 1659. It was powered by the fresh water stream that flows into the head of the North Mill Pond.

More than a hundred years would pass before the town would grant Peter Livius the privilege of damming the outlet of the North Mill Pond for the purpose of running a tidal mill, in 1764. By 1850, that operation was functioning as both a grist and woodworking mill.

> When word got around that Wards' distillery was about to open on Christian Shore, it was suggested that perhaps the area needed a new nickname – **Diabolical Shore.**

IN 1664, THE LAND beyond "Strawberry Banke Creek" – Christian Shore – was divided up and granted to various colonists. Richard Jackson, the son of an immigrant cooper and himself a woodworker, farmer and seaman, was given twenty-six acres running down to the Mill Pond on one side and to the Piscataqua on the other. The area soon became known as Jackson Hill; hence, **JACKSON HILL STREET**. The Jacksons went on to become shipbuilders, with a shipyard on the North Mill Pond.

*Seven generations of **Jacksons** lived in this historic home for more than 250 years. PA*

Richard Jackson built what is now the oldest extant wood frame dwelling in New Hampshire. The **JACKSON HOUSE** was purchased in 1924 by preservation pioneer William Sumner Appleton and delivered into the stewardship of the Society for the Preservation of New England Antiquities, which lately underwent a name change of its own – it is now known as Historic New England.

CHARLES BREWSTER SPEAKS of **FREEMAN'S POINT** as "one of the most beautiful locations in Portsmouth for river proximity, extensive prospect and varied landscape." Located above the Sarah Mildred Long Bridge, it was known through the 17th and 18th centuries as **HAM'S POINT**, being the family seat of William Ham and other early settlers by that name. After the Hams, one Peyton R. Freeman took over farming the fertile promontory, at which time the area came to be called Freeman's Point.

*It's hard to imagine, but in 1902, Freeman's Point, was home to the 22-acre **White Mountain Paper Company** plant, producing 500 tons of paper per day. During WWI, the area was transformed into the Atlantic Shipyard. From CS Gurney's* Portsmouth, Historic and Picturesque.

AROUND THE NORTH MILL POND
Bartlett* Street – Burkitt Street – Clinton Street
Cutts ** Avenue/Street – Dearborn Street/Lane
Dennett Street – Marsh Lane – Morning Street
Pine Street – Prospect Street – Sparhawk Street – Stark Street
Walker* Street – Woodbury Avenue

Josiah Bartlett attended to affairs of state while his wife Mary held down the fort on the family farm back in Kingston, caring for eleven children – with one more on the way. From the collection of the State of NH, Division of Historical Resources.

KNOWN AS **CAMBRIDGE STREET** until the sale of the City Farm, **BARTLETT STREET** was most probably named for New Hampshire patriot Josiah Bartlett (1729-1795), great-grandson of Richard Bartlett (1575-1647) who immigrated to Newburyport early in the 17th century. Josiah Bartlett came to New Hampshire to seek his fortune, first as a doctor, and then, as a statesman, the first president and governor of the state (1790-1794) and a signer of the Declaration of Independence.

Politics ran in the family. Son Josiah Bartlett Jr. (1768-1838) was also a physician, state senator and congressman. Grandson Josiah Bartlett Jr. (1788-1853) was a doctor/politician, practicing medicine in Stratham and serving as a member of the U.S. House of Representatives from 1811 to 1813.

John H. Bartlett (1869-1952) served Portsmouth as a schoolteacher, and principal of the Whipple and Haven schools, as well as the Portsmouth High School, while also studying for the law. He acted as Portsmouth's postmaster from 1899 to 1908, and played a large role in town's hosting of the conferees to the 1905 Russo-Japanese Peace Conference. He went on to become governor of the state from 1919 to 1921, then served as Assistant U.S. Postmaster General, administering the first transcontinental air mail service. He also sat on the international boundary commission.

Early in the 20th century, Gov. Bartlett could give the following complete set of directions to a driver bringing Bartlett's car up from Florida: "Get on Route 1, follow it about 1500 miles to Portsmouth, take a right at the second traffic light and into the first driveway on the left." Bartlett's Miller Avenue property is today's parking lot for the Masonic Lodge.

AN 1893 ISSUE OF the *Portsmouth Journal* laments, "...In those days, it was the custom to name the streets after people living or owning and adjacent, or for something pertaining to our local history, or some great personage. I am sorry to say that this good custom has in later years being sadly changed. We have a street called BURKITT, because a man who built a house there had a friend in some distant land whom he wished to honor. *Such should not be the case.*" At the time of the sale of the City Farm, in 1875, Burkitt Street was slated to be renamed PITTS STREET, but the change never went into effect.

NO TRACE IS LEFT today of the original Great House of Strawbery Banke, once owned by John Cutt, but there are plenty of Cutts descendents in the area to remind us of this important early family. Today severed into two separate entities by Market Street Extension, CUTTS STREET and CUTTS AVENUE began life as a single Christian Shore thoroughfare.

Brothers John (1625-1681), Richard (1627-1676) and Robert (1628-?) Cutt came to this country in the 1640s, first settling at the Isles of Shoals to take advantage of the booming fishing trade there. Later, with the benefit of sizeable land grants, they went into the equally lucrative lumber business in Portsmouth. Richard became a prominent boat builder in Kittery, while John and Robert pursued mercantile opportunities – including trading in slaves – in Portsmouth. By 1680, the Great House holdings were theirs, and the Cutts family's influence was vast. Appointed president of the province in 1679 by Charles II, John Cutt was reputed to be, at the time of his death, the wealthiest man in New Hampshire.

*The federal-style **Cutts Mansion**, overlooking Maplewood Avenue, was built in 1805 by Edward Cutts. Photo by John Grossman.*

Ursula Cutt, John Cutt's second wife and widow, established a farm on property willed to her by her late husband. Known at the time as "the Pulpit" (today's Spinnaker Point and Osprey Landing), she built herself a fine home which only succumbed to fire in 1912. Ursula herself lost her scalp, her hands, their rings and her life to Indians marauders in 1694.

*An eccentric pair of cherubs above the front door once welcomed visitors to the **Ursula Cutt** house. The cherubs made their way into the collections of the Portsmouth Historical Society. PA*

TODAY WE HAVE a **DEARBORN STREET** and a **DEARBORN LANE**, and years ago we had a **DEARBORN STREET EXTENSION** as well. For the sake of more efficient emergency response, the latter became **MILL POND WAY** in 1994, the new name suggested by former shipyard employee Fred Harrington, who has long resided on the street.

There are no early references to any Dearborns in Portsmouth, neither on the list of Mason's 1630 colonists nor on the 1727 taxpayers' rolls. But grocer Asa Dearbon is listed in 1827 as living at the intersections of the North Road and **DEARBON'S LANE**. Perhaps this early spelling developed into the Dearborn Street we know today.

*New Castle's **Fort Dearborn** was also named for physician-turned-soldier, hero of both the Revolution and the War of 1812, and Secretary of War **Henry Dearborn**. From the collections of the State of NH, Division of Historical Resources.*

The street itself appears unnamed on the 1813 map. On the 1850 city map, we find it misspelled "**DEABORN STREET**." It again appears unnamed on the 1876 map. Jonathan Dearborn took office as mayor in 1867. Perhaps he took it upon himself to straighten things out. It's been "Dearborn" ever since.

We do have more Dearborns of note with Portsmouth connections, however. Major Henry Dearborn (1751-1829) grew up in Hampton and studied medicine in Portsmouth with Dr. Hall Jackson. He set up practice in Nottingham in 1772 and also organized a company of militia as the colonies moved towards war; his company was folded into the 1st New Hampshire Regiment under Col. John Stark and fought at Bunker Hill. He also distinguished himself fighting Burgoyne at Ticonderoga, spent the winter of 1777-78 with the Continental Army at Valley Forge, and fought with Washington at Monmouth, NJ, and at Yorktown, VA, the final battle of the war. He served as Thomas Jefferson's Secretary of War through Jefferson's two terms as president.

But an early Dearborn with much closer Portsmouth ties would be one Benjamin Dearborn, a renaissance man who served as schoolmaster in the mid-1700s. Brewster tells us of this Dearborn who maintained a house in town, the first floor of which was a shop where Mrs. Dearborn pursued retail interests on what sounds to be a small scale. Apparently, Benjamin Dearborn was the first schoolmaster willing to instruct young ladies so that they might receive "that education which fitted them for ornaments to society." After some time, he built a structure to accommodate an academy behind his home and hired assistant teachers so that all branches of learning might be addressed. The building also included a hall for dancing; it is entirely probable that Dearborn provided instruction in the gavotte to dancing students as well.

The schoolmaster was also the inventor of, among other things, Dearborn's Patent Balances and "an engine for throwing water." He also addressed the problems of musical notation, publishing a system requiring only letterpress characters to indicate pitch and duration, in his Scheme for Reducing the Science of Music to a More Simple State. And it's hard to imagine this man having the time, but he also was the Benjamin Dearborn who took over Daniel Fowle's *New Hampshire Gazette* from 1776 to 1778, changing its name to *The Freeman's Journal* for the duration. Surely a man of such accomplishment deserved to have a street named for him.

The same **Benjamin Dearborn** was also a visionary city planner, with a scheme to develop a community at the Durham end of the Piscataqua Bridge. The name he proposed for his new town: **Franklin City**.

WHEN JOHN DENNETT built his home on the North Mill Pond in 1680, his only neighbor was Richard Jackson. Expanded by Ephraim Dennett, one of the founders of the Portsmouth Mill Company in 1821, the home eventually reached the proportions of a mansion. It became known as "The Beehive" – a Widow Dennett kept bees.

*The Christian Shores **Dennett House** as it appeared in the late 19th century. From a watercolor by Sarah Haven Foster, courtesy of the Portsmouth Public Library.*

By 1821 Portsmouth was home to a Jeremiah Dennett, shipmaster; Mark Dennett, farmer; Richard and Joseph Dennett, gentlemen; John Dennett, joiner; and George Dennett, a boat builder, who lived on **DENNETT STREET**.

*The **Marsh House** on State Street sits one door to the west of Temple Israel. PA*

IN A CRYPT BUILT into the retaining wall of the burying grounds surrounding St. John's Church rests one Matthew S. Marsh, perhaps the namesake for **MARSH LANE**. Brewster tells us Matthew Marsh owned at least one ship and was partial owner of another engaged in the India trade in the early years of the 19th century.

The Abraham Lincoln Presidential Library and Museum holds a pair of obscure documents relating to Portsmouth's Matthew S. Marsh. In 1835, "Honest Abe" was appointed postmaster of New Salem, Illinois, a job which earned the man who would one day be the nation's sixteenth president $60 a year, plus a percentage of his postage sales. According to one biography, "he ran an informal post office, often doing favors for friends, such as under-charging them for mailing letters."

Apparently, on Wednesday, September 16, 1835, our Matthew S. Marsh called at the New Salem post office. What Marsh didn't know was that Lincoln manned the office only two days a week, on Saturdays as the mail made its way north to the Warren County Court House in Monmouth, and on Thursdays for its return trip.

According to the description of the first of the Marsh documents: "Lincoln is absent from his post office. Matthew S. Marsh calls, and not finding Lincoln, looks through mail and takes home letter from his brother, George H. Marsh of Portsmouth, NH."

Reputedly the earliest known photograph of **Abraham Lincoln**, *c. 1846, the year he was elected to the U.S. House of Representatives.*

The following Tuesday, Marsh returns to the post office. "Lincoln franks letter from M. S. Marsh to his brother in New Hampshire. Marsh writes that Lincoln is very careless in leaving office open and unattended, and that he could have charged double the postage he marked on cover of recent letter. But Lincoln, says Marsh, would not have done that even if he had noticed [an] incorrect amount."

Was Lincoln trying to smooth ruffled feathers by undercharging a disgruntled Yankee?

WALKING ALONG **PROSPECT STREET**, it only takes a bit of imagination to put yourself back two centuries and envision the view that inspired the namers – down to the North Mill Pond, across the city, to the river beyond. A fine prospect indeed.

SPARHAWKS HAVE POPULATED Portsmouth, as well as nearby Kittery, from the early days – a John Sparhawk maintained a shop on State Street from 1771. But you must never pass **SPARHAWK STREET** again without say-ing a quiet thank-you to one Mary Sparhawk, a young lady who charmed a soldier and saved Portsmouth.

According to Ray Brighton, Capt. Henry Mowatt and a small fleet of British ships held Portsmouth Harbor in full blockade in 1775. But this maintaining of blockades was a tedious business. Capt. Mowatt grew weary of what company he had on board, and came ashore intent on visiting old acquaintances, the loyalist Sparhawk family of Kittery Point. And there he met and fell under the spell of our Mary Sparhawk.

When Mowatt received orders to "burn, destroy and lay waste" to a number of New England seaboard towns, Portsmouth included, Mary dissuaded him. Determined to burn *some* town to the ground, he set sail for Falmouth – today's Portland, Maine – which he proceeded to bombard for eight hours on October 24, 1775, then went ashore, torching what remained.

ORIGINALLY KNOWN AS **MYSTIC STREET**, today's **STARK STREET** took its present name when new streets were laid out and old ones renamed following the above-mentioned sale of City Farm land in 1875. Both the street and New Castle's Fort Stark honor Londonderry native John Stark (1728-1822), commander of New Hampshire forces at the Battle of Bennington.

A member of Rogers' Rangers in the French and Indian Wars, General Stark fought at Bunker Hill and took part in the New Jersey campaign, commanding Washington's right wing at Trenton. While recruiting troops back in New Hampshire, however, he was passed over for a brigadier generalship and resigned. Four months later, he was commissioned by the Exeter legislature as brigadier general of the New Hampshire militia.

General John Stark. From the collection of the State of New Hampshire, Division of Historical Resources.

Stark had a way with memorable phrases. His "live free or die" (the complete quote was "live free or die – death is not the worst of evils") was adopted as the state motto, and his famous exhortation, "There are the Red

Coats and they are ours, or this night Molly Stark sleeps a widow," preceded his victory at Bennington in 1777, a battle considered a major turning point of the war, leading as it did to the Battle of Saratoga and Burgoyne's defeat.

PREDATING THE DAYS of the coal baron Walker brothers as it does, **WALKER STREET** most likely takes its name from what Ray Brighton refers to as "a line of Gideon Walkers, one of whom signed the Association Test in 1776." A Captain Walker was listed in the 1727 census figures as owning four slaves, and a Colonel Gideon Walker (1766-1829) is buried in the North Cemetery. This Walker was a miller who had obviously also seen military service. Presumably, he is the same Gideon Walker who, in 1821, incorporated with Mark Laighton and Ephraim Dennett as the Portsmouth Mill Company, producers of woolens.

ONE OF THE BUSIEST thoroughfares in Portsmouth started out in life as **NEWINGTON ROAD**. In 1850, it was known as **CREEK STREET**. Today's **WOODBURY AVENUE** carries the name of one of this town's most accomplished citizens – and *only* an avenue would do for this man. The mansion Levi Woodbury (1789-1851) built may have been razed to make way for Woodbury Manor, but the great man's legacy echoes down through the years.

In 62 years of life, Levi Woodbury served as clerk of the state senate, associate justice of the state Supreme Court,

Levi Woodbury holds the honor of being the first Supreme Court justice to have attended law school, and the last secretary of the Treasury to pay off the national debt. Had he not died in 1851, it was likely that he would have been the Democratic party's nominee for president the following year. Courtesy of the Department of the Navy, Naval Historical Center.

Levi Woodbury's mansion, site today of the **Woodbury Manor** *apartments. From C.S. Gurney,* Portsmouth, Historic and Picturesque.

governor of the state, member and speaker of the state House of Representatives, United States senator, secretary of the Navy, secretary of the Treasury, and justice of the Supreme Court of the United States. His record of public service is unmatched in this state.

Born in Francestown, Woodbury came to Portsmouth in 1819. He had graduated with honors from Dartmouth in 1809, studied law briefly at Tappin Reeve's Law School in Litchfield, CT, then continued his studies privately. He was admitted to the bar in 1812.

Fourteen hundred miles from here, the city of Woodbury, Minnesota, credits the derivation of its name from that of Portsmouth's Levi Woodbury as well. A close friend of Woodbury's, one John Colby, chaired a county board which was given the task of renaming the town of Red Rock, when it was discovered that the name was already taken elsewhere in the state.

Downtown's Island
Nobles Island

I T'S BEEN A LONG time since **Noble's Island** stood apart from the shore on its islandly own. In 1822, Market Street was extended, crossing onto the island to carry vehicular and then train traffic across the island to the new bridge to Maine. Sometime after 1850 another causeway was built to continue rail lines to Newington and beyond.

The Ham family was the earliest owner of the island; in their day, of course, it was called **Ham's Island**. Five Hams can be found on the 1727 tax rolls. Twelve Ham households, consisting of "19 males over the age of 16,

18 males under the age of 16 and 32 females" are enumerated in the 1790 census for Rockingham County. None of these Hams held slaves. An Edward A. Ham joined the California gold rush in 1849.

Moses Noble failed to sign the Association Test in 1776. Mark Noble, on the other hand, was part of a mob that attempted an attack upon suspected Tory sympathizer John Stavers' Earl of Halifax hotel, sustaining a blow in the ensuing melee that rendered him insane for the rest of his days, according to Brewster. Captain Robert Noble, listed in the 1821 directory as "shipmaster," and his brothers built a fleet of 14 fishing vessels.

DOWNTOWN WEST OF MAPLEWOOD AVENUE
Bridge Street – Islington Street – Maplewood Avenue

PERHAPS TODAY'S oddly named **BRIDGE STREET** skirted the shoreline of the North Mill Pond in Colonial times, leading directly onto the bridge across it. What we do know is that by 1813 it dead-ended at a distillery at the corner of Deer Street, beyond which lay a ropewalk. By 1850 both of those were gone, replaced by railroad tracks, a station and a depot – and saddled with a name that no longer makes much sense and must cause a few visitors to scratch their heads.

*The **Boston & Portland Railroad** station and depot. The railroad came to Portsmouth in the late 1830s. TG.*

EARLY IN PORTSMOUTH'S history, Peter Livius was granted milling privileges on the North Mill Pond, originally referred to as **LIVIN'S CREEK**, most probably a corruption of the Livius name. The mill business must have been good – it wasn't long before Livius had built himself a mansion on the North Mill Pond as well. The area around the Livius mill quickly developed into a little community in its own right. According to Sarah Haven Foster's 1896 *Portsmouth Guide Book*, "quite a little village collected here, which was called ISLINGTON, giving its name to the road and creek."

There are no family names or family ties to explain the presence of an ISLINGTON STREET in colonial Portsmouth. Rather, I believe we can take this as another example of Bruce Ingmire's Anglicization theory at work. Islington Street led to that community of hearty souls who took up residence out at Portsmouth Plains.

Ray Brighton reports that hobos were known to take a break from road and rail to camp along ISLINGTON CREEK, presumably through the years of the Great Depression. The land between the tracks and the North Mill Pond, he tells us, comprised a well known "hobo resort."

EARLY IN NOVEMBER of 1887, the town planted a total of 138 maples down both sides of the NORTH ROAD (once known as MILL STREET) so it comes as no surprise that within fifteen years, the North Road was being called MAPLEWOOD AVENUE. It also should come as no surprise that the town would go to such an effort to beautify what was in effect the driveway leading straight to the front gate of business tycoon, political heavyweight and one-time mayor Frank Jones' palatial "farmhouse" at the intersection of Maplewood and Woodbury Avenues.

The street leading off the bridge then led directly into Vaughan Street, making it one of the primary arteries into downtown. By 1925, the Portland, Saco & Portsmouth Railroad was coming through the north side of town, drawing the center of business activity westward

A 1930 map refers to Islington Street as **King's High Way.**

from the river front. Maplewood as we know it today, however, would not appear on an official map until 1975, another brainchild of urban renewal.

OFF ISLINGTON
Autumn Street – Brewster* Street – Cornwall Street
Dover Street – Frenchman's Lane – Hill Street – Langdon* Street
McDonough Street – Parker Street – Pearl Street – Rock Street
Rockingham Street – Salem Street – Sudbury Street – Tanner Street

SOMETIME BETWEEN 1813 and 1850, ROCK STREET and BREWSTER STREET swapped names. We will start with the story of BREWSTER LANE, which later came to be called Rock Street. In 1813, Brewster Lane sat one street to the west of Pearl Street.

Journalist/historian Charles Brewster comes to mind as the logical inspiration for the name of this street, except for one small problem – Brewster Lane appears on the 1813 map; it could hardly have been named for a boy who was turning an unremarkable eleven that year. But we should take pause and recognize the man who forged the link between Revolutionary Portsmouth and the Portsmouth of today. Writing in the mid-19th century, he still had access to people with living memory of far earlier times, and he brought them to vivid life in his weekly newspaper columns, titled *Rambles About Portsmouth*, a key resource for historians from that day forward.

No, the Brewster who must certainly be commemorated here has to be the indomitable Mary Brewster.

On June 26, 1696, calamity struck a group of independent-minded settlers who lived far beyond the outskirts of town, in an area known then as the Portsmouth Plains – today the section where Route 33 meets Islington and Peverly Hill, site of the Plains ball park and Calvary Cemetery.

The prolific 19th-century journalist and historian Charles Brewster. Portsmouth – and this writer – owe this chronicler of his day a tremendous debt of gratitude. PA

In what has been described as "the most murderous attack by the Indians that our local history records," five houses and nine barns were destroyed, fourteen inhabitants were killed and numerous others were wounded. Four were captured. But a number managed to escape and make their way to the nearest garrison and safety, where a detail was put together to attempt a rescue of the captured. The Indians were trailed through the GREAT SWAMP (today we call it the GREAT BOG) and overtaken as they breakfasted on a hill to the south, known to this day as BREAKFAST HILL.

Back at the site of the massacre, Mrs. Mary Brewster lay scalped and left for dead. But Mary recovered and went on to give birth to seven children, from whom, we are told by Hazlett in 1815, "most of the Brewster families in this vicinity have descended." Do think of Mary the next time you pass Brewster Street.

TODAY'S CORNWALL STREET first appears on the 1813 map as CREEK STREET, a reference to Islington Creek. Perhaps its renaming to Cornwall is another example of nostalgic Anglicization.

TWO VERSIONS OF the tale of the death of a Frenchman come down to us, the more colorful directly from Charles Brewster, the less detailed via a correction Brewster offers in a later edition of his *Rambles*. The first, we are told, on the word of an eyewitness, details a three-month-long visit to Portsmouth Harbor by five ships of the French fleet in 1782. Two thousand Frenchmen – officers, soldiers and marines – became part of the local landscape. Commander of two regiments of marines, the Marquis de Vaudreuil was grandly fêted. Splendid balls in honor of the town's visitors were attended and, as time went on, the foreigners became known at some of the rowdier

The Marquis de Vaudreuil (1698-1778).

drinking establishments at the head of the North Mill Pond. And one night, a dead Frenchman was discovered, the victim of a tavern quarrel it is supposed, in the vicinity of today's FRENCHMAN'S LANE.

No one was ever arrested in connection with the murder, and Brewster tells us that the Frenchman in question was laid to rest in Maplewood Avenue's North Cemetery. However, later Brewster brings to light information gleaned from Dr. Joshua Brackett's journals, to the effect that the Frenchman, by name one John Dushan, died four years *prior* to the visit of the ships of the French fleet, in 1778. Regardless of the date, the story inspired Benjamin P. Shillaber to write the *Ballad of Frenchman's Lane* a century later.

> Most lovely the spot, yet dark was the tale
> That made the red lips of boyhood pale,
> Of the Frenchman's doom and the bitter strife,
> Of the blood stained sword and the gleaming knife,
> Of the gory rock set the wrong to speak,
> In Frenchman's Lane, up by Islington Creek.
> ~ B.P. Shillaber

MODEST LANGDON STREET is first seen on the 1850 map as ANN STREET. By 1877, it carried the name of yet another powerful Portsmouth dynasty.

Tobias Langdon (?-1664) is the common ancestor of the many prominent Langdons of Portsmouth. A native of Cornwall, he had found his way here by 1656, when he married Elizabeth Sherburne. Elizabeth's father, Henry Sherburne, who came over as one of John Mason's men, settled at Strawbery Banke in 1632.

Tobias and Elizabeth had four children. Their eldest, Captain Tobias Langdon (1660-1725), married Mary Hubbard of Salisbury, NH; they had nine children. Their youngest, John Langdon (1707-1780)

Woodbury Langdon. Painting by John Singleton Copley. www.john-singletoncopley.org.

married Mary Hall of Exeter. John and Mary had six children; their two sons, Woodbury and John rose to prominence in the region and the young country they helped wrest from the English.

Woodbury Langdon (1739-1805) grew up to become a merchant, judge of the Supreme Court of New Hampshire and a delegate to the Continental Congress, and an unquestioned patriot who took part in the 1774 raid on Fort William and Mary. Accused of seeking French aid to undermine English embargos at the outbreak of the Revolution, he was imprisoned by the British for several months in New York. He served as the first president of the New Hampshire State Senate in 1784 and 1785.

Sitting on the supreme court of New Hampshire in 1782, Woodbury Langdon served again in this capacity from 1786 to 1790. William Plummer, governor of New Hampshire from 1816 to 1819, wrote of Langdon: "He was a man of great independence and decision – bold, keen, and sarcastic, and spoke his mind of men and measures with great freedom."

It is said that Woodbury's brother John (1741-1819) was thrown out the window of his parents' burning house (located on the farm we know today as the Urban Forestry Center) as a baby. If there is any truth to the story, it was a fortuitous rescue, for this man would go on to become a framer of the Constitution and New Hampshire's first governor. Starting out his career in the offices of a merchant, he came to command a ship of his own, but eventually gave up the sea for the life of a highly successful merchant ashore.

New Hampshire's first elected governor, John Langdon. From the collections of the State of NH, Division of Historical Resources.

Well established when English taxation ignited the small, persistent fires that would lead to the full blown conflagration of revolt, he was one of the ring leaders of the 1774 attack on Fort William and Mary. In 1775 and 1776, he served as a delegate to the Continental Congress, and was a member and speaker of the provincial legislature in 1776 and 1777. He commanded a troop of volunteers and was present for Burgoyne's defeat in Saratoga. With public credit exhausted, John Langdon outfitted General Stark's troops out of his own pocket.

Langdon owned a boat yard on Badger's Island. In 1778, Congress appointed him an agent of the government for the building of ships of war. As such, he had the difficult job of supplying materials for both the *Ranger* and the *America*; John Paul Jones (see Jones Avenue, page 138) would express great frustration with the pace of construction on the ships that were to be under his command.

> George Washington, writing in 1789 of Portsmouth and his visit to the Langdon Mansion on Pleasant Street in particular, had this to say:
> *"There are some good houses (among which Col. Langdon's may be esteemed the first)."*

Through the 1770s and '80s, Langdon served both his state and the emerging nation. He was elected president (governor) of New Hampshire four times, holding office off and on from the age of 46 to 73. 1788 saw him a delegate to the convention framing the Constitution, and a member of the state convention that ratified it.

Samuel Eliot Morison, in his *John Paul Jones: A Sailor's Biography*, tells us that John Langdon was not an eloquent man; rather, it was his "disinterested devotion to the interests of his country, sacrificing his property and risking his life in the cause of liberty" that explained his popularity. George Washington stopped by Langdon's Pleasant Street mansion for tea during his visit to the city in 1789.

PARALLELING ISLINGTON IS McDONOUGH STREET. Sarah Foster describes the scene before the days of the street and the railroad that came to front it: "It was a delightful spot, much frequented by boys and pedestrians ... a shady little retreat in the neighborhood, called McDONOUGH'S DELL, through which flowed the brook, now polluted and dried up." And Brewster tells us about one James McDonough, an entrepreneurial gentleman who arrived in town with "some trading capital" around 1757 or so. He must have been successful in business, as his property taxes went from a mere £2 in 1758 to £27 ten years later. By 1768, as a man of wealth and position, he and Abigail Sheafe, eldest daughter of the illustrious Jacob Sheafe, made plans to marry. However, with absolutely no explanation, Abigail was left standing at the altar and James McDonough was never seen again.

THE STORIES OF **PARKER STREET** and **TANNER STREET** go hand in hand. Tradition has it that in 1703 one William Parker married Miss Zerviah Stanley, purportedly the daughter of the Earl of Derby – apparently, without having gained the Earl's permission. The two found it necessary to flee to this country and settled in Portsmouth. Parker took up as a tanner; the tanning yard near his residence was used for the same purpose for more than a century. Both a Tanner Street and a Tanner Court attest to this fact.

A second William Parker (1703-1781), the eldest son of William and Zerviah, was a self-made man. Raised to the tanning trade, he chose rather to be a schoolmaster. Later, having studied the law, he was admitted to the bar. He was appointed registrar of probate, a judge of the Admiralty, a notary public (the only notary to be found in the province for many years), a member of the general assembly from 1765 to 1774, and a judge of the Superior Court, continuing in this office until the Revolution. He is often referenced as "Judge Parker."

John Parker (1732-1791), Judge Parker's second son who was most often referred to as "Sheriff Parker," was the gentleman who read the Declaration of Independence from the balcony of the State House in Market Square. Appointed sheriff of the Province by Governor John Wentworth in 1771, he went on to become the

John Parker Jr., the son of Noah Parker, paired up with Nathaniel Adams, of *The Annals of Portsmouth* fame, to survey and map the town in 1778.

Sheriff of Rockingham when the Province was broken up into counties. After the Revolution, Washington appointed him marshal of the District of New Hampshire.

Samuel Parker (1744-1804), Judge Parker's third son, became rector of Trinity Church, Boston, and in time, Episcopal bishop of the eastern diocese.

Noah Parker (1734-1787), the only son of Sheriff Parker, was a black-and-white smith, which is to say he worked in metals requiring both the application of heat (blacksmithing) and those that can be worked cool. He was also the first Universalist preacher in Portsmouth. This was the same Noah Parker whose large, oddly shaped house on the corner of Daniel and Penhallow Streets was called the Ark.

AT ONE TIME, the street running just to the west of what was then known as Parker's Lane was called **BARTLETT STREET**, but some time between 1830 and 1840, Bartlett changed names to **PEARL STREET**. The Bartletts we've already met, but whence the name Pearl Street remains a mystery.

Today known as **THE PEARL OF PORTSMOUTH**, the church on the corner of Pearl and Hanover started life in 1859 as the Free Will Baptist Church. In 1915, it became home to the multi-denominational People's Baptist Church, an all black congregation which disbanded in the 1970s. In the 1980s, The Pearl became "72," a fine dining establishment. Today, The Pearl has returned to its roots, as a wedding chapel and function hall, and takes its place on the National Register of Historic Places.

*Once home to the **People's Baptist Church** on Pearl Street.. PA*

Nathaniel Holloway, founder and chairman of the Seacoast Martin Luther King Jr. Coalition, campaigned for twenty years to see the Reverend

*23-year-old Boston University doctoral student **Martin Luther King Jr.** spoke here in 1952, on the People's Baptist Church's 59ᵗʰ anniversary. Coretta Scott, a student at the New England Conservatory of Music, was a featured soloist singing with a guest choir from Malden, MA, that day.*

King's birthday observed in New Hampshire. In 2003, he approached the City Council to rename a street in honor of the fallen civil rights leader. The Council referred the matter to the Planning Board, and Pearl Street surfaced as the most obvious choice.

IN BREWSTER'S *Rambles About Portsmouth*, we learn that 18th-century ROCK STREET was nothing but a cow pasture. In the midst of the pasture was a particularly lofty rock. The pasture was known locally as ROCK PASTURE, and from this, Rock Street took its name, as did today's ROCK PARK. By the mid-19th century, the area was the site of the Sagamore Mill, a manufactory of cotton.

WE LIVE IN ROCKINGHAM COUNTY, and we also have a ROCKINGHAM STREET, and with good reason. The second Marquis of Rockingham, Charles Watson-Wentworth (1730-1782) was a friend of democracy in the court of George III. (His likeness appears on page 1.) Appointed First Lord of the Treasury (prime minister) in 1765, he undid the work of Lord Grenville by repealing the detested Stamp Act. This and other pro-colonist stands saw him replaced within the year by William Pitt the Elder. Rockingham was appointed prime minister a second time in 1782, and his first official act was to recognize the United States of America. Fourteen weeks later he died of influenza.

Rockingham Street is first seen on the 1850 map as PENN STREET, perhaps named after Quaker visionary William Penn (1644-1718), who obtained the charter to settle Pennsylvania in 1681, though I can find no connection between him and Portsmouth. But a quick look at two streets further to the west – SALEM STREET and DOVER STREET – may give us the clue: both Salem and Dover have clear Quaker connections as well.

THE OUTSKIRTS OF TOWN
Middle Road – Portsmouth Plains – Plains Avenue
Banfield* Road – Peverly** Hill– Spinney Road
Sherburne** Road – Ocean Road – Lang* Road – Gosling Road

LYING TWO MILES from Market Square as the crow flies, PORTSMOUTH PLAINS was far enough from the heart of Portsmouth to warrant having its own public houses. The first scheduled stage began running between Portsmouth and Boston in 1761; by 1764, it was making a stop at the Plains Tavern. The Globe Tavern once stood on the site of today's Calvary Cemetery, while a Falstaff Tavern lay closer to downtown, near the intersection of Middle Street and Mendum Avenue. In 1893, a writer to the *Portsmouth Journal* expressed the opinion that the section of highway from Middle Road where it joins South Street, the site of the Orange Tree Inn (also known as the Pound Tavern), to the Plains should simply be called TAVERN ROAD.

The **Orange Tree Inn** took its unusual alternate name, **The Pound Inn**, from the fact that the innkeeper also served as the keeper of an actual animal pound. The elective position paid no stipend, but the keeper was entitled to the fee required to reclaim wayward horses, cows and pigs.

As already recounted, the Plains was the site of the fearsome Indian raid in 1692. PLAINS AVENUE recalls the bloody occurrence.

ONCE KNOWN AS REBELLION ROAD, though why I have not been able to discover, BANFIELD ROAD was named for a family of Banfields who show up in town records as early as the 17th century, if under variant spellings of the surname. Hugh Banfill, the first child of Portsmouth residents John Banfill and Mary Pickering, was born in 1673. On the list of taxpayers in 1727 were Hugh, George and a Capt. Samuel Banfield.

THOMAS PEVERLY (c. 1620-1670) held 110 acres south of the Plains, extending from Sagamore Creek to what

A 19th-century scion of the family, **Freeman Peverly** *was listed as a laborer, living at 97 Water Street, in the 1860-1861 city directory. PA*

was known as PEVERLY'S HILL back in Brewster's day, just as it still is today. Peverly held the position of surveyor of highways, so it is particularly apt that he should lend his name to PEVERLY HILL ROAD.

SPINNEYS OF NORMAN descent made the crossing to England with William the Conqueror in 1066. Brewster credits one Thomas Spinney with being the first of the name to come to this country from England, in the mid-1600s. According to a family genealogy, Thomas Spinney "came to 'Piscataqua Colony' (in Captain Fernald's ship) at Strawberry Banke, now known as Portsmouth, New Hampshire," settled in Eliot, became the first schoolmaster in the area and married in 1650. Thirty years later, a Joseph Spinney took up residence on the Kittery side of the Piscataqua at a point soon called SPINNEY'S NECK – today SPINNEY COVE. In time, these Spinneys would seek each other out and discover that they were brothers, Thomas having left England when Joseph was still a babe in arms.

A **James Spinney** made it into the town book covering 1720 as 'Jams Spiney.'

Brewster credits these brothers as the forebears of Portsmouth's later Spinneys. These would include Ebineezer Spinney, a farmer with land on the North Road in 1821, and Daniel Spinney who "enjoyed a large reputation as an orchardist and farmer." He was particularly famous for his fine pears. Daniel lived on WHITE'S ROAD, which would later take the name of SPINNEY ROAD.

THEY'VE BEEN PLAYING baseball at PLAINS FIELD since the first game was scheduled in 1866, when Portsmouth's best took on a team from Concord. Concord took the match, 31 to 26.

IN 1759, A ROAD WAS cut through then heavily forested land in a perfectly straight line from the Great Bay to the Piscataqua and named the **RIVER ROAD**. Felled pines, some reputedly as great as two hundred feet in length and two to three feet wide at the base, were most probably hauled along this road as they made their way from the interior to the river for transport to England, where they would be used in the making of masts for His Majesty's Royal Navy. In the 1930s, River Road's name was changed to **GOSLING ROAD**.

THE SHERBURNE FAMILY dates to the early days of Strawbery Banke. **SHERBURNE ROAD**, far beyond the outskirts of Portsmouth proper, remembers this founding family.

According to a Langdon genealogy, the first Henry Sherburne arrived with the Mason party in 1630. By the end of the 17th century, the second Henry Sherburne, Portsmouth's first tavern-keeper, had made his fortune in the vicinity of today's Prescott Park. His influence extended far beyond the doors of his tavern. Brother-in-law of Lieutenant Governor John Wentworth, Sherburne enjoyed a seat on the Governor's Council. He also served on a commission entrusted with the building of a State House in 1758.

*The **Sherburne House** at Strawbery Banke was home to Captain John Sherburne, his family and servants. Built in 1695, it survives as the oldest stud-framed house in the Piscataqua region.*

This Henry's son Edward, an aid to General John Sullivan, died in the Revolutionary War of wounds suffered in battle. His brother, Samuel, inherited and became a successful merchant. His contribution to the Revolution was to sit on a committee tasked with the creation of a government for New Hampshire.

A John Sherburne was one of the 31 citizens of Portsmouth who refused to sign the Association Test in 1776. On the other hand, John Samuel Sherburne (1757-1830) served as an aide-de-camp to General William Whipple. The loss of a leg fighting under General Sullivan did not prevent him from pursuing a legal career after the Revolution, a stepping stone to becoming a congressman, a U.S. Attorney and a judge of the U.S. District Court of New Hampshire.

Judge John S. Sherburne. From the website of the US District Court, District of New Hampshire.

Sherburnes ruled on sea as well as on land. Captain Nathaniel Sherburn, who had taken the helm of the *Amhurst* in 1761 and the *Fox* the following year, perished on his way to Granada in the *Abigail* in 1770. A Captain Daniel Sherburne served as the secretary of the local Masonic lodge in 1765.

As life became more centralized and mechanized, entrepreneurial dairy farmer Andrew B. Sherburne pioneered selling milk to the urban population of Portsmouth in 1840. This Sherburne also served as surveyor of highways. Perhaps it was he who laid out Sherburne Road.

OCEAN ROAD was once called SODOM ROAD. I really don't want to know why.

DANIEL AND ROBERT LANG were both 18th-century sea captains. No fewer than seven Langs signed the Association test in 1776. One hundred years later, Thomas M. Lang was living, and most probably farming, on LANG ROAD.

CHAPTER 5

19 TH CENTURY EXPANSION

*Late 19th-century construction along **Miller Avenue**. PA*

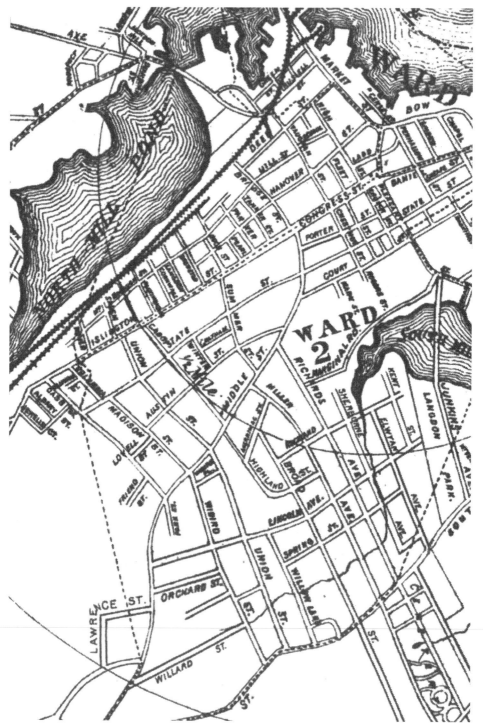

From Map of the City of Portsmouth, N.H.   *W.A. Greenough & Co., Publisher, 1903. PA*

FROM COW LANE TO RICHARDS* AVENUE

B ACK IN THE EARLY days of Portsmouth, a dirt road made its way from Middle Street down towards South. Along this dirt road ambled cows on their way to pasture, or eventually, on their way to the slaughterhouse that awaited them at the corner of South Street. This dirt path was aptly named COW LANE.

By 1813, Cow Lane bore the more dignified name of JOSHUA STREET (though the slaughterhouse would remain until 1871). Ray Brighton tells us it honored yet another member of the powerful Wentworth clan, Joshua Wentworth (1742-1809) "who lived in the brick house at the head of the street." By the age of 28, this Wentworth was so successful as a merchant that he ranked as one of the wealthiest citizens of Portsmouth, but he was never considered an "inner-circle" member of the family.

> Unlike the majority of the Wentworths, **Joshua Wentworth** was a staunch supporter of the Revolution. A signer of the Association Test, he oversaw the often difficult job of supplying New Hampshire's troops for the duration of the war.

In 1838, the powers that be decided that the road leading directly to the entrance of a newly opened burial ground should now be called AUBURN STREET. In 1831, the beautifully landscaped Mt. Auburn Cemetery had opened in Cambridge. Founded by the Massachusetts Horticultural Society, Mount Auburn marked a new development in cemeteries sometimes referred to as the "Rural Cemetery Movement," a move away from crowded, aging urban graveyards to park-like, naturalistic spaces on the outskirts of towns.

Brighton surmises that "some person thought it was worthwhile to copy Boston names and the street was renamed Auburn for its mortuary associations." The new

*A contemporary view of Cambridge's park-like **Mt. Auburn Cemetery** by British photographer S.J. White.*

burial ground followed suit – it became known as AU-BURN CEMETERY.

What many think of as one cemetery at the corner of Sagamore Avenue and South Street is actually five. Once the cow pasture belonging to a family by the name of Cheevers, it was eventually developed into the complex of cemeteries we know today. Part is still called AUBURN CEMETERY. The beautifully landscaped 13 acres of the PROPRIETORS' BURYING GROUND is the final resting place of Captain Daniel Marcy, among others. Leonard Cotton (?-1839) is buried in a vault along the South Street wall of COTTON'S CEMETERY, designated a burial ground in 1671. It adjoins the Proprietors' Burial Ground along its eastern side. Still active today are the SAGAMORE CEMETERY and HARMONY GROVE, the section backing up to Little Harbor Road. Resting peacefully in the latter are Supreme Court justice Levi Woodbury, New Hampshire governor John H. Bartlett, and brewer Frank Jones.

The Proprietors' Burying Ground dates back to 1831.

Fast-forward thirty years to the spring of 1861. The Civil War has broken out with the Confederate attack on Fort Sumter. In Portsmouth, far to the north, a young man described as somewhat shy and sensitive – resembling Lord Byron "in his best days," Brewster tells us – spends his spring that year setting and staking embryonic elm trees down Auburn Street. Perhaps he and his friend Dr. Robert Odiorne Treadwell work together planting each sapling; perhaps the young man matches the good doctor's efforts on the opposite side of the street. Within two years, the tender trees will be well established – and Henry Lakeman Richards will be dead at Gettysburg.

The young man with the soul of a poet went to war late that summer. Fourteen months later, he returned home to recover from wounds sustained on the battlefield at Antietam, but as soon as his health permitted, he rejoined the Army of the Rappahannock. On July 2,

1863, the second day of the Battle of Gettysburg, he was cut down by a rifle ball. He passed the night on the battlefield, "the rebels…treating him kindly, bringing him water and giving him food." The next day he was removed to a field hospital, where his leg was amputated "under the influence of chloroform." He died July 4th, age 39. With a civic outpouring of sorrow and speeches, Auburn Street was renamed **RICHARDS AVENUE** in his honor.

In an 1881 editorial, Richards was recalled thus: "Few who remember him well can walk under the shadow of the trees which his helping hand planted without recurring to the memory of his life and the sterling character he bore from his early youth to his glorious but untimely end." The writer goes on to recollect afternoons of fishing together, when "as the boat lay motionless upon the placid tide, glowing like molten gold from the reflection of the gorgeous sunset sky, in the stillness of such an hour and with such poetical surroundings, it was his wont to repeat long passages from his favorite poets, always in a low murmur, but with an unction that told how deeply he felt the spirit of the poetry." Spare a thought for Henry Richards the next time you stroll down the street that bears his name, under a newer crop of trees, his elms having long since fallen to the Dutch elm disease of the 1960s.

In the 1870s, Mrs. Mary Cutts left $17,000 for the improvement of Richards Avenue which funded the widening of the street and its paving from one end to the other in brick. Sidewalks were installed – on *both* sides. Such public works projects are never trouble-free; it took a full six years to see the plan from its conception to the reopening of the street to carriage traffic.

All the while, during this period of snail-paced improvement, skaters were enjoying a skating rink located a short distance down Richards. And in all weather, the fine straight road attracted another kind of sport: horse racing, under saddle or burdened with conveyances.

Some of the bricks from the 19th-century restoration of Richards Avenue today form a patio around a gazebo on the Griffin farm at the corner of Richards Avenue and South Street.

LAFAYETTE ROAD

IN 1782, THE FRENCH FLEET lay in Portsmouth harbor. The Marquis de Lafayette (1757-1834) came from Providence, Rhode Island, to pay a call on his principal officers who were boarding at the William Pitt tavern, presumably enjoying the greater creature comforts that life ashore can offer. According to Brewster, it was a "happy meeting, enjoyed with all that enthusiasm which characterizes the habits of the French."

Marie Joseph Paul Yves Roche Gilbert du Motier, the Marquis de Lafayette.

PHS

Lafayette made his second visit to Portsmouth in 1824. Accompanied by his son, George Washington Lafayette, the French hero of the Revolution was escorted into town by a two-mile-long grand procession of the town's worthiest inhabitants, on horseback and in carriages. A thousand school children lined the streets, shouting "Welcome, Lafayette!" as the general proceeded into the downtown to the accompaniment of a military band and the cheers of the citizenry. A dismal September rain did nothing to dispel the excitement. After much speechifying, an emotional reunion with soldiers of the Revolution and an elegant reception at the home of the late Governor John Langdon, the largest assemblage to ever dine together in Portsmouth gathered in Jefferson Hall, followed by a ball given in Lafayette's honor.

LAFAYETTE ROAD, then more grandly known as LAFAYETTE HIGHWAY, was opened to travel the same year as the general's last call on our city.

DOWN BY THE SOUTH MILL POND
Langdon Park
Junkins Avenue – Parrott Avenue

IN 1867, JOHN LANGDON ELWYN gave the city five rolling acres of land for the creation of LANGDON PARK, which opened to great fanfare in 1876. Easy access to the park from the downtown area, however, was not available until **JUNKINS AVENUE** was laid out in 1894. Dr. William O. Junkins, Portsmouth's mayor in 1895-96, was among the mix of simple townsfolk and dignitaries who welcomed William Howard Taft as he stumped for re-election in 1912. The itinerary for that visit reads like those of any of today's presidential hopefuls: a stop at the Portsmouth Naval Shipyard and the Sparhawk Mansion in Kittery, the Elks Lodge, lunch at the Rockingham Hotel, capped off with a speech at the South Playground.

Dr. William O. Junkins. His portrait hangs in the City Council chambers.

THE STREET THAT SKIRTS the northwestern margin of the South Mill Pond began life in 1882 as **MARGINAL ROAD**, traversing an area created by one of the town's first land-fill operations. Planning for the project began seven years earlier, in the midst of a general uproar about stench abatement. Some things never change.

Ray Brighton tells us, with such authority that it never crossed my mind to doubt him for a moment, that Marginal Road was renamed **PARROTT AVENUE** early in the 20th century in honor of the Portsmouth native, Rear Admiral Enoch G. Parrott (1816-1879), in-

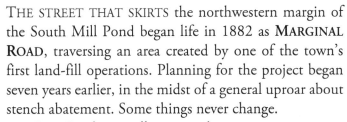

The iron-clad monitor USS **Monadnock** *was built in 1863; Enoch G. Parrott was commander. Steam-powered iron-clads date back as far as 1855.*

ventor of the Civil War Parrott rifle. Well, it turns out that the Parrott rifle was no rifle – it was a cannon. And the patent holder on it was one Robert Parker Parrott, a cousin of the Rear Admiral, who haled from Lee, NH. Whoever designed it, nobody debates the influence this advance in armament had on the outcome of the Civil War. The Parrott rifle was inexpensive to manufacture, and it was deadly accurate.

You didn't lift a **Parrott rifle** *to your shoulder. Incorporating new safety features, the 'rifled' or grooved barrel of the cannon also allowed for greater accuracy. Courtesy of www.texasbeyond history.com.*

Admiral Parrott did play an important role in the Civil War, as commander of the Union ironclads USS *Canonicus, Manadnock* and the Portsmouth-built *Agamenticus.* (Two ironclads came out of the Portsmouth Naval Shipyard, the *Kearsarge* in 1862 [see page 164] and the *Agamenticus,* the following year.) Admiral Parrott lies buried beside St. John's Church. Engraved on his monument are the campaigns he took part in: Africa, 1832; Mexico, 1840; Port Royal, 1861; Fort Fisher, 1863; Charleston, 1865; and Asiatic Squadron, 1873; and the words, "A brave and loyal Officer."

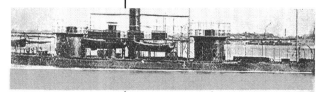

The 1863 ironclad USS **Aga-menticus***, later refitted and known as the USS* Terror.

However – according to papers of the Federal Fire Society, published in 1905 – Parrott Avenue was named for neither of these two Parrotts, but rather for one James Brackett Parrott (1817-1890), following his "handsome bequest upon his death in 1890 of $1000 to the city of Portsmouth to be used to embellish the borders of South Millpond."

"AUSTINBOROUGH"
Albany Street – Austin Street – Brewery Lane – Cabot Street
Cass Street – Cater Park – Chatham Street – Coffins Court
Columbia Street/Court – Friend Street – Jewell Court
Lovell Street/Chevrolet Avenue – Madison Street
Summer Street – Winter Street

THE EARLY 19TH CENTURY saw the first growth of developments beyond the original South End and the central downtown. Streets by the names of Austin and Cabot attest to the entrepreneurial spirit of the day. There should have also been a Boardman Street.

Langley Boardman is best remembered as New Hampshire's preeminent furniture maker; examples of his work hold places of honor in the finest museums and private collections today. However, Langley Boardman was more than just a furniture maker – he was also a speculator, a developer, a builder and a shrewd investor in a town brimming with investors, not all of whom made money on their investments.

In 1800, the land running from Pleasant Street to the South Mill Pond was subdivided and sold. Boardman bought up all the lots of the south side of Cottars Lane (today's Franklin Street; see page 39), reselling them to other speculators and builders/craftsmen who in turn developed the property. Again, in 1805, Boardman bought up all but the corner lots when Joshua Street, today's Richards Avenue, was opened up to development. In this case, he sold the lots to other craftsmen, taking payment in trade. This quickly became the pattern for other speculators as the town expanded.

DANIEL AND MARY AUSTIN moved to Portsmouth from Charlestown, MA, in 1800, Mary having inherited land on what was then the outskirts of Portsmouth, lying to the west and south of Haymarket Square. In 1802, Daniel Austin sold off lots on what can be seen on the 1813 map as AUSTIN STREET; as it crossed over today's Summer Street, its name changed to RUNDLET STREET, after James Rundlet (1772-1852), a rising member of the landed merchant aristocracy, whose vast holdings bordered it to the south. Rundlet's heirs would sell off his properties piece by piece through much of the 19th century.

*The **Rundlet-May House**, built in 1807. The entrance to Rundlet's pasture straddled the corner of Middle Street and Miller Avenue. A small pond – today the site of the Methodist Church parking lot – provided water for cattle. PA*

Rundlet was emperor of all he could see from his front door: pastures rolled away to the south, while property to the west extended to the slopes of 'RUND-LET'S MOUNTAIN,' the second highest promontory in Portsmouth. After the Civil War, the western pasture served as a baseball diamond, while the grassy banks of Rundlet's Mountain provided conveniently raked seating for spectators. Today, it is the site of the L. Verne Wood funeral home. More on that later.

*In its heyday, the **Frank Jones Brewery** boasted a workforce of over 500 employees. TG.*

BREWERY LANE DID NOT receive its current name until the 1990s, but the story of Brewery Lane is the essence of 19th-century Portsmouth, when breweries, along with the Portsmouth Steam Factory, the Sagamore Mill, the Morley Button Company and the Portsmouth Manufacturing Company, came to form the industrial backbone of the city. The Frank Jones Brewery, off Islington, was the nation's largest brewer of ale and clearly dominated the field, with the Eldredge Brewery on Bartlett Street and the Portsmouth Brewery on Bow Street providing strong competition.

Frank Jones was the acknowledged king of Portsmouth brewing. With 51 buildings and a private water supply coming in from Newington, Frank Jones Brewerye produced *half a million barrels* of the golden brew annually. Jones developed much of the west end to house his workers. Following in his footsteps, his brother, True W. Jones, was the undisputed king of brewing in Manchester.

*As a point of reference, **Smuttynose Brewery**, soon to move to Hampton (and named after the island of the same name at the Isles of Shoals), produced in excess of 23,000 barrels in 2009.*

But that's only half the story. In the early 1990s, what remained of the complex, then the Schultz Meat Company's headquarters, came up for sale. It was decided that the section of State Street that took a slight jog as it came into the Plaza 800 shopping center needed a name of its own. "EILEEN DONDERO FOLEY WAY," honoring our eight-term former mayor, was in the running, but most agreed that such a moniker would be as much of a mouthful as one of the Schultz family's famous hot dogs. Attorney Bernard Pelech looked around him at the real estate in question and suggested Brewery Lane. What could be more fitting?

WILLIAM CABOT AND Nathaniel Gookin became the owners of land once held by the Reverend Anthony Wibird. In 1802, Cabot bought out Gookin's interest in the property, and in 1807, he subdivided and sold house lots along what would become CABOT STREET.

ON THE CORNER OF Columbia and State Streets sits CATER PARK. William J. Cater served as a member of the state legislature in 1913, ran for the state senate in 1916, spent two terms on the city council, as well as serving on the staff of Governor John H. Barlett (1919-21). He also served as a delegate to the 1916 Republican convention, and an alternate to the conventions of 1924 and 1928. He gave the city the land for the park that bears his name in 1947. Cater died in 1954.

> Portsmouth has been home to many Casses over the years, but it has been suggested that CASS STREET may well have been named for Exeter-born Lewis Cass (1782-1866), the prominent soldier-turned-politician whose last appointment was as Secretary of State under President Buchanan. He resigned his post in 1860 in protest against the decision not to reinforce the forts of Charleston, SC.

THE MANY COFFINS still living in the greater Portsmouth area today can count sea captains and importers, fighting men, businessmen and even a sheriff among their ancestors of note.

In 1809 Edward Coffin, a painter who lived on Union Street, purchased the front half of a lot that had just been sold to Daniel Dearborn, a laborer, along what would come to be known as COFFIN'S COURT.

COLUMBIA. THE ALLEGORICAL female personification of the United States whose image generally fell out of use early in the 20th century, except perhaps by Columbia Pictures. The capital of South Carolina. The first ship of the United States Navy to circle the globe. The 1200-mile river that flows from the base of the Canadian Rockies through Oregon and Washington to the Pacific, first navigated by the above-mentioned USS *Columbia*, in 1792, and named for her. And long after the naming of Portsmouth's **COLUMBIA STREET** and **COLUMBIA COURT**, the name of the command module for the Apollo 11 lunar landing mission, watching from a ring-side seat, 69 miles above the moon's surface, as Neil Armstrong and Buzz Aldrin made their descent on July 20, 1969. And, of most recent memory, the name of a tragically ill-fated space shuttle (1981-2003).

Ichabod Goodwin served as governor of New Hampshire during the Civil War. From the collections of the state of New Hampshire, Division of Historical Resources.

THE GOODWIN MANSION, home of New Hampshire governor Ichabod Goodwin (1794-1882), once sat amidst numerous stately residences on Islington Street; pasturage opposite was known as Goodwin Field. Long before the mansion's 1963 move to Strawbery Banke, brewer and then-mayor Marcellus Eldredge purchased the field from Goodwin's heirs for use as a park, with the understanding that **GOODWIN PARK** would remain just that, in perpetuity. He in turn presented the land to the city as a site for a stately Civil War memorial.

Dedicated July 4, 1888, the monument that serves as the park's centerpiece underwent a $125,000 restoration and was rededicated in 2003. The Civil War memorial is now joined by memorials commemorating the sons and daughters of Portsmouth who gave their lives in both World Wars, in Korea and in "all wars."

Fourteen-year-old Ichabod Goodwin came to Portsmouth from North Berwick, Maine, and went to work in the counting house of merchant Samuel Lord. At 23, he was captain of one of Lord's ships. By his mid-thirties, he was deeply involved in both shipbuilding and shipping, transporting large quantities of salt among other goods. He founded the Portsmouth Whaling Company, owned two railroads, two banks, a gas utility and the Portsmouth Bridge Company, as well as the Portsmouth Steam Factory, a six-story textile mill that turned out 2½ million yards of cloth annually. And that was just his private record. Goodwin sat in the state legislature for six terms between 1838 and 1858, and was elected governor of the state in 1859 as the country reluctantly moved towards civil war.

The Monumental Bronze Company of Bridgeport, CT, mass produced sculpture to satisfy a growing national thirst for public statuary. **Goodwin Park**, *designed around the grand monument above, sits across Islington Street from the original site of the* **Goodwin Mansion**, *below, which today anchors the Hancock Street side of Strawbery Banke Museum. PA*

JEWELL COURT came into existence at some point between 1839 and 1851. No family by that name is listed in the 1827 city directory, the earliest available. Perhaps it carries a woman's first name?

I HAVE NO EXPLANATION to offer for the naming of **LOVELL STREET**, but I do have the story of the renaming of a section of it, straight from the renamer's attorney's mouth.

The Tacetta family owned property along the section of Lovell Street that runs into what we know today as the Plaza 800 Shopping Center. Vincent Tacetta once owned the Chevy dealership in Portsmouth. In fact, his first showroom was located just around the corner from **CHEVROLET AVENUE**. I rest my case.

THE 1850 MAP includes **MADISON STREET**, running parallel to Anthony/Union. Given the date that this area was being developed, I am willing to wager that this street was named for the country's fourth president, James Madison, who held office from 1809 to 1817.

RICHARD WINTER OWNED a Portsmouth ropewalk in 1745. Brewster remembers several ropewalks in the vicinity of Islington Street and the North Mill Pond, which might put Mr. Winter's in proximity to **WINTER STREET**, which took its name soon after 1844. I am going to guess that **SUMMER STREET**'s name was inspired by a desire for some semblance of seasonal symmetry, though it wasn't always known by that name. On the 1813 map, the first half of Summer from Islington to the top of the hill was called **MASSY STREET**; from the top of the hill down to Middle Street was known then as **ACKERMAN STREET**.

The main geographical feature of the area changed names as well. The hill at the intersection of today's Summer and State Streets was known once as **WINDMILL HILL** (John Pray built a towering windmill atop this hill, circa 1700, which stood for over fifty years) and **MASON'S HILL** (lawyer and landowner Jeremiah Mason built his house, today's Advent Christian Church parish hall, on the eastern side of the street). This prominence was the site of a tremendous bonfire in celebration of the repeal of the Stamp Act in 1766. The conflagration was topped by a bomb, according to the papers of the day, to "blast the joy of Portsmouth to the heavens when the flames touched it off."

Late 19th-century concern for safety was expressed in an editorial of the day which suggested that "a policeman ought to be standing on Islington at the intersection of Summer" to keep an eye on the youngsters who sledded down Mason's Hill.

Jeremiah Mason (1768-1848), U.S. Senator from New Hampshire from 1813 to 1817. A bust of Mason resides in the Special Collections room of the Portsmouth Public Library.

UP THE HILL TO SOUTH STREET
Broad Street – Chauncey Street – Elwyn Avenue
Hawthorne Street – Highland Street – Kent Street – Lincoln Avenue
Mendum Avenue – Merrimac Street – Miller* Avenue
Orchard St/Court – Park Street – Rockland Street – Sherburne Avenue
Spring Street – Union Street – Wibird* Street – Willow Lane

ONCE CALLED THE SEVEN PINES, the highest point in Portsmouth long served as a navigation landmark for men at sea until such time as the seven pines from which it took its name were felled. You will also find it referred to as RUNDLET'S MOUNTAIN, WIBIRD'S HILL, LINCOLN HILL or SPRING HILL, and kids called it BREAD AND CHEESE ROCK, for reasons lost to antiquity. Whatever you call it, the rise on South Street served as much as a magnet for 19th-century development as it had always been a magnet for children and sleds.

Streets in the triangle bounded by South, Miller and Middle fall into three rough categories of names: those tied to the history of the period (LINCOLN, MERRIMAC and UNION), those less imaginatively named as the developer looked around him and decided, "This one we'll call ORCHARD, and that one over there'll be WILLOW LANE" (a sixty-foot piece of evidence stands at its corner today), and those honoring citizens of note.

As Ray Brighton once put it, "Only in the flatlands of the seacoast could such a hillock gain such a heady status."

THE SOUTH END OF BROAD STREET, to the south of South Street, appeared on maps as NEW BROAD STREET in 1924.

THE EARLIEST CHAUNCEY to this area, Charles Chauncey (?-1809), came in 1748 to work for his uncle, the powerful Sir William Pepperell of Kittery. Charles owned 18 acres near the intersection of Middle Road and South Street, a short distance from the road that bears the family's name, CHAUNCEY STREET.

Samuel Chauncey (?-1815), one of twelve children born to Charles and his second wife, Joanna Gerrish, became a sea captain in the employ of Eliphalet Ladd, married Ladd's daughter Betsy and settled into a home on Islington Street. He was described in old age by a granddaughter as a highly respected, "small, very erect old gentleman, of quick movement, wearing a cocked hat, black silk hose, with diamond knee buckles."

Dr. Alfred Langdon Elwyn. His Glossary of Supposed Ameri- canisms, *published in 1859, can be downloaded at no charge at www.archive.org.*

THE NAME OF ELWYN crops up all over around Portsmouth, most often with a Langdon attached, all beginning with Governor John Langdon's only child Elizabeth's marriage to one Thomas Elwyn. Alfred Langdon Elwyn (1804-1884), a grandson of the governor, compiled and edited a volume of letters written to his grandfather both during and after the Revolutionary War by such notables as George Washington, John Adams, Thomas Jefferson and others. And as mentioned previously, John Langdon Elwyn gave the city the land for Langdon Park. The Urban Forestry Center was established in 1976, through the generosity of John Elwyn Stone. ELWYN AVENUE dead-ends at the South Playground, adjacent to Langdon Park.

EASILY THE MOST INTERESTING Kent with local ties for whom KENT STREET might be named has to be John Horace Kent. Born in Barnstead, in 1828, he lived briefly in Portsmouth and attended Portsmouth High School, before seeking his fortune first in New York, then in Pennsylvania, and ultimately in California; when news of gold made its way back east, the 21-year-old Kent joined the throngs headed west. Idled briefly in Panama while awaiting passage on to California, he put the time to good use, founding a newspaper, quickly selling out his interest in the paper when a berth became available. Within two years of reaching California, he was San Francisco's coroner, serving in this capacity from 1851 to 1857.

Returning east in 1860, Kent enlisted in a Massachusetts regiment and joined the Army of the Potomac. After the war, he held numerous positions: clerk at the Portsmouth Naval Shipyard; special officer and claims agent for the Eastern Railroad; special inspector of customs for New Hampshire; chief of customs for all of New England; colonel on the staff of Governor P. C. Cheney; sheriff of Rockingham County; and warden of the new state prison. He was elected Portsmouth's city marshal for two five-year terms, and was twice elected a state representative.

However, success is no guarantee against temptation. One biographer of the period tell us that, "possessing a social nature and having a large, open heart, he was gradually led into the habit of using intoxicating liquors to excess." He must have pulled himself up, however; he went on to become the president of the New Hampshire Total Abstinence Society. He died in Concord in 1888.

The multifaceted John Horace Kent.
From The History of Rockingham and Strafford Counties, N.H., *by D. Hamilton Hurd.*

MERCHANT AND SHIP OWNER C. M. Mendum maintained a store on Market Street and owned property off Middle Street which today is crossed by MENDUM AVENUE. His three-masted *Paul Jones*, built in 1877 by Portsmouth shipbuilder W. F. Fernald, went up in flames off the coast of Australia in 1886. His forebear, Captain John Mendum (1738-1806) lies buried in the North Cemetery. Brighton tells how French privateers captured the *Rebecca*, captained by this John Mendum, but turned her loose, as she was carrying no cargo at the time. For all their pains, they gained but one barrel of beer.

THE UNCERTAINTY OF THE Civil War years ended and expansion began in earnest. Newspaperman Frank W. Miller (? – 1880) purchased two sizeable lots atop Lincoln Hill, at the corner of South and Union. To this he soon added thirty acres known as Packer's Pasture, which he was able to acquire from John Elwyn. Miller intended to continue Summer Street on down to South through land that was still in the Rundlet family, but the Rundlet heirs refused to oblige; several years ensued before Portsmouth could lay out what was first known as SOUTH SUMMER STREET, then as MILLER AVENUE in honor of the one-time mayor and city visionary.

Journalism was in Miller's blood. Starting as a journeyman in the offices of the *New Hampshire Gazette*, he soon was working for his father, the Rev. Tobias Ham Miller, who was publishing *The Portsmouth Journal* along with partner Charles Brewster. The ambitious Miller, with help from his father and another partner, soon founded a paper of his own, *The Morning Chronicle*, and in due time became sole owner.

A Republican, Miller served as mayor of the city for a truncated six-month term. Shortly after stepping into office in 1874, ward boundaries were redrawn, followed immediately by another municipal election which saw Miller replaced by Democrat Moses H. Goodrich.

Marcellus Eldredge, Portsmouth's mayor in 1885 and 1886, built one of the first homes along the new Miller Avenue. The structure in the foreground was ldredge's barn and carriage house. PA

FOR THE DERIVATION of **SHERBURNE AVENUE**, please see **SHERBURNE ROAD**, page 115.

RICHARD WIBIRD (1702-1765) came to Portsmouth to seek his fortune. Serving as a ship's steward or poulterer (the proper terms for a provisioner of the officers' table), he had a long way up to climb, but climb he did. He married the owner of a small market on Market Street, and by the dint of hard work, amassed a fortune; by 1727, Wibird was one of Portsmouth's wealthiest, owning five houses and three slaves, and paying the highest tax in town. Appointed collector of customs for the port in 1730, he built himself a fine mansion of brick, the first of its kind in a city that would one day legislate building only with brick. He sat on the King's council and served as judge of probate. Upon his death, Richard Wibird left his wife Elizabeth "all my Negroes, Portsmouth [a male slave] who was hers before, Phillis, Sylvia and Venus." **WIBIRD STREET**, formerly **WIBIRD'S HILL STREET**, carries his name.

"WEBSTERVILLE"

MASTER CARPENTER, BUILDER, real estate investor and developer Benjamin Franklin Webster (1824-1916) left his stamp on Portsmouth's Victorian neighborhoods. From the elegant façade of the Kearsarge Building on Congress Street to the majestic Italianate/Renaissance Revival mansion we know today as the J. Verne Wood Funeral Home's Buckminster Chapel on Broad Street, numerous examples of Webster's work attest to the Epsom, NH, native's command of his craft.

B. F. Webster would be "put[ting] up several homes in **WEBSTERVILLE** next season," the *Portsmouth Journal* informed its readers in an article in

*Master builder and developer **Benjamin Webster**. PA*

1886. Webster built many one-family homes in the area bordered by Miller Avenue and Middle, South and Wibird Streets.

Webster built as much for the wealthy elite of Portsmouth as for the middle class, but his crowning achievement he built for himself, in 1878. Sited on the crown of 'Rundlet's Mountain' overlooking the many homes he had built, his mansion required three years and some 56,000 board feet of lumber to construct. Five yokes of oxen were needed to move the building's marble buttresses, each weighing seven to eight tons a piece.

*The magnificent Italianate Victorian mansion to which carpenter **Benjamin Webster** treated himself. Photo by John Grossman.*

James Rundlet had once erected a tall flagpole atop his mountain, but it had snapped off at five feet in a strong storm in the mid-1800s. Webster replaced it in 1885 with a 70-foot flag pole of his own.

So how did Webster's name come to be tied with that of a Buckminster, you may ask. Daniel Warner built a home on the corner of Islington and Bridge Street. Sixty-three year later, Eliphalet Ladd purchased the house. After his death, Ladd's widow married the Rev. Joseph Buckminster and the house came to be known as the Buckminster house. Eventually the property came into the hands of J. Verne Wood and George Ward, who for many years operated it as a funeral home called BUCKMINSTER CHAPEL. When Ward moved the business to the Webster mansion, he chose to retain the name.

For an image of the original Buckminster House, see page 214.

SOUTH OF SOUTH
Sagamore Avenue – Jones Avenue

BANDS OF GYPSIES rendezvoused along Sagamore Creek late into the 19th century, even as the first homes were being built along SAGAMORE AVENUE. The

1877 bird's-eye view map of Portsmouth shows an un-named thoroughfare trailing south across the Creek and on to Rye and the horizon, with one large estate and a handful of small homes along it.

The native populations of New England, organized along familial lines, designated the eldest son of the dominant family as their leader, or "sagamore." (To the south, this leader would be called a "sachem.") Twenty such sagamores ruled between the Kennebec River and Connecticut at the time of the early settlement of the region, and Brewster suggests that the sagamore who presided over settlements on the Piscataqua most proba-bly resided along what we know today as Sagamore Creek. Its earliest name was SACHEMORE CREEK. It can also be found referenced as SACKEN CREEK and WITCH-ES CREEK.

MEANDERING DOWN TO the shore of Sagamore Creek and the present-day home of the Benevo-lent and Protective Order of Elks, Lodge #97, JONES AVENUE came into existence before World War I, and must surely have been named on the death of Victorian beer magnate Frank Jones (1832-1902). A native of Barrington, NH, Jones came to Portsmouth at the age of sixteen, on the heels of two older brothers, going to work for one of them as a tin peddler. Three years later he joined this same brother in the hardware and stove business. Seventeen years later, in 1868, he was elected mayor, and six years after that he was elected to Congress for two terms. He only missed becoming the gover-nor of New Hampshire by two thousand votes, in 1880.

Frank Jones. The self-made man wore countless hats: merchant, brew-er, politician, hotelier, captain of industry. PA

Jones made his name in beer. From his entrance into the business in 1858, he grew an empire that by 1880 boasted the largest ale and porter storage cellars in the world. And that was just the man's brewing credentials. He was president of the Boston & Maine

Railroad, the Granite State Fire Insurance Company, the Portsmouth Fire Association and the Portsmouth Shoe Company. And he was the owner of the Rockingham Hotel, not to mention New Castle's Wentworth-by-the-Sea Hotel. His estate at his death was valued in excess of $5 million. His Maplewood Farm's thousand acres included a tennis court, croquet lawns, half a dozen greenhouses, stables and a racetrack.

> Ruth Griffin, formerly a member of the Governor's Council, recounts that her husband John used to wonder why they would 'honor' a man by naming a street for him that ran "from a cemetery to the city dump."

However, Frank Jones was hardly the only Jones of note in Portsmouth history. We cannot forget a visitor by the same name who may have only made two brief stays with us, but who left behind a slew of broken hearts and a rich legacy for the imagination.

Scotsman John Paul Jones (1747-1792) immigrated to the colonies as John Paul, adding the surname Jones some time thereafter. Commissioned a first lieutenant in the fledgling Continental Navy at the outbreak of hostilities, he came to Portsmouth in 1777 to oversee the completion of his first command, the frigate *Ranger,* nearing completion in John Langdon's Badger's Island boat yard. Before long, he was on his way to France, capturing the British sloop of war *Drake* off the coast of Ireland, and carrying out raids on the English coast. In 1779, the French loaned him the *Duc de Duras,* a decrepit ship which he refitted and renamed the *Bon Homme Richard,* from whose decks he attacked HMS *Serapis* off the coast of England. The battle having gotten off to a decidedly disastrous start, the captain of *Serapis* quickly called for Jones' surrender. His "I have yet begun to fight!" still rings in American ears today.

The perennially controversial John Paul Jones, "father" of the U.S. Navy. PHS

Four years later, Jones returned to Portsmouth a hero, ready to take the helm of the 74-gun ship of the line *America.* But seeing this ship through to completion would prove beyond even Jones' considerable political skills. Before its launch, Jones received word that Congress had opted to make a gift of her to France, to replace a ship our ally had lost in Boston Harbor.

Jones finished out the war years participating in the establishment of the Navy and writing extensively on the training of naval officers.

Jones' career was not without controversy. The brilliant theoretician, credited as the 'father' of the United States Navy, was capable of tactics worthy of a pirate. He went on to serve for two years as rear admiral in the Russian navy under Empress Catherine II, and died in obscurity in Paris after two last years of failing health. It wasn't until 1905 that his body was found and returned to this country with great fanfare. In 1913, he was finally laid to rest in the chapel crypt of the Annapolis Naval Academy.

The **John Paul Jones House**, *said to be where Jones boarded during his stays here, is today home to the Portsmouth Historical Society.*

THE SUMMER COLONY
Little Harbor Road
Wentworth*-Coolidge Mansion State Park
Belle Isle Road – Lady Isle – Martine Cottage Road
Sagamore Landing – Wentworth House Road

L EADING DOWN TO the harbor for which it is named, quiet LITTLE HARBOR ROAD also leads to the architecturally amazing Wentworth-Coolidge Mansion. The eccentric 40-room mansion was home to New Hampshire's first royal governor, Benning Wentworth. As mentioned earlier, from 1741 to 1767, Wentworth inconvenienced all who needed to see him by removing to the family seat on Little Harbor.

In 1816, Charles Cushing, the son of a Boston senator and wife of Anne

The eccentric **Wentworth-Coolidge Mansion**, *and the 65 acres that surround it, are maintained today by the New Hampshire Division of Parks and Recreation. PA*

Sheafe of Portsmouth, purchased the mansion; their family owned it for seventy years and were the first family known to open its doors to public visitors, as early as 1846.

Some of the mansion's more curious wings were the later additions of wealthy Bostonian patron of the arts, J. Templeman Coolidge III, who purchased the estate as a family summer retreat in 1886. He built the carriage house that today functions as an art gallery, and also added wings to accommodate his numerous guests.

In 1887, Arthur Astor Carey purchased acreage along Sagamore Creek from Coolidge and hired Boston architect (and nephew of the poet) Alexander Wadsworth Longfellow to build 'Creek Farm,' the classic New England shingle-style summer home and estate that once abutted the Wentworth-Coolidge property. In 1902, Carey also founded the "undenominational" Little Harbor Chapel down the road, serving as lay minister between 1903 and 1922.

J. Templeman Coolidge, a patron of the arts in Boston, entertained such cultural luminaries of the day as Isabella Stewart Gardner, John Singer Sargent and Edmund Tarbell. PA

Above left, **Creek Farm,** *the summer home of Coolidge's friend, fellow Harvard classmate and trustee of the Boston Museum of Fine Arts, Arthur Astor Carey, now the property of the Society for the Protection of New Hampshire Forests. The Careys hosted the delegates to the Russo-Japanese Peace Conference here in 1905. Courtesy of SeacoastNH.com. Right, the bell tower of Carey's* **Little Harbor Chapel.**

IN 1890, ARTHUR CAREY sold some of his Sagamore frontage, including the MARTINE COTTAGE, to Boston architect R. Clipston Sturgis. Martines came early to Portsmouth. In a town meeting in 1693, "the Selectmen, together with Mr. Richard Martine, Capt. Walter Nele and Mr. Marke Hunking" were appointed to "regulate and order the seating of the people in the meeting house." The farmhouse that this Richard Martine built on the north shore of Sagamore Creek around 1700 would stay in the Martine family for more than 150 years.

In 1798, France's Prince Louis-Philippe and his brothers, in the company of the French foreign minister Charles de Talleyrand, traveled America on an extended tour while revolution raged back home. At one point, the exiled royals spent a week as guests at the Martine farm. The young princes were forced to continue their wanderings until Napoleon's abdication and exile in 1815. When Louis-Philippe became king of France in 1830, flowers from the Martine gardens, sent to mark his ascendancy, were planted in the Tuilleries Gardens in Paris. Presumably, the road known today as MARTINE COTTAGE ROAD took the royal visitors right to the farmhouse door.

The seemingly humble Martine farmhouse on Sagamore Creek that played host to French princes in exile. Watercolor by Sarah Haven Foster, courtesy of the Portsmouth Public Library.

MOST FOLKS HEADING SOUTH on Sagamore Avenue, crossing the bridge over Sagamore Creek and taking their first left will tell you that puts them on ROUTE 1B, and it does. Very few will know that they are actually on WENTWORTH HOUSE ROAD, as it appears on the official city map, or simply WENTWORTH ROAD, as it is more often named on unofficial maps. Needless to say, this is the road that leads to the famed hostelry built by Boston rum distiller David Chase in 1874. The name evolved over the years, from WENTWORTH HOUSE, to WENTWORTH HALL, to the WENTWORTH HOTEL, to the WENTWORTH-BY-THE-SEA HOTEL (see page 215).

*The **Wentworth Hotel** as it appeared in 1892 under the ownership of Frank Jones.*

CHRISTIAN SHORES EXPANSION
Boyd Road – Cate* Street – Franklin Drive
Morning Street – Myrtle Avenue/Kane Street – North School Street
Thornton Street/Hunter's Hill Avenue – Whipple Street

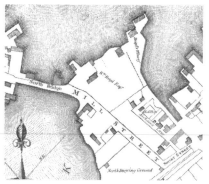

COLONEL GEORGE BOYD was a successful merchant and prolific shipbuilder on the North Mill Pond, turning out upwards of ten ships a year prior to the Revolution. Born in Newington, his first position upon coming to Portsmouth was as a lowly house boy in the employ of Henry Sherburne. Just how he came by his

*Above, **Boyd** properties as detailed on the 1813 map. According to Brewster, "It was a magnificent seat, such as a nabob might envy, enclosed within a white open fence, and at regular intervals of some forty or fifty feet, those handsomely carved towering Grenadiers' heads were placed on posts, and presented a very unique appearance." PA*

fortune is a matter of question, appearing to coincide suspiciously with the departure from Portsmouth of two individuals with whom Boyd was associated.

Cautious not to be taken as a Loyalist, thereby losing business, Boyd set sail for London in 1775, remaining there until 1787. On his return voyage, he shipped many items back with him which he had purchased while abroad, including a coach and an elegant sarcophagus which I am sure he hoped would be for use at some far future date. Brewster describes his "just reaching the scene of his magnificent mansion and spacious gardens in season to occupy a tenement six feet by two in the North Cemetery, on the opposite side of the way, and to be covered by the cold stones which had accompanied him on his voyage." Perhaps **BOYD ROAD** remembers the sad tale of George Boyd, Esq.

*Boyd's sarcophagus, above, reads "**George Boyd, Esq.**, former merchant of this town who after many years embarked at London for his native town in August 1787. But to the great grief of his wife, children and friends he departed this life on the 6th day of October 1787, age 54, two days before making port."*

THE 1850 MAP OF Portsmouth shows a stub of a street servicing a cluster of industrial buildings that took their power from the stream coming into the North Mill Pond. By 1903, **CATE STREET** had taken on the rest of its current course, though without the benefit of a name, and **COTTAGE STREET**, into which it runs, did not yet exist.

Carpenter James Cate (c. 1634-1677) was the first of the Cates to be mentioned in early Portsmouth documents, in 1657. Not to gossip, but James was well known to the local constabulary – some of his offenses included excessive drinking, breach of the peace and fornication – with his wife. On his death, his son Edward (c. 1655-1732), also a carpenter, inherited his "dwelling house, outbuildings, land, pewter, Indian corn, iron and brass, carpenter tools, furniture, cow, horse, sow, a pair of shoes and two guns." However, Edward lived on Sagamore Creek, nowhere near today's Cate Street.

Joseph Cate was recorded as a landholder in 1660; a Widow Cate was listed as an inhabitant in 1678. John and Edward Cate held seats in meeting as of 1693. William Cate Jr. lost his life in the Indian massacre at the Plains in 1696. In 1776, patriots Samuel Cate, Samuel White Cate and William Cate, Jr., signed the Association Test. The 1831 directory lists Cates who were joiners, carpenters and farmers. In 1849, a restless Joseph J. Cate sailed for the California gold rush. Plenty enough reason to explain the presence of a Cate Street in Portsmouth.

NORTH SCHOOL STREET takes its name from the 19th-century school house that sits at one end. Like many of the other fine old school buildings in town, the North School has been converted to condominium apartments.

FRANKLIN DRIVE HAS played host to an elementary school since the early 1900s. The original two-story building, built on the site of the old City Farm, burned down in 1981, though an addition added in 1967 survived. A one-story version of the older part was appended to the addition to become the school we know today.

BEFORE THE DAYS OF the Route 1 Bypass, MYRTLE AVENUE traveled from Dennett Street due west to the City Farm. In 1994, the easternmost part of the bifurcated street was renamed KANE STREET.

Tylene Jousse lives at 197 Dennett Street. In the 1880s, her great-grandmother immigrated to this country from Ireland and moved into 198 Dennett Street, across the street from her brother and their mother. In due course, she met and married a gentleman by the name of George Kane. For a wedding present, he bought her 197 Dennett Street. The house has been in the family ever since, and the family name now graces the street at the corner.

ANOTHER OF THE NEW streets that came into being in 1875 was **THORNTON STREET**. Thorton had been used earlier for a street paralleling Dennett one block to the north, along part of today's Route 1 Bypass.

A number of Thorntons can be found in the pages of Portsmouth city directories from 1831 on, but my guess is that this street, like its neighbor Whipple Street, was meant to honor the third of the New Hampshire signers of the Declaration of Independence. Even though he never resided in Portsmouth, it is likely that his name and reputation were still as highly regarded in 1875 as they were in 1775.

Matthew Thornton (1714-1803) was born in Ireland and came to this country at the age of three, his family settling in Worcester, Massachusetts. He studied medicine, later establishing a practice in Londonderry where he rose to social, financial, military and political prominence. He was president of the Fourth Provincial Congress in 1775, which assumed governmental authority as the colonial government fled, chaired the Committee of Safety through this turbulent year, and presided over the Fifth Congress which in 1776 implemented the first constitution in the colonies.

Thornton arrived in Philadelphia two days after the adoption of the Declaration of Independence, signing a document he had long worked for as he began the first of two terms in the Continental Congress. He continued over the next ten years to juggle his work in state government, a seat on the Superior Court, chief justice of the Court of Common Pleas – and his medical practice.

Matthew Thornton, doctor, legislator and government chief. Thornton lived out his days as a gentleman farmer and owned a ferry that crossed the Merrimack River at a point still known as Thornton's Ferry. From the collection of the State of NH, Division of Historical Resources.

THORNTON STREET WAS bisected when the Route 1 Bypass went in, creating a spur that was given the name **THORNTON STREET EXTENSION**. As with many other such "extensions," the city decided to rename this section of street in 1994. A family named Hunter lived at the top of a favorite sledding hill on this section of Thornton which neighborhood children always referred to as Hunters' Hill. When new names were solicited, the choice of HUNTERS HILL AVENUE was a natural.

General William Whipple, signer of the Declaration of Independence. From the collection of the State of NH, Division of Historical Resources.

ANOTHER OF THE NEW streets created after the 1875 sale of City Farm property, I like to think of WHIPPLE STREET as being named not just for William Whipple, one of those courageous men who pledged their lives and fortunes as signers of the Declaration of Independence, but also for another family who bore the Whipple name – as slaves. Their stories are intertwined.

Captain William Whipple (1730-1785) went to sea as a young boy, was master of a ship before he was old enough to vote, and having become wealthy in the slave trade, retired from the sea at the age of 29. Settling into life ashore, he became active in town affairs, and married his cousin Catherine Moffat, daughter of Captain John Moffat (see Moffat Street, page 219-221). Though a man of little formal education, Whipple became an industrious public servant. He was a member of the Committees of Safety for both Portsmouth proper and for New Hampshire, and spoke for the province in the Continental Congress of 1775. In fact, a Whipple descendant describes him as "one of its major workhorses, recognized by his peers as one of its leaders." Commissioned a brigadier general in 1777, he commanded the first New Hampshire brigade at Saratoga, reinforcing the troops of General Gates, and participated in Burgoyne's surrender. Returning home, he served as a member of the state assembly and as an associate justice of the superior court until his death.

After leaving the sea, Captain Whipple went into business with his brother Joseph; they were partners as merchants until the time of the Revolution. Afterwards, Joseph was appointed collector of customs duties and superintendent of lighthouses – for a state with only 18 miles of shoreline.

ACCORDING TO 19TH-CENTURY SOURCES, Prince Whipple (?-1797) was born in the town of Amabou, perhaps today's coastal town of Anomabu, in Ghana. Of an obviously prosperous family, possibly royalty, his parents sent him to this country for his education at the age of ten, following in the footsteps of an older brother who had returned from America four years prior. He traveled with a cousin. The boys' first lesson upon their arrival in this country was one of treachery: in Baltimore, the ship captain entrusted with their passage sold the two into slavery. Prince was purchased by William Whipple, and served his master for many years as a trusted servant and bodyguard.

Prince's wife, Dinah Chase Whipple (1760-1846), was born a slave into the home of New Castle's Reverend Chase and his wife; she received her freedom at the age of 21, came to live in Portsmouth and married Prince the same year. Both Prince and Cuffee Whipple (Brewster believes the two were brothers and sons of an African prince, while Russell Lawson asserts that Cuffee was actually Dinah's brother) and their families lived in homes on lands that were given to them at the west end of the Whipple property, in houses which still stand on High Street today. Dinah ran a school for the town's African-American children after Prince's death, from 1800 to 1832.

Whipple School, also converted to condominium use today, could serve as a fitting memorial to school teacher Dinah Whipple, as well as to the Revolutionary War leader. TG

Washington Crossing the Delaware, 1851, by Emanuel Leutze. It was Captain John Blunt of Little Harbor who navigated the boat in 1776, according to Charles Brewster. The iconic image was chosen for the back of the New Jersey state quarter.

Slaves didn't come just from Africa. In 1654, John Pickering bought the remaing five years of service of an Irish "servant man" who had been brought over as a captive.

For generations, the story had circulated that Prince Whipple was the lone African-American figure depicted in Emanuel Leutze's famous 1851 epic painting of George Washington crossing the Delaware. However, recent research has placed both Whipples, master and servant, in Baltimore on Christmas night, 1776.

But Prince did attend his master everywhere. When Whipple was ordered to go after Burgoyne in 1777, Prince was expected to be at his side. Upon receipt of the news of their imminent departure, Prince is said to have told Whipple, "You are going to fight for your liberty, but I have none to fight for." Other accounts word his reply as: "I have no wish to fight and no inducement, but had I my liberty, I would fight in defense of the country to the last drop of my blood."

Whatever the wording, Prince Whipple so moved his master that his freedom was promised – though it would be four more years until he was allowed the rights of a free man, and another three before William Whipple granted him legal manumission. Prince was one of twenty slaves who petitioned the New Hampshire Legislature in 1779 for their freedom and an end to slavery in the state.

Prince Whipple is described as having been a leader of his people and a man well respected by both black and white. It is said that after the Revolution, Prince often went by the name of 'Caleb Quotem,' from a popular expression of the day referring to a jack-of-all-trades.

WEST OF THE ROUTE 1 BYPASS
Barberry Lane – Rockingham Avenue – Rutland Street
Melbourne Street – Greenland Road

THE NAME OF **BARBERRY LANE** brings to mind pirates with sharp swords and shrubs with sharp spines. Whether the namers had either – or neither – of these in mind, I cannot say. But for more Portsmouth connections to Barbarry pirates, see entries concerning the USS *Crescent*, on page 161, Commodore Edward Preble, on page 163, and Commodore Steven Decatur, page 175.

FARMLAND BELONGING TO members of the Sheafe family was subdivided into building lots. Late in the 19th century, **RUTLAND** and **MELBOURNE STREETS**, and later **VINE STREET** and **ESSEX AVENUE** were created to serve the new neighborhood.

MOST LOCALS THINK OF it only as the shortcut from Woodbury Avenue onto the Spaulding Turnpike heading north, but on the map this street appears as **ROCKINGHAM AVENUE**. In 1876 it was called **NEW ROAD**, and traversed the entire distance from today's Woodbury Avenue to Sherburne Avenue and beyond. The 1950s and the construction of the Route 1 Bypass/Spaulding Turnpike brought an end to all that.

AND **GREENLAND ROAD** leads to – Greenland.

OLD IRONSIDES

Oliver Wendell Holmes, Sr.

The earliest known photograph of the USS Constitution. *Overhauled at the Portsmouth Naval Shipyard in 1858., she had been slated for demolition in 1830. Outraged, Oliver Wendall Holmes, age 21, wrote a poem and rallied a nation to save what is now the world's oldest floating commissioned naval vessel.*

Ay, tear her tattered ensign down!
Long has it waved on high,
And many an eye has danced to see
That banner in the sky;
Beneath it rung the battle shout,
And burst the cannon's roar;
The meteor of the ocean air
Shall sweep the clouds no more.

Her deck, once red with heroes' blood,
Where knelt the vanquished foe,
When winds were hurrying o'er the flood,
And waves were white below,
No more shall feel the victor's tread,
Or know the conquered knee;
The harpies of the shore shall pluck
The eagle of the sea!

Oh, better that her shattered bulk
Should sink beneath the wave;
Her thunders shook the mighty deep,
And there should be her grave;
Nail to the mast her holy flag,
Set every threadbare sail,
And give her to the god of storms,
The lightning and the gale!

CHAPTER 6

TWENTIETH-CENTURY DEVELOPMENT
HISTORY TAGS ALONG TO THE SUBURBS

Atlantic Heights, under construction in 1918. PA

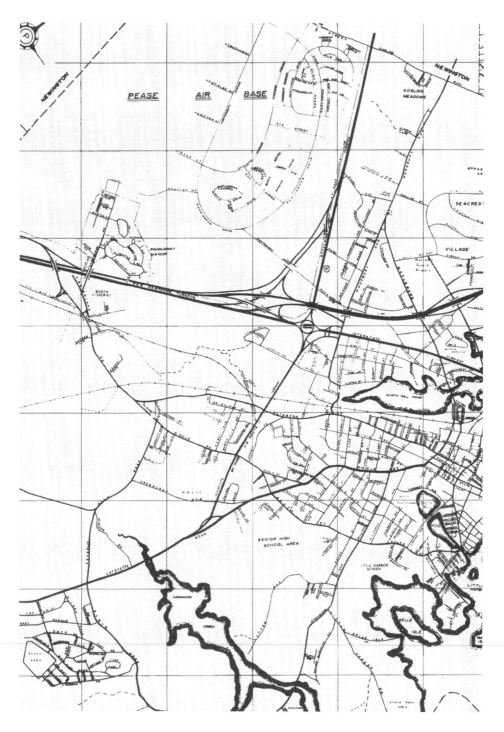

From the Planning Department's 1972 Portsmouth, NH Street Map. *PA*

BY THE TURN OF THE 20th century, new streets were being laid out between the main thoroughfares of South Street and Islington Street. Bungalows and other popular styles of single-family houses quickly lined them, expansion served by the town's network of electric trolleys. Growth would come steadily, punctuated by staccato bursts of housing put up in haste to accommodate rapid influxes of defense workers, during the First and Second World Wars and on through the Cold War years.

1900 – 1910
Cottage Street – Greenleaf Avenue – Lawrence Street – Leavitt Avenue Lois Street – Marjorie Street – Marston Avenue – McNabb Court Monroe Street – Newton Avenue – Sheridan Avenue – Swett Avenue Willard Avenue – Woodworth Avenue

STEPHEN GREENLEAF AND John Pray conducted an inventory of the "Polls and Estates of the Town of Portsmouth" in 1727. John Greenleaf opened the Bell Tavern prior to the Revolution; it soon became known as a gathering place for patriots, and continued to serve the local populace for the best part of the next hundred years.

But the namers of streets probably had Abner Greenleaf (1785-1868) in mind when they named GREENLEAF AVENUE. A native of Newburyport and a brass founder by trade, Greenleaf went to work at the Navy Yard during the War of 1812, then went on to teach school. He became postmaster, briefly published the *People's Advocate* in 1816 and 1817, and served in both houses of the state legislature, presiding over the Senate in 1829. In 1850, he was elected the first mayor of Portsmouth. One of the founders of the Democratic Party, he later was a contributor to the *New Hampshire Gazette*.

Abner Greenleaf served as Portsmouth's first mayor. A skilled coppersmith, operated a copper and brass foundry on State Street in the vicinity of the Unitarian Church. PA

IN 1796, SEVEN SHREWD men incorporated as the New Hampshire Turnpike Proprietors and laid out a toll road from Portsmouth to Concord. Among them was one Thomas Leavitt. Gilman Leavitt was an incorporator of the New Hampshire Fire and Marine Insurance Company in 1803; he was also an incorporator of the Portsmouth Bank, in the early 1820s. Frank E. Leavitt took a seat on the Police Commission in 1912, too late to be the inspiration for **LEAVITT AVENUE**, just west of the Portsmouth Plains.

Joseph Marston, farmer. PA

JOSEPH MARSTON LIVED and farmed on the north-facing slope of Lincoln Hill in 1850. In 1871, Simon Marston erected a new icehouse by **MARSTON'S POND**, on the edge of his premises. It's said that by January in the winter of 1873, he had removed 750 *tons* of 15-inch-thick ice from this pond. This icehouse, which burned in 1887, was rebuilt in 1889.

By the end of the first decade of the 20th century, **MARSTON AVENUE** had been added to the map. By then Charles, Marcellus and Sidnie Marston lived in three homes on Joseph's subdivided property, along which ran the new thoroughfare named to honor their forebear.

SURELY THE DEVELOPER of **MCNABB COURT** gave his own name to the street, which runs one short block south from Lincoln Avenue. Everett McNabb, the owner of E. N. McNabb, Contractors & Builders, lived almost directly across Lincoln at 36 Kent Street.

JAMES MONROE (1758-1831) served in the Virginia assembly and the Continental Congress, as a Virginian senator, as minister to France, as the governor of Virginia, as a negotiator in the Louisiana Purchase, as James Madison's secretary of state and, concurrently, his secretary of war. In 1816, he became a two-term president of the United States. His "Monroe Doctrine" insisted on an end to European involvement in the Americas (and the beginning of America's involvement with other nation states of the western hemisphere).

Portsmouth's **MONROE STREET** surely remembers America's fifth president, who made a presidential visit to Portsmouth in 1817, reviewing troops at Portsmouth Plains, visiting the local forts, attending St. John's Church and dining with senator Jeremiah Mason.

NEWTON AVENUE EXISTED for only fifty years. Created on the completion of filling in Puddle Dock, it ran through the area comprising today's Strawbery Banke Museum, from Washington Street to Water (later Marcy) Street. By the 1950s, Newton had deteriorated into a thoroughfare of scrap metal yards, junk dealers and used auto shops.

Newton Avenue hardly lived up to the aspirations of its namesake. PA

Impending urban renewal led to the creation of Strawbery Banke and the loss of the avenue named for Elvin Newton. An Isles of Shoals fisherman, Newton came to the mainland in 1873. Soon after, he founded the firm of E. Newton & Company, running a sizeable fleet of fishing vessels. Newton himself proposed the creation of the street that would carry his name in 1903.

Elvin Newton's son, Sherman T. Newton, was a member of the New Hampshire state house of representatives in 1893, a collector of customs and one of three generations of Newtons to act as proprietor of the Kearsarge House hotel on Congress Street.

Another Newton also left his mark on Portsmouth, and only a matter of yards from Newton Avenue. Gary Newton (1935-2000) was founder and artistic director of the Player's Ring Theatre, which opened in 1992. The Ring's historic home served the Portsmouth Marine Railway from 1833 to 1855.

*General **Philip Henry
Sheridan**. From the
Civil War Soldier Pho-
tograph Exhibit, Indi-
ana State Library.*

CONTINUING THE TRADITION of naming streets for Civil War heroes is SHERIDAN AVENUE. A graduate of West Point, General Philip Henry Sheridan (1831-1888) fought the Indians in the west, and was a brigadier general in command of a division of the Army of the Ohio by the age of 31. As commander of all the cavalry of the Army of the Potomac in support of General Grant, his ability to turn a rout at Cedar Creek into a victory for the Union earned him Grant's unqualified admiration. In 1883, he succeeded General William Tecumseh Sherman as commander-in-chief of the Army.

Charles Brewster lists a James, a David and a John Swett as signers of the 1776 Association Test, declaring their willingness to take up arms against the British. Few of the 496 signers' names have come down to us on street signs, but perhaps SWETT AVENUE on Portsmouth Plains was one of the exceptions.

IN 1795, THE REVEREND Joseph Willard succeeded the Reverend John Cosens Ogden as pastor of St. John's Church and served in that capacity for the next eleven years. Could it be that the Reverend's sermons were still remembered a hundred years later, when WILLARD STREET appeared on the map?

1910 – 1920
Foch Avenue – Versailles Avenue – Joffre Terrace
Lens Avenue – Marne Avenue – Verdun Avenue

THE HARSH REALITIES OF World War I resonated through the streets of early 20th-century Portsmouth. In a scene that repeated itself in town after town across America, the cream of Portsmouth's youth enlisted and sailed for Europe. Many never returned.

The history of World War I resonates still, through many of Portsmouth's street names. The ink was barely dry on the Treaty of Versailles before the first new roads took names to commemorate "the War to End All Wars." As with the downtown approach to the new Memorial Bridge (see Wright, Dutton and Scott Avenues, pages 171-4), the war was very much on the minds of the namers of our streets.

FOCH AVENUE AND VERSAILLES AVENUE were the first. Ferdinand Foch (1851-1929) rose from commander of France's Ninth Army early in 1914 to commander of the Northern Army on the Western Front in October of the same year. By 1918, he was Allied Supreme Commander, with overall control of the Allied forces. Stopping the advancing Germans at the July 1918 Second Battle of the Marne, he mounted a counter-attack that finally turned the tide of the war. In November, 1918, by then elevated to the rank of Marshal of France, Foch had the privilege of accepting the German surrender.

Marshal of France
Ferdinand Foch.

JOFFRE TERRACE WOULD not take its name until the 1940s, but its explanation belongs along with the other streets commemorating World War I. Chief of the French general staff at the outbreak of the First World War, Joseph Jacques Cesaire Joffre (1852-1931) was distinguished by a remarkable capacity for calm and absolute refusal to accept defeat. Joffre was credited as the savior of France after the 1914 First Battle of the Marne, and continued as chief of staff until the initial success of the Germans at the 1916 Battle of Verdun brought about his downfall within the military.

Joffre's popularity was such, however, that he was immediately made Marshal of France, and he continued to serve in ceremonial roles, traveling to this country in 1917 as head of the French military mission, encouraging America's imminent entrance into the war, and acting as president of the Supreme War Council in 1918.

Affectionately known as
'Papa Joffre,' **Joseph**
Jacques Cesaire Joffre,
Marshal of France.

Allied delegates witness the German delegation's acceptance of the terms of the Treaty of Versailles.

VERSAILLES AVENUE honors the 1919 treaty signed by Germany with the Allies at the Paris Peace Conference in the Hall of Mirrors at the Palace of Versailles, just outside Paris.

LENS AVENUE, named later in the 1920s, remembers the French coal-producing village that lay along the trench lines of the Western Front, occupied and devastated by the Germans for the greater part of the war. It would suffer a similar fate in the Second World War.

*Looking like a child's lead toy soldiers, troops in the 1st Division of the American Expeditionary Forces take the offensive in the **Second Battle of the Marne**.*

MARNE AVENUE marks the 1914 battle that brought the German advance across France to a halt. Both sides dug in and the trench warfare that would come to characterize World War I began.

VERDUN AVENUE recalls the ancient French fortress town of Verdun, attacked by the German Fifth Army in an attempt to break the deadlock along the Western Front in early 1916. The Germans sought a prolonged struggle, their intent to "bleed the French dry." Ten months later, at tremendous cost to both sides, the French finally succeeded in repulsing the Germans. Between the opposing forces, almost a million soldiers gave their lives in a battle that gained neither tactical nor strategic advantage for either side.

ATLANTIC HEIGHTS
Falkland Place – Bedford Way – Raleigh Way – Ranger Way
Crescent Way – Porpoise Way – Concord Way – Preble Way
Saratoga Way – Kearsarge Way
Birch Street – Mangrove Street – Oak Street – Orange Street
Big Rock Park – Hanscom Park – Hislop Park – Maynard Park

FOR PORTSMOUTH, the second decade of the 20th century's most remarkable undertaking in home construction was that of **ATLANTIC HEIGHTS**. Built in 1918 to house workers employed at the nearby Atlantic Shipyard, architect Walter H. Kilham Jr.'s garden community was designed in ten days flat. It remains to this day a charming, functioning example of the "city beautiful" movement.

Atlantic Heights, from the 1925 map. PA

Atlantic Heights' streets honor ten Portsmouth-built ships-of-war. These streets will be presented in chronological order of the ships for which they are named.

The first ship to be built in American waters of American lumber was the **HMS** *FALKLAND*. Fabricated for the British navy by British craftsmen in 1690, the 54-gun frigate carried a full complement of 226 men and appears to have continued in active service until at least 1768.

H.MS Falkland *proved a most successful experiment for the British. Some say she was built in New Castle, while other sources credit her to a shipyard on the North Mill Pond.*

THE BRITISH ADMIRALTY, pleased with *Falkland,* put the **HMS** *BEDFORD* into work in 1696. A 32-gun galley, the *Bedford* carried 135 men and probably saw action during King William's War (1689-1697), the first of the French and Indian Wars.

USS *RALEIGH,* Portsmouth's first contribution to the Continental Navy, went to sea in 1777, with Portsmouth's Captain Thomas Thompson at the helm. Constructed on the North Mill Pond in 1776 in an astonishing sixty days, another year and a half would go by before its frustrated builders could take delivery on its 32 cannons. In her day, *Raleigh* was considered the fastest ship of her size. She was named for English explorer Sir Walter Raleigh.

The USS **Raleigh***, the first ship commissioned by the Continental Navy, is the same ship featured on the New Hampshire seal, below. PA*

A second *Raleigh*, a cruiser built in 1894, took part in the Battle of Manila Bay under Admiral George Dewey. The fourth *Raleigh* (LPD-1), one of a new class of amphibious transport docks or landing ships, came on line in 1962. A website has been put up to remember her – dedicated to "the Engineers who endured this Abomination of Ship Building by New York Naval Shipyard." A veteran of Desert Storm/Desert Shield, she was decommissioned in 1991 and disposed of by being used for target practice in 1994.

USS *RANGER* also took to the seas in 1777, though her builders allowed themselves a leisurely 114 days to complete this 308-ton sloop-of-war. Though *Ranger* was designed for 20 six-pound guns, her captain, John Paul Jones (see Jones Avenue, p. 117), chose to arm her with 14 long nines and only four six-pounders instead. Built for speed, she was heavily sparred, and with fewer cannon than planned, proved top-heavy and hard to handle in heavy weather. However, as described by one eye-witness, with "...her masts raked two or three degrees more than any other ship of the day, she was on the whole the

A model of the USS **Ranger** *overlooks the harbor of her birth. PA.*

sauciest craft afloat." She was named in honor of Rogers'
Rangers (see Rogers Street, page 77).

The Navy has put a total of eight *Rangers* in the
water over the years. The first American aircraft carrier,
built in 1934, was the seventh *Ranger* (CV-4). The Nazis
mistakenly claimed to have sunk her in 1943; Adolf
Hitler personally decorated U-boat commander Otto
von Bulow for his supposed achievement. She would
survive the war in tact, however, not to be decommissioned until 1947. The eighth *Ranger* (CV-A61), also an
aircraft carrier, was launched in 1957. Her planes flew
more sorties and logged more hours (10,542) than those
of any other carrier in the 1991 Gulf War.

THE UNITED STATES was able to get along without a
formal navy of her own until the outbreak of
revolution in France and depredations by
raiders from North Africa's Barbary Coast
began interfering with American shipping
and trade.

Congress approved the building of six
frigates. The effort was underway when peace
was negotiated with Algiers in 1796. The
settlement agreement included building Algiers a 32-gun frigate.

> The *Crescent* was not the only
> locally-built ship to be bestowed
> on the government of another
> country. John Paul Jones had to
> swallow a lot more than his pride
> as the 74-gun ship-of-the-line
> *America* was presented to the
> French in 1783 in a grand gesture
> of appreciation for their critical
> assistance in our revolution.

The **USS** *CRESCENT* sailed from Portsmouth harbor in 1798, a gift to the Dey of Algiers,
designed to provide "sufficient inducement to observe
his treaty with the United States." Nathaniel Adams
described her as "the finest specimen of naval architecture that ever floated on the waters of the Piscataqua."

THE NAVY COMMISSIONED the **USS** *PORPOISE* in 1820.
The shallow-draft schooner was constructed in four
months at a cost of about $25,000. It would later sail
against West Indian pirates.

Numerous *Porpoises* followed. The fifth *Porpoise* (SS-172) came out of the Portsmouth Naval Shipyard in 1935. She was in the Philippines, torn apart for an overhaul, when the Japanese bombed Pearl Harbor. Fourteen days later she was on war patrol. She prowled the world's oceans until 1945, then put in another nine years of service as a training vessel.

The fifth ship to bear the name USS Porpoise. In fact, this ship lent her name to an entire class of torpedo subs. All three images on these pages are from the collections of the U.S. Naval Library.

IN 1828, THE 24-GUN sloop-of-war **USS CONCORD** took to the waters of the Piscataqua. Whether she was named for the Massachusetts town that saw the first armed action of the American Revolution in 1775 or the capital of the state of her construction is anybody's guess. She carried a crew of 190 men, and spent many of her years policing the Caribbean, the Gulf of Mexico and coastal Florida before running aground in 1842 on the western coast of Africa.

Another USS *Concord* (1891-1909), older sister to the cruiser *Raleigh* above, also served as part of Admiral Dewey's Asiatic Squadron at Manila Bay.

And yet another *Concord* (CL-10), a 7000-ton *Omaha*-class light cruiser built in 1923, performed as flagship for the explorer Rear Admiral Richard E. Byrd as he traveled to survey the southeastern Pacific islands in 1943. She was decommissioned in 1947.

SIX NAVY SHIPS have been named for Revolutionary War naval officer Edward Preble (1761-1807), commander of the *Constitution* and commodore of a seven-ship squadron that sailed against the Barbary pirates between 1803 and 1805. The Commodore has descendents living in Portsmouth today. The *COMMODORE PREBLE*, an 80-ton sloop of war and the first of the name, took part in the Battle of Lake Champlain in 1814.

Commodore Edward Preble.

The second, the 556-ton sloop-of-war USS *Preble*, was built here in 1839. She sailed the world for 24 years, participating in the blockade of the Mississippi River in 1861. The third *Preble* (DD-12), a destroyer, was built in San Francisco in 1901. Assigned to the Pacific fleet, she was back in her homeport for the earthquake of 1906. Surviving World War I as part of the Pacific Torpedo Flotilla, she was taken out of service in 1919. The following year, the fourth *Preble* (DD-345) left the yards of Bath Iron Works. She was also in Pearl Harbor undergoing an overhaul in December of 1941, but survived the Japanese attack unscathed. A minelayer, escort and anti-submarine vessel, she ended her service in 1945. Also from the Bath Iron Works, the fifth *Preble* (DLG-15) served from 1959 to 1991, providing naval gunfire support in Vietnam.

The sixth of the name, today's USS Preble is a guided missile destroyer that has been defending American interests around the world since 1996.

THE SLOOP-OF-WAR *SARATOGA*, the third US Navy vessel so named, left the ways of the Portsmouth Naval Shipyard after being commissioned here in 1843. The next day she returned to us, her mast smashed in a gale. Two months later she left again, to become flagship of Commodore Matthew C. Perry, commander of the Africa Squadron, primarily in support of the new nation of Liberia, founded as a haven for freed slaves from the United States twenty years earlier. Over the years, this *Saratoga* sailed the Gulf of Mexico, the Caribbean, the coast of South America, the western Pacific and the waters of Japan and China. In 1847, Commander David G. Farragut (1801-1870) took her helm. Fifteen years later he would distinguish himself at the Battle of New Orleans, while *Saratoga* spent the war patrolling – and raiding – the coasts of Delaware and the Carolinas.

David G. Farragut, commander of the third USS Saratoga, was actually referring to mines when he spoke the famous words, "Damn the torpedos! Full speed ahead!" Portsmouth has named two school buildings after the Civil War hero (see also, Farragut School, page 177). Photo from the collections of the Library of Congress.

Farragut's *Saratoga* ended her career first as a school ship training U.S. Navy apprentices, then on loan as a state marine school ship in Philadelphia. Farragut would die with the rank of admiral in 1870 at the Portsmouth Naval Shipyard.

LAST OF THE PORTSMOUTH-built ships commemorated at Atlantic Heights is the USS *KEARSARGE*, the first of four Navy vessels to carry the name. Sent down the ways in 1862, the 1550-ton steam sloop-of-war *Kearsarge* took her name from the mountain in Merrimack County. Ordered into production under an emergency Civil War shipbuilding program, she was commissioned in 1862 and immediately sent in search of Confederate raiders, successfully engaging the 1050-ton Liverpool-built CSS *Alabama* in 1864 outside Cherbourg, France, in one of the most famous naval battles of that war. After thirty years sailing the world, her career came to an abrupt end on Roncador Reef in the Solomon Islands.

The second *Kearsarge* (BB-5), a flagship of the North Atlantic Fleet from 1903 to 1905, was decommissioned, then refitted as a crane ship, playing an important role in the raising of the ill-fated submarine *Squalus* in 1939. Her name was passed on to an aircraft carrier that sailed from 1946 to 1974. This *Kearsarge* (CV-33) took part in Korea and Vietnam, and was on hand to pluck astronauts Wally Schirra and Gordon Cooper out of the Pacific in 1962. Yet another *Kearsarge* (LHD-3), a Wasp-class amphibious assault ship, took to the high seas in 1993.

The USS Kearsarge v. the CSS Alabama, 1864. From the collections of the U.S. Naval Library.

ALBERT HISLOP, FOR whom **HISLOP PARK** is named, bought the old Eldridge Brewery at the onset of Prohibition, intending to convert the buildings into a cold storage facility. In 1936, with the repeal of Prohibition, he went into brewing himself, putting up ale brewed on the premises under the Frank Jones label. As the city's mayor in 1920, Hislop was accused of allowing "commercialized vice" to run rampant. He was said to have owned two houses of ill repute himself.

Hanscom Park in Atlantic Heights, an area developed in response to World War I, is named for Russell Hanscom, one of the first casualties of World War II.

A SUBDIVISION OF POETS AND AUTHORS
Aldrich Road/Court – Fields Road – Thaxter Road
Sewall Road

A SHORT STUB OF asphalt labeled **WEST STREET** appears on the 1913 map of Portsmouth. By 1920, that street extended through to Islington as **ALDRICH ROAD**. It would be several more decades before its companion, **ALDRICH COURT**, would appear. Both streets remember one of Portsmouth's great contributors to American literature.

Born in Portsmouth, poet, novelist, essayist and humorist Thomas Bailey Aldrich (1836-1907) grew up in the South and in New York City. However, he lived with his grandfather, Thomas D. Bailey, on Court Street during the formative years of thirteen to sixteen, a period immortalized in his *Story of a Bad Boy.* (Aldrich would later fictionalize his elder relation as 'Grandfather Nutter,' from which today's Thomas Bailey Aldrich Memorial derives its name, the 'Nutter House').

First published by Ticknor and Fields, Aldrich is described as "a gently mirthful New Englander, who felt eminently at home in the company of

*Author **Thomas Bailey Aldrich** spent his youth in Portsmouth. From the 1907 biography of Aldrich by Ferris Greenslet.*

[Henry Wadsworth] Longfellow, [James Russell] Lowell, [Oliver Wendell] Holmes, and others whom he met through Fields." And like James T. Fields (below), he did a stint with the *Atlantic Monthly*. Its fourth editor, he held this post from 1881 to 1890.

> October turned by maple's leaves to gold;
> The most are gone now; here and there one lingers;
> Soon these will slip from the twig's weak hold,
> Like coins between a dying miser's fingers.
> – from Thomas Bailey Aldrich's "Maple Leaves"

PORTSMOUTH NATIVE James T. Fields (1817-1881) began life on Gates Street in the South End. Going to Boston at 17 to clerk in a booksellers shop, by 29, he'd became junior partner in the publishing house of Ticknor & Fields, later known as Fields, Osgood & Company. Fields published many of the leading writers of the day.

> We were crowded in the cabin;
> Not a soul would dare to sleep:
> It was midnight on the waters
> And a storm was on the deep.
>
> Tis a fearful thing in winter
> To be shattered in the blast,
> And to hear the rattling trumpet
> Thunder "cut away the mast!"
> – from James T. Fields'
> "Ballad of the Tempest"

Fields succeeded James Russell Lowell as the second editor of the *Atlantic Monthly* in 1862. A poet and author in his own right, Fields enjoyed friendships with many major talents of his day, including such luminaries as Charles Dickens, Nathaniel Hawthorne, William Wordsworth and William Makepeace Thackeray.

Fields' wife, Anne Adams Fields, also an accomplished writer, was an intimate friend of Celia Thaxter. A tip of the hat to Mr. and Mrs. Fields as we wander down **FIELDS ROAD**. Fields Road, which was opened during the 1930s.

*Prominent publisher, author and poet **James Thomas Fields**, right. From the collections of the Portsmouth Public Library. **Anne Adams Fields**, above, wife of James and close friend of South Berwick writer Sarah Orne Jewett. PA*

POET, ESSAYIST, ARTIST, island gardener and the intellectual magnet that drew many of the most prominent writers, musicians, artists and poets of the day to her island home, Celia Thaxter's Portsmouth roots are remembered in the naming of **THAXTER ROAD**, which joined the others of this group in the 1920s. Born on Daniel Street in 1835, Celia was four when her father, Thomas Laighton, took the job of lighthouse keeper on White Island and moved his family out to the Isles of Shoals. In 1847, Laighton began building the Appledore Hotel, in partnership with Levi Thaxter, who would marry the 16-year-old Celia four years later. Thaxter soon tired of island life and moved his wife and their first child back to the mainland, to the town of Newtonville, MA, west of Boston, where two more children were born into an increasingly troubled marriage.

Celia Thaxter counted literary figures James and Annie Fields, John G. Whittier and Sarah Orne Jewett, and artists Childe Hassam, John Appleton Brown and William Morris Hunt as personal friends. PA

In 1860, Celia poured her frustration into a poem, "Land-locked," which her husband found and gave to his friend James Russell Lowell, then the first editor of the *Atlantic Monthly.* Lowell published it to immediate critical acclaim, marking the beginning of a celebrated literary career.

The Thaxter family moved to Kittery Point in 1880, within view of the Isles of Shoals, ten miles across the sea. Celia died on her beloved Appledore, where she still summered, in 1894.

Not only a poet, Celia Thatxter was also an accomplished painter of watercolors and pottery.

> O happy river, could I follow thee!
> O yearning heart, that never can be still!
> O wistful eyes, that watch the steadfast hill,
> Longing for level line of solemn sea!
> – from Celia Thaxter's "Land-locked"

THE LESSER-KNOWN Revolutionary War poet Jonathan Mitchell Sewall (1748-1808) lent his name to **SEWALL ROAD**. Born in Salem, MA, Sewell was raised in Portsmouth and studied the law under Judge John Pickering. He practiced in this city all his life, but it is for his poems, orations, parodies, patriotic lyrics and wit in general that he was most esteemed. His Revolutionary War song, "Washington and War," was said to have been sung in every camp across the rebellious colonies. Sewell Road appeared on the maps in the 1930s.

> *To S.S., Esq.*
> *On his joining the American Army in 1777*
>
> When once the die is cast, vain all regret!
> Sense, virtue, duty, teach us to submit.
> Go then, dear friend! in quest of glory go,
> Defend your country, and repel the foe.
> With native fortitude and valor blest,
> Let your example animate the rest.
> – Jonathan M. Sewall

WASHINGTON & WAR

VAIN BRITONS, boast no longer with proud indignity,
By land your conquering legions, your matchless strength at sea,
Since we, your braver sons, incensed, our swords have girded on,
Huzza, huzza, huzza, for war and Washington!

Urged on by North and vengeance, those valiant champions came,
Loud bellowing Tea and Treason, and George was all on flame,
Yet sacrilegious as it seems, we rebels still live on,
And laught at all their empty puffs—huzza for Washington!

Still deaf to mild entreaties, still blind to England's good,
You have for thirty pieces betrayed your country's blood.
Like Æsop's greedy cur, you'll gain a shadow for your bone,
Yet find us fearful shades indeed, inspired by Washington.

Mysterious! Unexampled! Incomprehensible—
The blundering schemes of Britain, their folly, pride and zeal.
Like lions how ye growl and threat! Mere asses have you shown,
And ye shall share an ass's fate, and drudge for Washington!

Your dark, unfathom'd counsels our weakest heads defeat,
Our children rout your armies, our boats destroy your fleet,
And to complete the dire disgrace, coop'd up within a town,
You live, the scorn of all our host, the slaves of Washington!

Great heaven! Is this the nation whose thundering arms were hurl'd,
Through Europe, Afric, India? Whose navy ruled the world?
The lustre of your former deeds, whole ages of renown,
Lost in a moment, or transferred to us and Washington!

Yet think not thirst of glory unsheaths our vengeful swords,
To rend your bands asunder, and cast away your cords.
'Tis heaven-born freedom fires us all, and strengthens each brave son,
From him who humbly guides the plough, to godlike Washington.

For this, Oh could our wishes your ancient rage inspire,
Your armies should be doubled, in numbers, force and fire.
Then might the glorious conflict prove which best deserved the boon,
American, or Albion; a George, or Washington!

Fired with the great idea, our fathers' shades would rise;
To view the stern contention, the gods desert their skies.
And Wolfe, 'mid hosts of heroes, superior bending down,
Cry out with eager transport, God save great Washington!

Should warlike weapons fail us, disdaining slavish fears,
To swords we'll beat our ploughshares, our pruning hooks to spears,
And rush, all desperate! On our foe, nor breathe till battle won;
Then shout, and shout America! And conquering Washington!

Proud France should view with terror, and haughty Spain revere,
While every warlike nation would court alliance here.
And George, his minions trembling round, dismounting from his throne,
Pay homage to America, and glorious Washington!

Sewell was also known for his epitaphs, some of which got right to the point. 'Phthisic,' in the example below, is an archaic reference to any illness of the lungs or throat, such as asthma or a cough.

On a Quack Who Died of Asthma
Here lies death's caterer, breathless with the phthisic,
Who lived by what killed all his patients – PHYSIC.

OTHER NEW STREETS OF THE 1910S
Ash Street – Ashland Road – Central Avenue – Durgin Lane
Essex Avenue – Meadow Road – Monteith Street – Rands Court
Ridges Court – Sagamore Grove

WILLAM DURGIN FARMED land he owned along Newington Road in 1901. **DURGIN LANE** most probably took its name from this Durgin family. Later in the 20th century, the Durgin farmland would be eclipsed by and lend its name to a shopping area.

ROBERT MONTEITH, a carpenter, lived at 11 Dennett Street in 1861, just around the corner from present day **MONTEITH STREET**. Monteith Street wasn't opened until the 1910s, but it is conceivable that a prudent tradesman acquired land and eventually he, or perhaps an heir, developed it, as so many carpenter-turned-developers did before him.

IT IS APPROPRIATE that **RANDS COURT** be named in the plural (though its current street sign only acknowledges one Rand) – in 1875, the town directory listed 35 Rands. Francis Rand was one of the fifty men John Mason sent to establish a settlement at Strawbery Banke in 1630. And along with the fifty men, the *Annals of Portsmouth* tells us, Mason sent "eight Danes and twenty-two women." Presumably, Francis found favor with one of the twenty-two women; by the early 1700s, the births, deaths or marriages of 38 Rands living in Portsmouth and Rye had been recorded.

*A handsome young **Rand** of Civil War vintage.*
PA

IN THE LATE 1800s, the corner of South Street and New Castle Avenue belonged to one Rienzi Ridge. Ridge had leased the land to the Portsmouth Athletic Club for use as a baseball field, complete with grandstands sufficiently commodious to seat 500 spectators. In 1896, Ridge bought back the lease, intending to expand the complex to include both a quarter-mile bicycle track and a trotting track.

The bicycle track came to fruition, the trotting track apparently not, though there was great local interest in the sport at the time – Frank Jones's Maplewood Farm was fielding some of the great trotters of the day.

As for bicycle racing, it seems to have been a great draw in its day. Over a thousand spectators cheered on their favorites at the first bicycle meet on the new track in 1897, with the Portsmouth Cadet Band parading between races.

But in 1901, the bike park was plowed up and returned to pasturage, and Ridge made plans to subdivided the land into house lots. The City entertained the possibility of purchasing the tract in 1904, but when those plans came to naught, Ridge's scheme went forward, and so today we have RIDGES COURT.

*Rienzi Ridge's popular **Bicycle Park** still appeared on the 1903 map, above. Left, a group photo of the New Hampshire Wheelsmen, c. 1895. PA*

1920 - 1930
THE MEMORIAL BRIDGE APPROACH
Dutton Avenue – Scott Avenue – Wright Avenue

YOU WON'T FIND ANY street signs for DUTTON, SCOTT or WRIGHT AVENUE, though they still exist as pavement and on maps. To get to Bow Street from State, you follow State onto Dutton, under the Memorial Bridge approach and then onto Scott – or at least you will again, we're told, by the summer of 2012.

Like any fundamental alteration to the infrastructure of a town, the grafting of a major artery into its very heart requires significant change. By 1920, there was little argument over the obvious benefits of a roadway crossing into Maine at this point along the river; the automobile-owning public was on the move and an alternative to ferry service was eagerly awaited. Federal funding was secured, buildings were condemned and new streets were laid out. The approaches on both ends of the bridge would be designated as veteran memorial parks – and neither park escaped controversy.

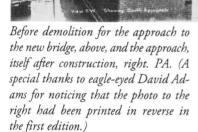

Before demolition for the approach to the new bridge, above, and the approach, itself after construction, right. PA. (A special thanks to eagle-eyed David Adams for noticing that the photo to the right had been printed in reverse in the first edition.)

On the Portsmouth side, the debate questioned just *which* veterans were to be memorialized. Veterans of the Civil War's Grand Army as well as those of the 1898 Spanish-American War wanted their brethren included; the American Legion felt this memorial should commemorate only those who fought in the World War, hostilities history has renamed World War I. The American Legion prevailed and the World War Memorial Park was created.

While Portsmouth dealt with veteran politics, Kittery redesigned its former militia training ground into the beautiful John Paul Jones Memorial Park. Maine governor Percival Baxter selected Boston artist Bashka Paeff (1894–1979) to provide a monumental bronze relief as the centerpiece of its Soldiers and Sailors Memorial, but by the time the piece was ready for installation, a new governor had taken Baxter's place. Governor Ralph Brewster had no use for a monument that he felt gloried pacifism, and refused to pay for it. Concessions were made and Paeff completed "The Sacrifices of War." Apparently even the name was controversial – she had originally titled the anguished study "The Horrors of War."

But let us return to our forgotten avenues. SCOTT AVENUE was named for Francis A. Scott, a Portsmouth native killed in action in France on September 11, 1918, at the age of 27. DUTTON AVENUE was named in memory of Harold L. Dutton, who died of wounds sustained in the Battle of the Argonne Forest the same year. WRIGHT AVENUE, which connects the two, was named for the most celebrated of Portsmouth's World War I fighting men, John Brandon Wright.

First Lieut. J. Brandon Wright distinguished himself in service with the 14th Aero Squadron, American Expeditionary Forces in France, as well as with the Army of Occupation in Germany, and continued in aviation in the service after the war's end. A year later found him among 20 teams of aviators selected from a field of 500 applicants to participate in a "big aeroplane race" from Minneola, NY, to San Francisco. Two weeks of front page headlines in the autumn of 1919 chronicled the competition – a round-trip transcontinental contest at speeds ranging from 120

*A stationary section of the **Memorial Bridge** moves toward its piers in 1923. Shortridge Hardesty designed the bridge; partner J.A.L. Waddell designed and engineered the central lift. The pair were credited with the designs for bridges all over the country.*

Due to deterioration, the Memorial Bridge was closed in July, 2011; demolition took place in February, 2012. Its replacement is due to open to traffic in the summer of 2013. PA

*Portsmouth's World War I flying ace **Lieutenant J. Brandon Wright**. The* Portsmouth Herald, *October 21, 1919.*

to 150 mph that had claimed the lives of 5 of the 62 starters before the race was half run. Wright piloted a DeHavilland 4 biplane powered by a 413 horsepower Liberty motor. Though not a winner, he was credited as being among "the successful flyers," no mean feat in itself. He died of disease two years later in Colorado and was returned to Portsmouth for burial.

PANNAWAY MANOR
Colonial Drive – Decatur Road – Georges** Terrace
Hall Court – Mason** Avenue – Schurman Avenue
Victory Road – Whipple Court – Worthen Road

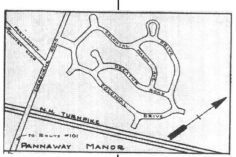

Pannaway Manor as it appeared on the 1956 city map. PA

ONE OF THREE neighborhoods quickly constructed to house World War II Naval Shipyard workers, PANNAWAY MANOR's 159 homes were completed and rented before material and time shortages began to affect the quality and detail of such housing. Monthly rents ranged from $40 for a 4-room cape to $55 for the 6-room model. All 159 homes still stand, though their original tenants would hardly recognize them today. The development off Sherburne Road takes its name from that of David Thomson's 1623 settlement and trading post at Odiorne Point.

PANNAWAY MANOR'S HOUSING was neo-colonial in design, perhaps the inspiration for the name of COLONIAL DRIVE.

MASON AVENUE most probably derives its name from one of the grant holders for the region, Thomson's employer, Captain John Mason (1586-1635), the merchant-adventurer and founder of New Hampshire who served under both James I and Charles I. In 1615, Mason was appointed Royal governor of the five-year-old colony of Newfoundland, and in 1622, he and partner Sir Ferdinando Gorges were granted patents to develop a colony between the Merrimac and Kennebec Rivers. Mason sent a contingent of settlers to his land under the leadership of David Thompson, a Scot, in 1623.

DECATUR ROAD most likely honors Commodore Steven Decatur (1779-1820), famous for, among many other exploits, ending hostilities in 1815 with Algeria and the Barbary pirates. His proclamation regarding the negotiations ("Our country! In her intercourse with foreign nations may she always be in the right; but our country right or wrong") rings down the intervening years.

Eleven cities and five counties have been named for naval hero **Stephen Decatur,** *who died in 1820 from wounds received in a duel. Stephen Decatur IV would marry Mabel Goodwin, daughter of NH governor Ichabod Goodwin, in 1884. From the U.S. Naval Library.*

I'D LIKE TO THINK that the street namers of Pannaway Manor had the other grant holder to the region, Mason's partner Ferdinando Gorges, in mind when they christened GEORGES TERRACE. My guess is that they anticipated just too many misspellings. Gorges was one of the principal owners of the Plymouth Company, who sent over their first explorers in 1606. His servant, the Native American Squanto, is best remembered as the man without whose aid the Pilgrims at Plymouth might never have survived their first winters.

REVOLUTIONARY WAR HERO Elijah Hall (1746-1830) could conceivably be the inspiration for the naming of HALL COURT. A lieutenant under John Paul Jones on board the *Ranger*, Hall returned home to Portsmouth to take his place among the successful ship captains of his day. Prosperity permitted him to participate in numerous business opportunities. He was one of the principals in the 1795 incorporation of the Portsmouth Pier and

New Hampshire Hotel, and of the New Hampshire Union Bank in 1802. In 1804, he signed on as a proprietor of a new public bathing facility, and in 1810 joined others forming the Union Insurance Company. He also represented Portsmouth in the state legislature.

Hall married Elizabeth Stoodly, who had inherited her father James Stoodly's Daniel Street hostelry. The Halls made what is known again today as Stoodley's Tavern their private residence.

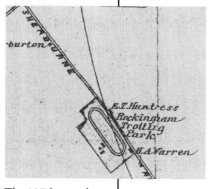

The 1876 map shows a trotting track in the vicinity of what Ray Brighton describes as a county fairgrounds. PA

AN ARTHUR SCHURMAN was a member in good standing of the Portsmouth Driving Club in 1914. Ray Brighton tells us the club raced at the old Rockingham track at fairgrounds off Sherburne Road. Another big stretch, but perhaps this gentleman took an interest in property in the area and became the inspiration for the naming of SCHURMAN AVENUE.

VICTORY IS CERTAINLY what the country was hoping for in 1941; VICTORY ROAD reflects the sentiment of the day.

WHIPPLE COURT, which bears no physical proximity to Whipple Street, is yet another example of Portsmouth's odd predisposition to double up on names. (See Whipple Street, page 146.)

*Signatory to the Declaration of Independence **William Whipple** is remembered all over town. This monument stands near the South Mill Pond.*

EZEKIEL WORTHEN IS LISTED by Ray Brighton as one of a short list of "key men" working under General John Sullivan to ready defenses of Portsmouth harbor in the fall of 1775. Others on the list: "surgeon turned soldier," Dr. Hall Jackson, Major George Gaines and Pierse Long. This Worthen sounds entirely worthy of having WORTHEN ROAD named for him.

OTHER NEW STREETS OF THE 1920S
Beechwood Street – Benson Street – Boss Avenue – Fletcher Street
Forest Street – Garden Street – Kensington Road – Pearson Street
Sims Avenue – Sylvester Street

A "BOSS FIELD" EXISTED before 1930, by which time BOSS ROAD, today's BOSS AVENUE, had come into existence. A farmer by the name of Joseph Boss lived on Gosling Road in 1875.

PORTSMOUTH MAY HAVE started out as a secular under-taking – we are often reminded that the original inhabitants came in search not of religious freedom but of fish – but by the late 17th century, a puritanical ethic had caught up with the locals. In 1678, 'Tythingmen' were appointed, "whose duty it was to look after the good morals of their neighbors, ... every individual or family, excepting that of the minister, who probably was a sort of supervisor of the Tythingmen," according to Brewster.

A Dr. Fletcher was listed as one of thirteen "honest men" appointed by the selectmen "to inspect their neighbors, as the law directs, for preventing drunkenness and disorder." He bore the weighty responsibility for the souls of the families of "Mr. Jno. Cutt, Sen'r, Mrs. El. Cutt, Lt. Vaughan, Mrs. Cowell, Mr. Tho. Harvey, Jno. Cutt, Jun'r, Jno. Tucker, Mr. Martin, Mr. Shipway [and] Clem't Merserve." I am going to give the good doctor one more responsibility, for the naming of FLETCHER STREET.

*A watercolor of a closed door by **Helen Pearson**, in this case that of the Langdon House. Portsmouth Public Library.*

PORTSMOUTH ARTIST Helen Pearson (1870-1949) is best remembered for her 1913 *Vignettes of Portsmouth*, a collection of pen and ink and pencil drawings of the historic homes and vistas amidst which she grew up. Her drawing, 'The Open Door,' was featured widely through the early 20th century in promotional brochures, eventually lending its name to Portsmouth's nickname, 'the city of the open door.'

Pearson was also an avid golfer and classical pianist who played at one time with the Schnectady, NY, Symphony Orchestra. Perhaps **PEARSON STREET** remembers this multi-talented woman.

1930 – 1940
ELMWOOD
Harvard Street – Princeton Road – Oxford Avenue

ACCORDING TO A *Portsmouth Herald* of the day, a development called ELMWOOD was proposed in 1902, which would consist of half a dozen streets named for different colleges. Of the names proposed, only HARVARD STREET, PRINCETON ROAD and OXFORD AVENUE were actually developed, three decades later.

THE FLATIRON LOT
Lafayette School – Ward Playground – Ward Place

THOMAS WARD'S HOME stood across South Street on the site of today's Lafayette Professional Park. He and his brother, Fred H. Ward, were partners in William Ward and Sons, distillers of "Pure Molasses Rum." The town's only distillery was located at 23 Dennett Street, with offices at 93 Market Street.

Ward purchased the small triangle formed by the intersection of South Street, Middle Road and Lafayette Road at auction in 1898. In 1914, the city negotiated to purchase the plot on which **Lafayette School** would sit, owned at the time by the Consolidation Coal Company. At the same time, Ward offered to present the city with his adjoining property – with the stipulation that there be no further building on the land and that no roads be built across it. The city council, uncomfortable with Ward's restrictions, voted to reject his offer. However, they did finally come to terms, agreeing to purchase the land from him for $3,500, a bit more than half its appraised value, with the guarantee that no building would be considered for 18 years, and that the area would be known as the WARD PLAYGROUND.

The playground remains intact today, as Ward had hoped, and WARD PLACE remembers the city's generous benefactor. The neocolonial Lafayette School opened its doors in 1915, and was named, of course, for the major thoroughfare that heads south from one corner of its playground.

And after sitting vacant for years, including years the city spent convincing the neighborhood, the old Lafayette Elementary School finally reopened as housing for seniors in 2009.

OTHER NEW STREETS OF THE 1930S

**Artwill Avenue – Baycliffe Road – Brackett Road/Lane
Cliff Road – Dodge Avenue – Fairview Drive/Lane – Haven Road
Hillside Drive – Jenkins Avenue – Lookout Lane
McClintock Street – Pinehurst Road – Rockaway Street
Summit Avenue – Walker Bungalow Road
Sarah Mildred Long Bridge – Incinerator Road**

BROTHERS ARTHUR AND William Hopley developed – and named, presumably – ARTWILL AVENUE. Arthur (1912-2000), a Navy veteran, saw action in Africa, Sicily and Iwo Jima during World War II. Joining the U.S. Postal Service as a substitute mail carrier in 1938, he attained the rank of Postmaster of Portsmouth in 1971.

A poster of the day advertising Colonel W. F. Cody's **Wild West** *extravaganza.*

JOSHUA BRACKETT (1733-1801) must be considered one of the great renaissance men of colonial Portsmouth. Educated at Harvard in theology, he preached for a short period before deciding to study medicine with Dr. Clement Jackson, one of the foremost medical practitioners of his time. As the young country moved toward revolution, the young doctor participated as a member of the state committee of safety, signed the Association Test and, during the Revolution, presided as a judge of the New Hampshire maritime court, determining the disposition of ships captured by local privateers. In 1793, he was elected president of the New Hampshire Medical Society. Though in declining health himself, he nevertheless administered to the sick during an outbreak of yellow fever in 1798.

Dr. Brackett once owned the area encompassing Little Harbour School and the residences thereabout. BRACKETT'S FIELD was often the site of itinerant circuses and Buffalo Bill's Wild West Show, when they came through town. BRACKETT LANE and BRACKETT ROAD remember the good doctor and judge, and the late 19th-century crowds that gathered in his field.

THAT A LESTER DODGE was one of the first four homeowners on DODGE AVENUE is, most probably, not a coincidence.

Portsmouth has spawned a Dodge of note, however. Journalist and insurance man Samuel Dodge's work was of sufficient importance to rate an entry *and* a photograph in Hazlett's *History of Rockingham County.* Born in 1844, Samuel Dodge served as a correspondent for Boston newspapers, as well as a number of national publications.

Journalist **Samuel Dodge.** *From Hazlett's* History of Rockingham County, NH.

WE KNOW THAT Haven Park is named for the Reverend Dr. Samuel Haven (see pages 31-33), thanks to clear documentation, but we cannot be as certain about **HAVEN ROAD**. Several generations produced Havens of note, two more of whom we'll meet now.

Nathaniel Appleton Haven (1762-1831), son of the Reverend, graduated from Harvard with a degree in medicine in 1779 and practiced his trade in Portsmouth, while pursuing commercial interests as well. He was employed as a ship's surgeon during the Revolutionary War, and represented New Hampshire's 4th District in Congress from 1809 to 1811.

Nathaniel Appleton Haven (1790-1826), the above-mentioned Reverend's grandson, also graduated Harvard, studied the law and set up a practice in Portsmouth. Known as much as an orator, journalist and poet as a lawyer, he was editor of the *Portsmouth Journal* from 1821 to 1825, and contributed to the *North American Review*.

> I love the dews of night
>   I love the howling of the wind
> I love to hear the tempest sweep
> O'er the billows of the deep!
> For nature's saddest scenes delight
>   The melancholy mind.
>   – from the younger N. A.
>   Haven's poem "Autumn"

IN 1871, THE *Portsmouth Journal* received a letter to the editor advocating the construction of a look-out tower, ideally "on the highest point of land in the field south of the elegant residence of F. W. Miller Esq. on Lincoln Hill, commanding a view north to the White Mountains." Instead, a residence was built on that prominence, known in 1884 as **LOOKOUT ROCK**, which today serves as the centerpiece of the Edgewood Centre complex. My guess is that this selfsame Lookout Rock is the inspiration for **LOOKOUT LANE**. Likewise, **SUMMIT AVENUE** straddles the highest point in the area.

MCCLINTOCK STREET must certainly have been named for Captain John McClintock (1760-1855) – he was the kind of man for whom streets *should* be named. Ninety-five years of age at his death, Captain McClintock was still in active service to his country as a purchasing agent for the city of Portsmouth. Charles Brewster tells us that McClintock assured him, the very week of his death, that in the preceding five years he had missed only a single day attending to his duties – due to a snowstorm.

Patriotic duty came naturally in the McClintock family. His father, the Reverend Samuel McClintock of Greenland, served as a chaplain at Bunker Hill. Just a lad when the colonies revolted, John McClintock went to sea on a privateer, quickly moving up the ranks to commander. By the end of the 18th century, he both commanded and owned his own ship. Like many before him, he became a merchant when he left the sea, was a justice of the peace for fifty years, a general commissioner of bankruptcy for the state of New Hampshire under Jefferson, and was a founder of the Portsmouth Aqueduct, among many other distinctions. It is only natural that such an illustrious citizen's name would be put forward for recognition.

> SAGAMORE LANDING forms a cul-de-sac at the terminus of Walker Bungalow Road.

The bustling **Walker Coal Pockets** *were a feature of the thriving Portsmouth waterfront of the late 19th century. PA*

NONE OF THOSE summer "bungalows" that sprang up along Little Harbor Road during the late 19th century lie on today's **WALKER BUNGALOW ROAD**, but old timers remember a beauty of a summer home in those parts, built of stone, by A. W. Walker.

Walker was a prominent name in Portsmouth. Charles E. Walker and J. Albert Walker, conducting business jointly as Walker & Co., took part of the Portsmouth Pier as a coal wharf in 1879.

The partnership seems not to have flourished. J. Albert announced that *his* coal pockets were ready for business in 1880, while Charles, "late of the firm of Walker & Co.," opened a large coal pocket under his own name in 1881. By 1893, J. Albert and A. W. Walker were operating what was then known as the Portsmouth Coal Pockets.

And let us not forget Horton D. Walker, who served as mayor of Portsmouth from 1853 to 1855, and once again in 1872.

THE SARAH MILDRED LONG BRIDGE, most often referred to as the ROUTE 1 BYPASS BRIDGE or just the MIDDLE BRIDGE, was started in 1938 and opened for business in 1940. A toll was required to pass in the early days; it was then known as the DIME BRIDGE. Tolls were collected until 1972 and the arrival of the I-95 bridge.

The new bridge replaced the first structure to span the Piscataqua between Portsmouth and Kittery. Built in 1822 to carry foot and wagon traffic, it was retrofitted to handle rail in 1842. That bridge sat some 60 feet upstream of the one we use today. The Memorial Bridge further downstream took some of the pressure off the aging structure when it came on line in 1923.

It wasn't until the Middle Bridge's 50th anniversary that it was dedicated to the woman who served as executive secretary, as well as in other capacities, for the Maine/New Hampshire Interstate Bridge Authority for all those fifty years.

Sarah Mildred Long, "*the mainstay of the authority since its formation," and "the captain of the team." From Woodard Openo's* The Sarah Mildred Long Bridge, *with permission of the publisher, Peter E. Randall.*

THE NAMER OF INCINERATOR ROAD, off Jones Avenue, gets no points for creativity. The area opened in the 1930s as a city dump. The original incinerator on the site, constructed of brick, was replaced in the 1960s with a metal structure described as resembling a giant tipi. This system was scrapped in 1972, due to environmental concerns, though the site continued to function as a landfill until dumping moved to the infamous Coakley Landfill, a sand and gravel quarry on Breakfast Hill Road. Coakley was closed in 1985, with the EPA designation of Superfund Waste Site.

1940-1950
WENTWORTH ACRES
Dovekie Way – Staysail Way – Spinnaker Way – Osprey Drive
Blue Heron Drive – Shearwater Drive – Sanderling Way – Dunlin Way
Granite Street – Circuit Road/McGee Drive – Portsmouth Boulevard

TODAY KNOWN AS SPINNAKER POINT and OSPREY LANDING, and SEACREST VILLAGE and MARINER VILLAGE through the intervening years, this area began its modern existence as WENTWORTH ACRES (after Mark H. Wentworth, who owned and farmed the area first settled in the late 17th century by John Cutt's ill-fated widow Ursula – see page 96). The 750 units that comprised the original development were built by the Navy as wartime housing in six months flat, along with Admiralty Village in Kittery and Clay Village in Eliot – the Navy can be remarkably efficient when it sets its mind to it. But it turns out that the Navy is also capable of making remarkable blunders: plans for similar housing for the Norfolk Naval base located in Portsmouth, *Virginia*, were inadvertently switched with those to be built here. Virginia's installation got the insulation that was meant for New Hampshire.

Originally Seacrest Villiage, today's Spinnaker Point and Osprey Landing, as it appeared on the Planning Department's official map in 1972. PA

Originally designed as temporary housing, the neighborhood remained after the war, continuing on as Seacrest Village, an area of affordable housing with a diverse population. With its latest reincarnation as Osprey Village and Spinnaker Point, its affordability is no longer a given.

Two of Spinnaker Point's streets borrow their names from pieces of nautical equipment, the rest from shore birds.

THE LARGE, BALLOONING, kite-like sail that precedes a sailboat as it runs before the wind is known as a spinnaker. **SPINNAKER WAY** was originally part of **CIRCUIT ROAD**.

A STAY IS ANY ROPE or wire that stabilizes the mast, running from the top of the mast forward towards the bow of the vessel. A staysail is a triangular sail attached to such a stay. **STAYSAIL WAY** was also part of **CIRCUIT ROAD**.

THE SHORT BEAKED, short-bodied dovekie is also known as the sea dove or little auk. Abundant in arctic regions, it breeds in dense colonies in Greenland in the summer and spends its winters in southern Greenland, Labrador and Newfoundland. **DOVEKIE WAY**, which started out in life as **GRANITE STREET** and most certainly existed when I started this book, had disappeared from the 2005 Planning Department map. R.I.P.

*The **dovekie** favors life in the open seas, only coming ashore to breed. All images in this section come from John James Audubon's* Birds of North America.

THE S-CURVE-NECKED blue heron is a familiar sight in ponds, marshes and estuaries of the region, but makes itself to home almost anywhere in North America. Standing motionless in water, the blue heron will wait patiently for small fish or other amphibious snacks to stray within reach. If nothing presents itself, he'll finally take a few steps, then return to his perfectly immobile state again. **BLUE HERON DRIVE** was originally known as **ROCKHILL AVENUE**.

*The **great blue heron**, sporting a wingspan of almost six feet, feels equally at home in both salt and freshwater environments.*

THE OSPREY, a fish-eating raptor with a five-foot wing-span, is second cousin to the hawk, eagle and falcon. Diurnal feeders, they plunge feet-first into the water after their prey.

Almost extinct in the 1970s, New Hampshire's ospreys have made a dramatic recovery with the help of the Fish and Game Department, though they are still considered one of America's endangered species. They head for Central and South America in the early fall. OSPREY DRIVE was originally known as PROFILE AVE-NUE.

Osprey nests are remarkable for both their size (often three feet deep and five feet across) and the eclectic materials used to build them.

• THE SANDERLING, AN arctic-breeding cousin of the sandpiper, winters along both the east and west coasts of the United States. Darting along the shore after receding waves, they are distinguished by their pure white under-belly and jet-black bill, legs and feet. Only appearing on the city map in the 1960s, SANDERLING WAY is a newer addition to the neighborhood.

*The **sanderling** typically breeds and rears its young in the rocky arctic tundra.*

• THE DUNLIN, another familiar shorebird, is smaller, plumper and longer beaked than its cousin the sanderling. Endlessly busy at the shore-line, they typically dine on insects, sandhoppers and small crustaceans, probing the sand with the speed of little sewing machines. DUNLIN WAY is another section of the original CIRCUIT ROAD.

*The **dunlin**, also known as the 'red-backed sandpiper.'*

A section of the original Dunlin Way has recently been renamed **PORTSMOUTH BOULEVARD** at the request of developer Michael Kane. It now serves as the gateway to an industrial park, which will be well served with the grander name.

THE SHEARWATER spends its entire life at sea, coming ashore only to nest. Like the osprey, it winters in the southern hemisphere. Shearwaters are often found following fishing boats or accompanying whales, feeding on the same variety of fish the whales eat. **SHEARWATER DRIVE** was also part of the original **CIRCUIT ROAD**.

*Ideally adapted to life at sea, the **shearwater** drinks salt water, expelling the salt through its nostrils.*

TWO STUBS OF THE original streets of Wentworth Acres, Circuit Road and Granite Street, were left dangling with the further extension of Market Street Extension in late 1970s. We know them today as **GRANITE STREET** and **MCGEE DRIVE**. Granite Street kept its original name. McGee Drive is a story in itself.

Ray Brighton tells us that attorney and one-term mayor Calvin Page was "one of the men closest to Frank Jones," so it is not surprising that Jones tapped him to act as trustee of his $5 million-plus estate. Present day Portsmouth attorney Jack McGee's great-grandmother, Susan Flynn, purchased a parcel of land from the breakup of the Jones farm from Page, leaving the property to those of her grandchildren who were surviving at the death of the last of her children – which is how in 1954 Jack's mother, Louise McGee, and her husband, John P. McGee, Sr., came to build themselves a home at the corner of what would one day carry McGee Sr.'s name. It was renamed McGee Drive in 1985.

ELWYN PARK
Elwyn Road – Dondero School
Adams* Avenue – Arthur Road – Cleveland Drive – Coolidge Drive
Dwight Avenue – Fillmore Road – Garfield Road – Grant* Avenue/Way
Harding Road – Harrison Avenue – Hayes Place – Hoover Drive
McKinley Road – Nixon Park – Pierce Place – Polk Avenue
Taft Road – Taylor Lane – Truman Place – Tyler Place
Van Buren Avenue – Wilson Road

I**N CHARLES BREWSTER'S DAY**, John Elwyn, grandson of John Langdon, owned a large farm at the head of Sagamore Creek. One hundred sixty-two acres of the Elwyn farm have come down to us as the Urban Forestry Center, thanks to the generosity of descendent John Elwyn Stone (see Urban Forestry Center, page 208). **ELWYN ROAD** skirts the south side of the old farm.

John Elwyn, grandson of John Langdon, the first elected governor of New Hampshire. PA

Anticipating the housing boom that swept the nation at the end of the Second World War, developer John Golter started opening roads and breaking ground for the neighborhood that would become known as Elwyn Park. Erminio Ricci (1903-1982) would continue developing the area through the 1950s. The development was a hard sell, situated as it was so far out of town.

Born in Italy, Erminio Ricci boarded a ship bound for Philadelphia the day before he turned sixteen, rather than face conscription into the Italian army. Making his way to Portsmouth, he moved in with a family on Gates Street and started looking for work. He enrolled in night school to learn English and found jobs where he could. Often working double shifts, he sent the bulk of his pay back home to Italy. Among his many jobs was one working on the Memorial Bridge. He once even accepted employment in Exeter, at first commuting to and from work on foot. He sat on the City Council in 1960.

ERMINIO RICCI PROVIDED land for an elementary school to serve the children of Elwyn Park. **DONDERO SCHOOL** was named for Mary Carey Dondero (1894-1960). A beauty queen whose formal schooling ended before she completed the eighth grade, Portsmouth's first woman mayor, elected in 1944, was possibly the first woman *ever* to serve in that capacity east of the Mississippi. Starting in 1935, Dondero served ten terms in the New Hampshire House of Representatives. Her daughter, Eileen Foley, would follow in her mother's mayoral footsteps in 1968.

Mary Carey Dondero lost a 1946 bid for the state senate – by a single vote. Portrait hanging in the City Council Chambers.

THE STREETS OF ELWYN PARK (reportedly named by the wife of the surveyor on the project, John Durgin), celebrate twenty-four of America's past presidents. If the names chosen seem to favor Republicans over Democrats, it's not your imagination – a family member told me that Mrs. Durgin favored Republicans over Democrats in the voting booth, too. The presidents that made the cut are presented here in order of their terms of office.

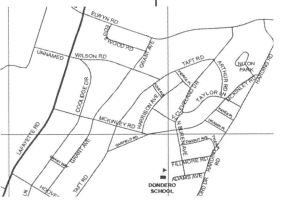

Elwyn Park was complete as we know at today when it appeared on the city's official street map in 1972. Taft Road has since been extended to meet Hoover Drive. Courtesy of the City of Portsmouth.

JOHN ADAMS (1797-1801), a Federalist who had served two terms as vice president under Washington, almost took the country to war against France. His son, Democrat-Republican **JOHN QUINCY ADAMS** (1825-29), the first son to follow his father in the presidency, had served as Secretary of State under Monroe. He faced criticism when he expanded the government's role into the development of the arts and sciences.

MARTIN VAN BUREN (1837-41), vice president under Andrew Jackson, was the first president born a U.S. citizen. A Democrat, he brought the nation through the economic Panic of 1837. However, his attempts to find a remedy only deepened the country's problems.

WILLIAM HENRY HARRISON (1841), Whig, the Indian fighter who took office in 1841, died of pneumonia before the month was out. (See also Benjamin Harrison, next page.)

JOHN TYLER (1841-45), Whig; on the death of Harrison the first vice president to find himself elevated to the role of president, presided over the annexation of Texas.

JAMES POLK (1845-49), Democrat, presided over both the Mexican-American War and the Gold Rush.

ZACHARY TAYLOR (1849-50), a Whig, was the first president prepared to hold the Union together by force if necessary. His death, due to a gastrointestinal illness, provided the slave states with an eleven-year grace period.

MILLARD FILLMORE (1850-53), also a Whig, stepped into the presidency upon Taylor's death, and signed the Fugitive Slave Act into law.

FRANKLIN PIERCE (1853-57), nine years a congressman from New Hampshire, was nominated by the Democrats on the 49th ballot and served as the nation's 14th president. On his watch, the Kansas-Nebraska Act brought the issue of slavery to the boiling point.

Franklin Pierce, a native of New Hampshire. By permission of the Franklin Pierce Homestead, Hillsborough, NH.

ULYSSES S. GRANT (1869-77), a Republican fresh from the battlefields of the South, presided over reconstruction in a presidency marred by scandals.

RUTHERFORD B. HAYES (1877-81), Republican, came into office after a fiercely contested election. Withdrawing federal troops from the South, reconstruction came to an end during his one-term presidency.

JAMES GARFIELD, a Republican and the last president born in a log cabin, served only six months before being assassinated in 1881.

CHESTER ARTHUR (1881-85), Republican, Garfield's vice president, championed civil service reform. The first federal immigration laws were enacted under his presidency.

GROVER CLEVELAND (1885-89, reelected 1893-97) is the only president to date to have served two non-consecutive terms. A Democrat, during his first term, he brought the railroads under federal regulation. His second term was marked by domestic unrest, economic woes, strikes and riots.

BENJAMIN HARRISON (1889-93), Republican and the grandson of William Henry Harrison, saw the Sherman Anti-Trust Act become law under his administration. (See also William Henry Harrison, preceding page.)

WILLIAM MCKINLEY (1897-1901), Republican, presided over the Spanish-American War and the annexation of Hawaii, the Philippines, Guam and Puerto Rico. He was assassinated less than a year into his second term.

WILLIAM H. TAFT (1909-13), a Republican, worked to rein in the powers of the presidency as expanded by Theodore Roosevelt.

WOODROW WILSON (1913-21), Democrat, saw America through the First World War, with the oft-stated intention of making the world "safe for democracy."

WARREN HARDING (1921-23), Republican, made sure that the United States did not enter into the League of Nations. The Teapot Dome scandal took place on his watch. He died in office, of a heart attack.

CALVIN COOLIDGE (1923-29), Republican, Harding's taciturn vice president, officiated over the 1920s boom years devoting himself to maintaining the status quo while turning a blind eye to growing problems in agriculture.

HERBERT HOOVER (1929-33), a Republican and Secretary of Commerce under both Harding and Coolidge, claimed in his 1928 campaign that America was "nearer to the final triumph over poverty than ever before in the history of any land." It was his view that caring for those left destitute by the stock market crash ten months after he took office should be the voluntary responsibility of local authorities.

HARRY S. TRUMAN (1945-53), a Democrat who briefly served as Franklin Roosevelt's vice president at the beginning of his fourth and last term, saw his predecessor's dream of a United Nations through to reality two months after Roosevelt's death. Another two months saw him bring World War II to an end with the dropping of atomic bombs on Hiroshima and Nagasaki. In 1950, he led the United States into limited war with North Korea.

DWIGHT D. EISENHOWER (1953-61), Republican, allied commander of D-Day forces as America entered World War II, warned America as he left office of the dangers of the "military-industrial complex." He ordered troops into Little Rock, Arkansas, to escort children to school when desegregation became the law of the land.

RICHARD NIXON (1969-1974), Republican, Eisenhower's vice president, resigned the presidency rather than face impeachment after the campaign scandals of his successful run for a second term. His historic summit meetings with China and the Soviet Union helped reduce Cold War tensions.

MAPLEWOOD ACRES
Clover Lane – Echo Avenue/Hill – Farm Lane – Hillcrest Drive
Longmeadow Lane – Maple Street – Woodlawn Circle

IN 1909, FRANK JONES' grateful widow gave the Maplewood Avenue farmhouse to her Boston psychotherapist, Boris Sidis. He and his wife operated the premises as a psychiatric sanitarium until his death in 1923.

The Frank Jones 'farmhouse,' which still stands today, at the corner of Maplewood and Woodbury Avenues. PA

Between 1941 and 1947, the Hampton Development Corporation created MAPLEWOOD ACRES from two tracts of land that were once part of the Jones farm.

The streets of Maplewood Acres, with names as bucolic as the terrain they replaced, are graced by architecture that has been described as 'eclectic colonial.'

OTHER NEW STREETS OF THE 1940S
Doris Avenue – Gray's Lane – Greenside Avenue
Hodgdon Lane – Holly Lane – Snug Harbor Avenue
Sutton Avenue – Vine Street – Witmer Avenue

FRED A. GRAY SAT on the Police Commission in 1912, and the City Council in 1917. He also sold paint and wallpaper on Daniel Street; his store is still there and thriving today. Fred and his wife Lillian lived at 191 Sagamore Avenue, almost at the corner of what appeared on the map in 1950 as GRAY'S AVENUE, changing names in the early 1960s to the more modest GRAY'S LANE.

John Golter, the original developer of Elwyn Park, also opened and developed an area off Sherburne Road that became known as Golterville. **Doris**, **Greenside**, **Sutton** and **Witmer Avenues** were all named for members of the Golter family.

THE NAME OF ONE Nathaniel Hodgdon was entered on the city's tax rolls in 1727. A George E. Hodgdon was serving as Portsmouth's mayor in 1887 and 1888. And Ray Brighton tells us of a carpenter by the name of

William A. Hodgdon (1849-?) who went to New York City to study architecture, then returned to Portsmouth to ply his new trade. This Hodgdon sat on the County Commission in 1909, and again from 1911 to 1914. Take your pick. Any one of them sounds like a likely candidate to have HODGDON LANE named after him.

1950-1960

PEASE AIR FORCE BASE

Airline Avenue – Ash Court – Ashland Road
Aviation Avenue – Corporate Drive – Country Club Road
Durham Street – Exeter Street – Flight Line Road – Goose Bay Drive
Grafton Road – Hampton Street – International Drive – Lee Street
Manchester Square – Maple Drive – Maplewood Terrace
Nashua Avenue – New Hampshire Avenue – Newfields Street
Newington Street – Northwood Road – Oak Avenue – Pease Boulevard
Pinecrest Terrace – Redhook Way – Rochester Avenue – Rye Street
Somerwsworth Street – Strafford Drive – Stratham Street – Willow Court

WITH ONLY A FEW exceptions, the names of the streets that crisscross today's Pease International Tradeport fit neatly into three categories: industrial/corporate, reflecting the area's economic significance; New Hampshire geographic; and ironically arboreal, considering that the once wooded property was pretty much stripped of trees when it became a military base.

Beginning its life as a 300-acre municipal installation in early the 1930s, Portsmouth's airport was taken over first by the U.S. Navy in the 1940s and then by the Air Force in the 1950s. Portsmouth Air Force Base was formally opened in 1956 as an expanded 3000-acre bomber base for the Strategic Air Command. The following year, the base was renamed in honor of Plymouth, NH, native, and University of New Hampshire graduate, B-17 pilot Captain Harl Pease, Jr.

Captain Harl Pease, Jr. (1917-1942). Courtesy of the 'Wings of Valor' web site.

MEDAL OF HONOR CITATION: For conspicuous gallantry and intrepidity above and beyond the call of duty in action with the enemy on 6–7 August 1942. When one engine of the bombardment airplane of which he was pilot failed during a bombing mission over New Guinea, Capt. Pease was forced to return to a base in Australia. Knowing that all available airplanes of his group were to participate the next day in an attack on an enemy-held airdrome near Rabaul, New Britain, although he was not scheduled to take part in this mission, Capt. Pease selected the most serviceable airplane at this base and prepared it for combat, knowing that it had been found and declared unserviceable for combat missions. With the members of his combat crew, who volunteered to accompany him, he rejoined his squadron at Port Moresby, New Guinea, at 1 a.m. on 7 August, after having flown almost continuously since early the preceding morning. With only three hours' rest, he took off with his squadron for the attack. Throughout the long flight to Rabaul, New Britain, he managed by skillful flying of his unserviceable airplane to maintain his position in the group. When the formation was intercepted by about 30 enemy fighter airplanes before reaching the target, Capt. Pease, on the wing which bore the brunt of the hostile attack, by gallant action and the accurate shooting by his crew, succeeded in destroying several Zeros before dropping his bombs on the hostile base as planned, this in spite of continuous enemy attacks. The fight with the enemy pursuit lasted 25 minutes until the group dived into cloud cover. After leaving the target, Capt. Pease's aircraft fell behind the balance of the group due to unknown difficulties as a result of the combat, and was unable to reach this cover before the enemy pursuit succeeded in igniting one of his bomb bay tanks. He was seen to drop the flaming tank. It is believed that Capt. Pease's airplane and crew were subsequently shot down in flames, as they did not return to their base. In voluntarily performing this mission, Capt. Pease contributed materially to the success of the group, and displayed high devotion to duty, valor, and complete contempt for personal danger. His undaunted bravery has been a great inspiration to the officers and men of his unit.

With more than two miles of runway, Pease International Airport was designated an alternate landing site for NASA space shuttles.

The Air Force's 100th and the 509th Bombardment Wings were joined in 1966 by the New Hampshire Air National Guard's 157th Military Air Lift Group. Nine years later, the base was designated as the 157th Air Refueling Group. In 1991, the base was the first of 86 Air Force facilities across the country to be closed down. Over ten thousand military personnel and dependants left the area. Pease continues to serve as home to the New Hampshire Air National Guard.

Prior to closure, the Pease Redevelopment Commission began its work, leading to creation of the Pease Development Authority whose job was to establish a nucleus of high technology business and aviation. Pease International Tradeport functions as a duty and customs free zone for foreign trade.

With 797 of the original 3000 acres zoned for airport use, Pease International Airport opened as a civilian facility in 1991. Another 448 acres were designated as an airport industrial zone, while 333 acres were zoned industrial, and another 466 acres were zoned business/commercial. The 1200-acre Great Bay National Wildlife Refuge formally opened in 1996. The 27-hole Pease Golf Course opened in 1901 as the Portsmouth Country Club. The Air Force operated it as a military course during its tenancy.

In terms of economic growth, the Tradeport has been an unqualified success: four *million* square feet of office/R&D/industrial space at the Tradeport is currently occupied by more than 225 companies, providing jobs for 7000 employees. Six colleges have facilities at the Tradeport. The Pease Development Authority also oversees the Division of Ports and Harbors.

PLEASANT POINT
Pleasant Point Drive – Moebus Terrace – Boyan Place – Robin Lane

I HAVE YET TO FIND an explanation for PLEASANT POINT's being known at one time as ELLEN or ELLIN'S POINT and at another by the intriguing name of GEORGE WALDRON'S TATTLE POINT. A George Waldron, perhaps a descendant of the Col. Richard Waldron who was listed on the 1727 tax rolls, signed the Association Test in 1776. Who tattled on whom and about what appears to be lost to history. But the explanation for the small outcropping of land's first name, FRAME POINT, is clear enough: fishermen erected frames for the purpose of drying their catch here. It certainly wouldn't have been described as pleasant in those days!

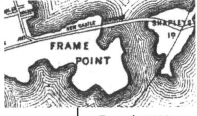

From the 1903 map.

BY THE TIME Robert Moebus (1916-2000), a native of the Bronx, came to Portsmouth in 1945, the point was pleasant indeed, and within a few years, Moebus set his mind to developing it. His obituary cited him as being the oldest living member of the Portsmouth Yacht Club – he'd been granted a life membership in 1985 – so clearly water views were a good part of the attraction.

Moebus left his family name on MOEBUS TERRACE. BOYAN PLACE was named for Moebus' wife, Ruth Boyan Moebus, and ROBIN LANE is named for his daughter.

BERSUM GARDENS
Leslie Drive

S HORTLY AFTER WORLD WAR II, Henry Weinbaum bought twenty to thirty small homes on the street behind the Cutts Mansion, which he already owned. An inventive man, Weinbaum named the area BERSUM GARDENS, creating 'Bersum' from the names of his two sons, Bernard and Sumner.

Nor was Weinbaum satisfied with just naming a neighborhood after his boys. In time, he purchased a home at 312 Miller Avenue for his own family's use, which was flanked on one side by a small private road connecting Miller to Broad Street. The city wanted to take over this street. Weinbaum agreed – on the one condition that the powers that be name it BERSUM LANE.

MAPLE HAVEN
Denise Street – Mariette Drive – Pamela Drive
Simonds Road – Suzanne Drive
Wallis Road – Winchester Street

Virginia Harvey, a longtime Maple Haven resident, tells me that the Manchester developer of the area, a gentleman of French descent, named the streets for his daughters, Denise, Mariette, Pamela and Suzanne.

PERHAPS WALLIS ROAD was named for an upstanding citizen who we only know as 'Mr. Wallis,' who was appointed to fill the roll of tythingman (see Fletcher Street, page 177) in 1678. Overseeing the behavior of the families of the following was his weighty responsibility: "Mr. Hen. Sherburne, James Rendle, Jno. Odiorne, Tho. Seavey, Mr. Tucker, Wm. Seavey, Robert Purrington, Sergt. Moses, Fardi Hoof, Tho. Creler, Joseph Walker, Hugh Leare, Robt. Lange, Goodm. Lucomb, Edw. Bickford, And. Sampson, John Bowman, Sa. Harris, Ric. Shortridge, Mark Hunking [and] Goodm. Goss."

MEADOWBROOK PARK
Coakley Road – Larry Lane

Larry Lariviere assures me it's only a coincidence that he lives on **Larry Lane.** He says the developer of Meadowbrook Park lent his first name to the street in question.

MARGARET O'CONNER tells me that her grandfather Cornelius Coakley's dairy cows had to negotiate a culvert to get from his Fox Hill Farm on Cate Street to pastureland beyond the four lanes of the new Route 1 Bypass. The cows are long gone, but the culvert remains, as do some of Coakley's original apple trees. COAKLEY ROAD remembers the dairyman and farmer.

OTHER NEW STREETS OF THE 1950S
Alumni Drive – Driftwood Lane – Edgewood Road – Fells Road
Fernald** Court – Hampshire Road – Inland Street
Sheffield Road – Sunset Road – Weald Road
Wedgewood Road – Windsor Road – Spaulding Turnpike

ALUMNI DRIVE, no doubt, was named with a tip of the hat to the public high school to which it leads.

A MRS. ELIZABETH A. FERNALD was the first resident of FERNALD COURT, when it was opened sometime in the 1960s. Fernalds have taken many important roles in the early history of Portsmouth.

Dr. Renald, or Reginald, Fernald came over with Mason's men as ship's surgeon (spelled "chirurgeon" in the earliest town records – and this must have been how Fernald himself spelled it, because he also served as the first town clerk). He was also the progenitor of a local family that rivals in sheer numbers that of any Wentworth or Pickering. Early spellings were also Furnald, Furnel or Furnell. John Furnal was secretary to Royal Governor John Wentworth.

Early Portsmouth Fernalds of note were predominantly men of the sea. Captain Daniel Fernald (1768-1866) lived at the corner of Manning and Howard Streets. At 98, he was the oldest living person in Portsmouth when he died. He played an active role in the Revolution, as well as the War of 1812, captaining a schooner whose commission included the smuggling of arms.

Frederick W. Fernald (1811-55) was considered major competition to any of the best shipbuilders in the region. Fernald and William Pettigrew set up shop on Badger's Island and turned out a total of thirty ships, including such notable vessels as the *Judah Touro*, the sailing packet *America*, and clipper ships *Typhoon* (also known as *The Portsmouth Flyer*), *Red Rover*, *Water Witch* and *Dashing Wave*. Fernald died suddenly in 1855, at which time Pettigrew went into partnership with Daniel Marcy, establishing the famed Marcy & Pettigrew ship-

> The term "fells" refers to rocky, upland pastures, which could well describe the terrain on which FELLS ROAD was built.

> Dixie McLean Tarbell tells us that **Driftwood Lane** was once known as **Red Lane**, "when my house, which was originally red, was the only house on the lane."

Captain William Fernald was listed as master of the sloop *Polly*, operating a packet service to Boston. He must not have been at the helm when *Polly* sank off the coast of North Carolina in 1793, as he later captained a privateer, the 74-ton schooner *Science*, whose participation in the War of 1812 was notably short-lived. Captured just off of Portsmouth, she was taken to Halifax, where her crew were imprisoned. This same William Fernald had a shipyard on the North Mill Pond and is credited with building the last 3-masted ship in Portsmouth.

yard at the foot of Pickering Street. Marcy & Pettigrew turned out four ships in their two years of operations, between 1857 and 1859.

Donald Normandeau purchased this property in 1975 for his Piscataqua Marine Laboratory. Normandeau Associates was one of the largest environmental consulting firms in New England at the time. And since then, the property has operated as Pickering Marine under Don's son Glenn, and Chandler's Loft under Glenn's wife Robin.

THE FIRST 23 MILES of the SPAULDING TURNPIKE were opened in 1957. The new highway honored not one but two Spauldings, brothers who both became governors of New Hampshire.

Rolland Spaulding (1873-1942) served as governor from 1915 to 1917, earning himself the reputation of a "progressive Republican" and a bureaucratic reformer, working to cut costs by streamlining government at both the municipal and state levels. One area of government in particular he sought to improve was the State Highway Department.

Rolland's younger brother, Huntley (1869-1955), chaired the New Hampshire Food Production Committee during World War I. In 1917, he was appointed New Hampshire's Federal Food Administrator. Later he chaired the European Relief Council and backed U.S. entry into the League of Nations. He took over as governor a decade after his brother's term, serving the state from 1927 to 1929.

The two brothers built themselves homes side by side in Rochester. Both estates today are operated in tandem as the Governors Inn.

*Brothers **Rolland**, above, and **Huntley Spaulding**, below. Originally from Townsend Harbor, MA, both Spaulding brothers settled in Rochester and worked in the family fiberboard business. Images from the collections of the state of NH, Division of Historical Resources.*

1960-1970
Diamond Drive – Onyx Lane – Opal Avenue – Ruby Road
Sapphire Street – Topaz Place – Edmond Avenue – Manor Drive
Martha Terrace – Mirona Road – Patricia Drive – Regina Road
The Piscataqua River Bridge

THERE WERE SOME distinct gems among the developments of the 1960s and 1970s – watershed years that redefined many things, street names included.

DIAMOND DRIVE, RUBY ROAD and SAPPHIRE STREET came into existence during the 1960s; OPAL AVENUE, TOPAZ PLACE and ONYX LANE would be added to the map in the following decade.

MARTHA TERRACE AND PATRICIA DRIVE appear on a 1986 map as OCEAN MANOR.

HENRY BEROUNSKY (1918-2001) gave us one of the most creative of our street names: MIRONA ROAD. Berounsky, the son of Czech immigrants, moved his father Ben's 1932 two-bay Parrott Avenue auto body shop into a larger space on Islington Street. Eventually outgrowing that facility, he opened what we know as Mirona Road and transplanted the thriving business into an even larger building there. Two letters apiece from the names of Berounsky's three children, Michael, Veronica and Nancy, were cleverly combined to name their dad's new road.

Henry Berounsky in 1962, then president of the Chamber of Commerce. PA

THE NEWEST SPAN over the Piscataqua, opening in the late 1960s, carried I-95 into Maine. Commonly referred to as the "HIGH BRIDGE" or the "HIGH LEVEL BRIDGE," it was officially named the PISCATAQUA RIVER BRIDGE when it opened for traffic in 1971.

The American Institute of Steel Construction gave the new bridge its annual Award of Merit, while the U.S. Department of Transportation labeled it the nation's most outstanding bridge that year, declaring that "the graceful shape and the way it fits into the site make it a pleasure for the eye to behold."

*Above, the **Piscataqua River Bridge** under construction in 1968, taken from the Kittery approach, looking south. Department of Transportation files, Portsmouth Public Library. Below, the result, a graceful backdrop to Portsmouth's skyline. Photo by John Grossman.*

1970-1980
COLONIAL PINES ESTATES
Anne Avenue – Joan Avenue – Ricci Avenue – Robert Avenue

ROBERT RICCI, SON OF Elwyn Park developer Erminio Ricci, broke ground on his COLONIAL PINES ESTATES in the early 1970s, on land once owned by his father. RICCI AVENUE, the main street into the area, bears the family name. ROBERT AVENUE he named for himself, while ANNE AVENUE was named for his mother. JOAN AVENUE was a corruption of his sister Joanne's name – the city would not permit two names in such close proximity that sounded as alike as 'Anne' and 'Joanne.' Joanne is long-time and much respected city counselor, Joanne Grasso.

THE WOODLANDS
F. W. Hartford Drive – T. J. Gamester Drive

THE FIRM OF WEEKS, Whalen and Gamester developed THE WOODLANDS, the subdivision off Elwyn Park, in the 1960s and '70s. Richard Gamester and Peter Weeks named the development's two streets after two of their grandfathers.

PETER WEEKS' GRANDFATHER was the powerful publisher, politician and businessman Fernando W. Hartford. Founder of the *Portsmouth Herald*, Hartford acted as the first manager of The Music Hall, from the time of its opening in 1877, and continued in that role under the brief ownership of Frank Jones, who took over in 1900. Upon Jones' death in 1903, Hartford and a partner, doing business as the Portsmouth Theatre Company, took over joint ownership of The Music Hall and ran it until 1916.

Frank Jones loaned Hartford the money to buy up all the competing papers of the day, which he promptly either took out of business, or in the case of the *New Hampshire Gazette*, folded into his own new creation, the *Portsmouth Herald*, thus guaranteeing its journalistic ascendancy.

Hartford took office as mayor of the city in 1930, and was honored by his grandson, mayor in 1982 and 1983, with the naming of F.W. HARTFORD DRIVE.

July 17, 1932. Fernando W. Hartford, in the top hat, greets Franklin Delano Roosevelt, fresh from his nomination at the Democratic Convention, at Hampton Beach, the first stop of his campaign for president. From the Lane Memorial Library, Hampton, NH.

THE NAME OF T.J. Gamester first appears in city directories in 1912, his profession at that time listed as 'boilermaker.' By the 1950s, Gamester was a master ship fitter and foreman at the naval shipyard. **T.J. GAMESTER DRIVE** remembers Richard Gamester's grandfather.

OTHER NEW STREETS OF THE 1970S

Borthwick Avenue – Calvin Court – Centre Street – Clark Drive
Clough Drive – Davis Road – Freedom Circle – Griffin Road
Heritage Avenue – Hillcrest Estates – Holiday Drive
Ledgewood Drive – Oriental Gardens – Post Road – Ruth Street
Shaw Road – Feaster Apartments – Keefe House
Margeson Apartments – Wamesit Place Apartments
Urban Forestry Center

PORTSMOUTH HISTORY IS FULL of Borthwicks for whom **BORTHWICK AVENUE** might be named. Both a James Borthwick, marble worker, and Robert Borthwick, farmer, lived on Greenland Road early on. The most likely candidate for the naming of Borthwick Avenue, however, would be Daniel F. Borthwick (1858-1936), who served several terms as police commissioner.

This Borthwick was one of those folks who preferred to pursue their civic and charitable good works in the background. Founder of the Market Street mercantile firm D. F. Borthwick, he served for nearly fifty years as treasurer of the Howard Benevolent Society. One of many local charitable organizations that flourished in this city in the 19th century, it ceased to exist in the 1980s, folding its remaining monies into the Greater Piscataqua Charitable Foundation.

Daniel Borthwick was succeeded in business by his brother, James F., who changed the name of the establishment to his own. PA

AND WHILE WE ARE on the subject of Borthwick Avenue, the landmark JACKSON GRAY MEDICAL BUILDING is named for two great Portsmouth physicians, Dr. Hall Jackson, already mentioned (see page 60) and Dr. Frederick S. Gray, a beloved and highly respected practitioner of the 20th century.

Dr. Frederick S. Gray. PA

IT WOULD BE ALMOST another century before a road would be cut further down into the old Brackett's Field to serve the new elementary school built at Little Harbour.

Arthur C. Clough (1913-2001) spent his working life as a custodian in the Portsmouth school system, but clearly this was a man who couldn't get enough of kids. Portsmouth's Father of the Year in 1959, he worked to see a sports program included in the elementary schools and volunteered many leisure hours with Portsmouth Youth Recreation. According to his obituary, "due to his commitment to Portsmouth's youth athletics, Portsmouth's CLOUGH FIELD and CLOUGH DRIVE were named after him."

IN 1861, BROTHERS Lewis G. (1833-1909) and Charles (1836-1911) Davis formed a partnership, placed an advertisement for their services as "Daguerrean artists" in the newspaper of the day and opened a studio on Daniel Street. From daguerreotypes (photographs fixed on silver plates), to ambrotypes (a similar process involving plain glass rather than silvered), to images on paper, they met the needs and tastes of the day, and in the process recorded a wealth of Portsmouth history. I should think that naming DAVIS ROAD to honor the Davis brothers would be a fitting way to remember their substantial contribution to our knowledge of days and ways gone by.

It has been suggested that CALVIN COURT, off Sherburne Road, might be named after Calvin McShane, a contractor who did a good deal of good work in the area. Until a better explanation comes forward, we shall honor Mr. McShane's contributions to Portsmouth's built environment.

*A **Davis Brothers'** image of the travails of what was known as the "Great Ice Storm of 1886." PA*

MICHAEL JOSEPH GRIFFIN was born in Ireland and immigrated at 13 to America in 1853, along with three siblings. A year later, young Michael made his way to Portsmouth, where he found employment as a laborer at the Auburn Cemetery. In time, he moved up the ranks in the burial business, eventually caretaking eleven different cemeteries, three Catholic, eight Protestant. In 1874, he married Mary Connery and fathered a number of children, four sons living to old age. Eventually he got into politics, serving as police and parks commissioner, plus four terms on the city council and a term in the state legislature.

Several generations of Griffins have gone on in the cemetery business. Later day Griffins have also become lawyers, doctors, nuns, priests, and politicians. Grandson John Griffin's wife Ruth Lewin Griffin sat on the Governor's Executive Council from 1987 to 2007. Elected to both State Senate and House of Representatives, her years of service to the state total well over thirty. Active in the Republican Party, she has attended seven national conventions as a delegate in the last 33 years.

GRIFFIN ROAD began, as many roads do, simply as an access for the Griffin Construction Company.

POST ROAD. Just the name conjures visions of the mail being carried at a gallop the 270 miles from Wall Street to Boston. And as if that weren't enough of an geographic image, over the centuries ithe Post Road has melded in with Route 1, the 2,390-mile road from Fort Kent, Maine, to Key West, Florida. Portsmouth's Post Road runs a humble 350 feet, from Heritage Avenue into one of 80-plus facilities that make up Thermo Fisher Scientific worldwide.

OWNED AND OPERATED by the Desfosses family, it's no wonder that one street bordering HILLCREST ESTATES should be called DESFOSSES AVENUE. Recently the mobile home park's streets were rechristened. Spinnaker Point/Osprey Landing has its shore birds theme. Hillcrest Estates has gone marine, with its BLUEFISH BOULEVARD, CODFISH CORNER ROAD, DOLPHIN AVENUE, MACKEREL AVENUE, OCTOPUS AVENUE, SALMON AVENUE, SQUID STREET, STRIPED BASS AVENUE, TUNA TERRACE and URCHIN AVENUE.

IT'S HARDLY LIKELY that **SHAW ROAD**, which lies near Sagamore Creek, was named with master privateer and entrepreneur Abraham Shaw (1775-1828) in mind, but he certainly was worthy of the recognition. While Abraham put up the capital to outfit privateers, his brother, South Ender Captain Thomas M. Shaw, took the helm. Abraham lived in the Federal style home to the east of the Rockingham House on State Street, and is buried at Point of Graves Cemetery with his wife, Elizabeth.

Emerson McCord's mother owned a field by the North Mill Pond which she sold to the city for use as a new street. Given the task of naming the new street, Emerson didn't have to look far: he named it **Ruth Street**, in honor of his wife.

THE **FEASTER APARTMENTS** remember the contributions of Army chaplain Captain William Newcomer Feaster, who died trying to save the life of a fellow soldier in Vietnam in 1966. But the naming of this building can be considered a two-fold honor; Feaster's father, the Reverend John N. Feaster, pastor of the North Church, was also a much loved and respected member of the community he served.

THE OLD HIGH SCHOOL on Islington graduated its last class in 1957, then stood vacant. Then the **FARRAGUT ELEMENTARY SCHOOL**, located on what's now known as The Hill, had to come down, a victim of urban renewal. The students and functions of the old elementary school moved into the old high school building, and the name came with them, but eventually that, too, closed and the structure once again stood vacant. There was talk of tearing it down.

City Councilman Bill Keefe refused to see that happen and went to bat for the fine old building, which finally reopened as subsidized housing under the name **FARRAGUT HOUSE**, but today it's known as the **KEEFE HOUSE**.

*Turning the old **Farragut School** into housing for the elderly earned **Bill Keefe**, above, his name on the sign out front. Above, PA. Below, TG.*

RICHMAN S. MARGESON, who served as mayor in 1950 and 1951, was honored with the naming of the **MARGESON APARTMENTS** after his death in 1972.

Richman and two of his three brothers partnered in Margesons' Furniture Store. Colonel Henry B. Margeson, U.S.A., Ret., was a West Pointer and professional soldier for thirty years. Donald H. Margeson, the youngest brother, was a three-time city council member and one of the founders of Strawbery Banke. He made his home for a period in the Oracle House on Marcy Street (see page 23). And Ralph C. Margeson, of New Castle, was a major in the Marine Corps and district governor of the Portsmouth Rotary in 1971 and 1972.

ORIGINALLY NAMED **RIDGEWOOD APARTMENTS**, today's **WAMESIT PLACE APARTMENTS** on Greenleaf Avenue are a classic example of the value of an unusual name. When the Portsmouth Housing Authority took over the complex, there was just too much confusion between the Ridgewood Apartments, the Ledgewood Apartments and the nursing home, Edgewood Manor. Something had to change. So they went to Sherm Pridham, then the director of the Portsmouth Public Library, and asked for a suggestion. Pridham handily produced the Abenaki word for a 'place to live.'

> The 170-acre **Urban Forestry Center** came into being in 1976, the gift of John Elwyn Stone, the last of the Langdon descendants in the area. Whatever it lacks for creativity in naming, it more than makes up for in beauty. Among the buildings on the property is the Langdon family farmhouse where John Langdon was born in 1741 (see Langdon Street, page 107). The Center is managed by the New Hampshire Division of Forests and Lands.

1980 – 1990
Alder Street – Andrew Jarvis Drive – Arthur Brady Drive
Constitution Avenue – Currier Cove Drive – Greenleaf Woods Drive
Heritage Hill – High Liner Avenue – The Hill
Michael Succi Drive – Oakwood Drive – O'Leary Place
Springbrook Circle – WBBX Road – White Cedar Boulevard

GREEK NATIVE ANDREW JARVIS (1890-1990) was another newcomer to this country who realized the American Dream in Portsmouth. In 1920, he was listed in the city directory as the proprietor of the Appolo Lunch at 17 Congress Street, which became the Jarvis Cafeteria in the 1930s. A Jarvis Tea Room was operating up the street at 5 Congress. By 1950, the cafeteria was now known as the Jarvis Restaurant.

In 1948, Jarvis served as a delegate to the New Hampshire state constitutional convention, representing Portsmouth's 2nd Ward. By 1957, he was a city councilman and assistant mayor, while also serving on the Planning Board. The following year, he was elected to a two-year term as Portsmouth's mayor. Two years later, he was selected to serve as an alternate delegate to the Republican National Convention.

Over the years, Andrew Jarvis owned six different eateries in Portsmouth.

Ray Brighton tells us Jarvis "attained the highest elective office in the state of anyone of Greek background" when he was elected to the Governor's Council. Fittingly, **ANDREW JARVIS DRIVE**, the street leading to the Greek Orthodox Church, was named to honor the successful transplant, who at the age of 80, was said to still enjoy his winter smelt fishing.

MAYOR ARTHUR F. BRADY (?-1989) was also a transplant from 'away.' Elected to the city's highest office in 1971, he played host to Great Britain's Prince Charles during the city's 350th anniversary in 1973. Today we have an **ARTHUR F. BRADY DRIVE**.

*Mayor **Arthur F. Brady**, left, with England's Prince Charles and the Lord Mayor of London. PA*

THE PATRIOTICALLY NAMED **CONSTITUTION AVENUE** lends the opportunity to acknowledge not only the 1789 document signed by New Hampshire delegates Nicholas Gilman of Exeter and John Langdon of Portsmouth, but also the ship of that name. '*OLD IRONSIDES*,' built in Boston and launched in 1797, was brought to Portsmouth in 1855 for the second overhaul of her career, a job for the navy yard that would take five years to complete. At that point, she became a training ship.

USS **Constitution** – *'Old Ironsides,' so named because her thick sides repelled even cannon shot – was undefeated in her 58 years of active service. See page 150 for more information about the Constitution.*

In 1882, the *Constitution* returned to Portsmouth Naval Shipyard for a 15-year retirement. Her deck was housed over, turning her into a sort of floating barracks for incoming sailors. On her hundredth birthday, she sailed for Charlestown, MA. Her birthplace would become her permanent home.

Excess timbers from a 1930-31 reconditioning of the stout old ship still float today in Meade Pond behind Building 136, the Shipyard's Defense Reutilization Marketing Office – one stop shopping for used military paraphernalia and seven-inch thick live oak beams that in the 1970s were deemed unfit for future use. According to Navy memos at the time, the wood was "so tough that it did considerable damage to the tools used, and it generated a stench which was offensive to those working with the material."

Children have been enjoying Currier's Cove as a swimming hole as far back as locals can remember. Though the cove is no longer formally named as such on nautical charts for these waters, its use will continue to be recalled with the naming of CURRIER'S COVE DRIVE.

HIGH LINER AVENUE takes you to the front door of High Liner Foods, Inc. One of the largest processors and packagers of frozen fish and Italian food products in North America, the publicly traded company was founded in 1899 as W. C. Smith & Co. Its head office is located in Lunenberg, Nova Scotia.

MARINE CORPORAL Michael Lawrence Succi (1947-1968) gave his life for his country in Quang Tri, Vietnam. His family once owned property in the vicinity of the street that honors his memory and his sacrifice, MICHAEL SUCCI DRIVE.

IN 1970, LESLIE CLOUGH transformed the old Ham farmstead on Maplewood Avenue into Flowers by Leslie. In the 1980s, attorney Jack McGee and his wife Diane decided they wanted to build a house, and persuaded Clough to sell them a piece of his property. Clough agreed, reluctantly – the spot they chose was where he grew his lilies. Peter Bresciano also wanted to build there, and finally Clough decided to build a house of his own as well. In due course, the three houses were built and Diane named the new street that served them **OLEARY PLACE**, in memory of Robert E. O'Leary, her father.

WBBX ROAD, first called the generic **RADIO ROAD**, no longer leads to the radio station with those call letters. WBBX came on the air in the early 1960s, and ceased to broadcast under that name sometime after 1983.

Ever wonder about radio call letters? Well, I started wondering as I was writing this, so I've done a bit of checking up on the subject. It turns out that a radio station's call letters are its official, international, legal name. In 1912, every country agreed to adopt specific letters as the first letter of their call letter names. Canadian stations use 'C.' Mexican stations use 'M.' The United States was assigned 'K' and 'W.' In 1923, the FCC decided to fine tune the system. From then on, any new stations east of the Mississippi would start with 'W,' while those to the west would use the 'K.' Now we all know.

Today, the utilitarian cinder block building houses the offices of the Housing Partnership.

1990-2000
TUCKER COVE
Gosport Road – Odiorne Point Road

THE NEW DEVELOPMENT of **TUCKER COVE** owes its name to the half-mile long dogleg off Sagamore Creek that wraps itself around the sprawling subdivision, though the name, like that of Currier's Cove, no longer appears on nautical charts. In colonial times, I am told, a family named Moses farmed this area; five households are listed under the name of Moses in Rockingham County's 1790 census.

Tucker Cove's two roads are named for important local coastal landmarks – neither of which lie within Portsmouth proper.

GOSPORT ROAD ferries our thoughts out to Gosport Harbor, which anchors five of the nine islands of the Isles of Shoals, ten miles off the coast of New Hampshire and Maine. The 17th-century fishing village on STAR ISLAND (named such because some have sufficient imagination to see the shape of a seven-pointed star in its irregular perimeter) was known as Gosport in its heyday, probably named after the 800-year-old Hampshire, England, fishing village by the same name.

Dennis Robinson has made his own educated guesses regarding the names of the other islands that make up the Shoals: DUCK, a wildlife refuge often visited by such; APPLEDORE, after a town in Devonshire, originally called Hog Island, possibly due to its rotund shape; MALAGA, which was most likely named by Spaniards; SMUTTYNOSE, whose name "may come from the image of a black 'smutch' on the nose or profile of the island," and which has been adopted as the name of a contemporary local brewing firm; CEDAR (Captain John Smith noted seeing cedars growing on this island in the 17th century); LUNGING, a corruption of its original name, Londoner's Island, after the London Company which was based there; SEAVEY, named for one of the Shoals' early inhabitants; and WHITE, home of the Shoals' lighthouse, also named for a resident, one Captain Joseph White (1750-1830).

Incidentally, it's anyone's guess as to whether the ISLES OF SHOALS were named for the shoals of rock that surround them, or for the prodigious shoals of fish that put the islands on the map in the first place. Fishermen had settled the islands on a seasonal basis decades before the first permanent colonists arrived in the region. The laws of this working community were straight-laced: no

The constellation of rocky outcroppings that comprise the Isles of Shoals.

woman, wife or otherwise, was permitted to reside on the island, nor was the importation of livestock to be sanctioned. Both rules were eventually flaunted, and finally abandoned altogether in 1650.

CHARLES BREWSTER WRITES evocatively and passionately about ODIORNE'S POINT, a location he reminds us should be "most venerated, not only by our own townsmen, but by every citizen of New Hampshire." This site qualifies as New Hampshire's Plymouth Rock. Locally, it is now honored with the naming of ODIORNE POINT ROAD.

> The 331.5 acres known today as **Odiorne State Park** make up the largest parcel of undeveloped land along New Hampshire's 18 miles of shoreline. In 1961, the federal government sold the property to the state for $91,000.

French explorer Samuel de Champlain stepped ashore here in 1605 and conferred with members of an indigenous tribe, most probably Pennacooks or Abenakis, learning all they could share with him of the immediate coastline.

Odiorne's Point also beckoned to David Thomson and his company as they chose where to establish the Laconia Company's Pannaway Manor in 1623. This is where they built their garrison – Brewster calls it MASON'S HALL or the MANOR HOUSE.

In the mid-1800s, Brewster tells us, Eben L. Odiorne was still farming land that had been in his family since 1660, when English immigrant John Odiorne (c. 1627-1707) came into possession of an original 42-acre parcel on the point.

Pulpit Rock Battery 951, a gun battery fire control tower at Fort Dearborn, one of many built during World War II to defend the coast of New England.

Post Civil War prosperity brought with it the development of a seaside colony of grand hotels and summer bungalows along the coast, including the Sagamore House which was built on former Odiorne farmland. By the outbreak of World War II, the point was home to 17 families, including 8th-generation Odiornes.

In 1942, the government seized the entire area by eminent domain, replacing most of the homes with the bunkers and artillery batteries of **FORT DEARBORN** (see Dearborn Street, pages 96-97) as part of a string of coastal defense installations. The area remained in government hands until the property was sold to the state of New Hampshire in 1961. Today we know it as **ODIORNE STATE PARK**, the home of the **SEACOAST SCIENCE CENTER**.

OTHER NEW STREETS OF THE 1990S
Buckminster Way – Campus Drive – Chase Drive
Commerce Way – Eastwood Drive – Heather Lane – Meredith Way

Buckminster House, at the corner of Islington and Bridge Streets, build c. 1720-30 by Daniel Warner and once owned by the Reverend Joseph Buckminster. From C. S. Gurney, Portsmouth, Historic and Picturesque.

BUCKMINSTER WAY dips a toe into the Great Bog off Ocean Road. It is said that it was named for Reverend Joseph Buckminster (1751-1812), a native of Rutland, MA, who took the pulpit of the North Church in 1779, remaining as the church's pastor until his death. He succeeded Dr. Ezra Stiles, who resigned in 1778 to take on the presidency of Yale.

CAMPUS DRIVE leads to the **COMMUNITY CAMPUS** and its universe of health, family and community services. It was built by the Foundation for Seacoast Health, which was created in 1984 with the proceeds of the sale of the Portsmouth Regional Hospital to its present owners, the Hospital Corporation of America. The complex currently provides program and office space for nine non-profit organizations, plus meeting space for the use of numerous other groups.

CHASE DRIVE GIVES US the opportunity to get to know some earlier Portsmouth Chases.

Captain John Chase was master and an owner of the 800-ton clipper ship *Danube*, built in 1848 at the Badger Island shipyard of Fernald & Pettigrew; a William S. Chase of Portsmouth traveled as a passenger on *Danube*'s Lisbon-New York run of 1857. Both the above-mentioned John and Charles H. Chase were masters at one time or another of the 600-ton clipper *Athens*, built by the Raynes shipyard in 1839.

Then there's the story of Daniel Chase of Somerville, MA, who built the original Wentworth Hotel in 1873. Building it bankrupted this Chase. Frank Jones purchased the hotel in 1879 and turned it into one of the great hostelries of its day.

*One of the great destination hotels of the 19th century, the **Wentworth-by-the-Sea** started life as simply the **Wentworth House**. The venture proved the financial undoing of its builder, Daniel Chase. PA*

After sitting vacant for twenty years and making the National Trust for Historic Preservation's 1996 list of America's Most Endangered Historic Places, the Wentworth reopened in 2003 as the Wentworth by the Sea Marriott Hotel & Spa.

And let us not forget the Chase Home for Children. What we know today as simply the Chase Home was founded on Mt. Vernon Street in 1877 by widower William H. Parks, a mariner who needed to provide a home for his motherless children when he was off to sea. In 1879, the publicly minded George W. Bilbruck (1818-1894), head brewer for Eldredge Brewery, donated what would come to be known as the Thomas Bailey

Aldrich house at 51 Court Street for the use of the town's growing orphan population. Within a few years, they moved next door into the Chase Home at 53 Court Street. In 1915 the trustees of the Chase Home purchased 22 acres fronting on Middle Road, and opened a newly built home for children that remains to this day, servicing the needs of at-risk youth and their families.

REALTOR/DEVELOPER MICHAEL KANE tells me that developer Arnold Katz named COMMERCE WAY for his Commerce Center, the complex to which it leads.

❧ A CENTURY OF SAIL, REMEMBERED TWO CENTURIES LATER ☙

View of the United States Navy Yard, at Portsmouth, N. H., from Gleason's Pictorial Drawing Room Companion, *1853. The Franklin Shiphouse, at the left, was completed in 1838 and lengthened in 1854, making it one of the largest in the country.*

The Fanny M., *launched from Adam's Point in Durham, NH in 1886 by Captain Edward H. Adams, was the last gundalow to operate commercially in the area.*

CHAPTER 7

PORTSMOUTH GREETS THE 21ST CENTURY
THE PLACES YET TO BE NAMED

The City of Portsmouth voted to create a public library in 1881. The Portsmouth Public Library had long outgrown its original home on the corner of Congress and Middle Streets before it was able to move to its new home in 2006.

D. The application of **Michael Brigham** for property located at **487 Cutts Avenue** wherein site plan approval is requested for the creation of a seven lot subdivision ranging in lot size from 15,078 s.f. ± to 25,612 s.f. ± with five of the proposed lots having access off a proposed cul-de-sac off Cutts Avenue. One proposed lot will have access off Chase Drive and the remaining proposed lot will have access off Michael Succi Drive with related paving, utilities, landscaping,

previously approved site plan, more specifically, the roadway plan. Said property is **John Bosa** for property located at **248 Peverly Hill Road** for an ame on Assessor Plan 243 as Lot 54 and lies within a Single Residence B district. (This Age item was tabled from the Board's July 17, 2003, meeting to this meeting.)

V. CITY COUNCIL REFERRALS:

1) City Council Referral: Request to accept Mo...

Mr. Holden recommended that the Board accept Moffat Street as a ...
recommended by the Department:

...m the Department of Public Works of their recommendation t...

1) Written notifi   C. **Work session requested by Attorney Bernard W. Pelech on behalf of Michael Clark**
    street;   a proposed subdivision off Little Harbor Road   ...lic Works that payments for all inspection services,
2) The submit   ...ve been completed.
3) Confirmati   The Board entered into a work session mode. Mr. Holden explained that Attorney Pelech w
    which have be   representing a client who owns the site more commonly known as Belle Isle including the m
                    land and the island. It was Mr. Holden's opinion that all would concur th... ...e area is a sens
Mr. Sullivan   parcel of land. He explained that the work session would c... ...xploration into
Street with '   low density development with a number of issue... ...t Moffat Street be accepted as a City
unanimous   indicated that he could not find a a... ...d   The motion passed , Mr. Holden.

...endment to the City's **Subdivision Rules and Regulations** regarding the
...nal plans presented for recording. Copies of the amendment
mit in a d   3.   The application of **Brora, LLC, Owner,** for property off **Portsmouth Boulevard** wherein Final Approval is requested
office of   **Brora, LLC, Owner,** ....This Agenda item was tabled at the Board's
...eeting.)   for a lot line relocation whereby property located at 325 Commerce Way would have a lot area of
            247,954 ± s.f. and 646.56' of street frontage and property located off Portsmouth Boulevard wou...
            have a lot area of 239,040 ± s.f. and 433.91' of street frontage, in a district w...
            of 3 acres and 300' of street frontage is required. Said ...
            Research/Mariner's Village distric...
            216 as I ot I or...   for property located at **235 Commerce Way** and

F. The application of **Parade Office, LLC,** for property located at **195 Hanover Street** wherein Preliminary Subdivision Approval is requested to subdivide one lot into three lots with the following: Lot 1 having a lot area of 28,515 s.f. and continuous street frontage off High Street and Hanover Street; Lot 2 having a lot area of 9,266 s.f. and continuous street frontage off Hanover Street; and Lot 3 having a lot area of 175,470 s.f. and continuous street frontage off Hanover S... Maplewood Avenue and Deer Street; and lying in a zone where a minimum ... continuous street frontage is required. Said pro... ...located **off Borthwick Avenue.** Assessor

are application of ...ral Business di... Woods, LLC for a lot located off **Barberry** ...ington Woods, LLC and for a lot located wherein Final
a...d at **66 Madison Street** wherein site plan approval ...ed by **Northern Utilities, Incorporated** wherein Final
ouses that are to be located on three proposed lots that ...vide two lots into three lots with the following:
...g two lots. Proposed lot 1 would contain two structures with ...ntinuous street frontage off Borthwick Avenue;
...lated paving, utilities, landscaping ...nuous street frontage off Borthwick
...es the demolition of the existing structure. Said prop... ...s to 3.624 acres and having access
01-001 and 001-000 (as reconfigured) and lies within an Apartment distr... ...e; and, with all proposed lots
Avenu... and 300 feet of continuous **...Edward W. Huminick, of CIF, Inc.** for property
...of **Joseph C. Tucker and** ...approval is requested for the construction of 11
lying in an Office ...two proposed lots that are being re-subdivided from the
street frontage are req... ...and associated site improvements. The proje...
...is shown on Assessor Plan 14?

Just a sampling of projects that come before the Planning Department and the Historic District Commission every month.

S OME PEOPLE MIGHT consider Portsmouth to be pretty much built out at the turn of the 21st century, but others would disagree. Plans for new developments, both downtown and on the fringes of the city, are on drawing boards as this book goes to press. Other developments, some consisting of only a street or two, have already been tucked ingeniously amidst existing neighborhoods.

NEW STREETS FOR A NEW MILLENNIUM
Albacore Way – Brigham Lane – Moffat Street – Nathaniel Drive
Weatherstone Road – Wholey Way

T HE NAME OF ANOTHER Portsmouth-built sailing vessel has been added to the roster at Atlantic Heights (see pages 159-165). **Albacore Way**, commemorates the pioneering research submarine USS *Albacore* (see picture on page 25). Commissioned in 1953, the experimental sub's teardrop-shaped hull represented the Navy's first attempt to design a boat actually meant to travel under water.

OFF THE OLD CUTTS AVENUE lies one of Portsmouth's newest streets, **BRIGHAM LANE**, named for Michael Brigham, realtor and the developer of **HARBOUR'S EDGE**, the seven house lots that will someday be served by this recent addition to the map.

IT PLEASES ME NO END to see a **MOFFAT STREET** appear on the map of Portsmouth's byways, providing as it does an excuse to delve into the history of the Moffats of Moffatt-Ladd fame. We've met the Ladd family. Now let's meet those Moffatts (or "Moffats" – the names seem to have been used interchangeably).

John Moffat (1692-1786) arrived in Portsmouth in 1723 as captain of an English vessel, resigned his commission and settled here. Before long, he had established himself as a ships' chandler and merchant, outfitting ships and exporting pine for masts to England, while importing molasses and rum and luxury goods for the wealthy of the region. He also dealt in slaves. Two years after his arrival in Portsmouth, he was accused and convicted of kidnapping a slave from his owner in Massachusetts as he set off for Portugal.

By 1763, Captain Moffat had married Katherine Cutt, the daughter of Robert Cutt, and had built the home we know today as the Moffatt-Ladd house, on Market Street, overlooking his own wharf and warehouse. Originally meant as a wedding gift for his son Samuel, the father took up residence after his son's business ventures ended in bankruptcy, forcing Samuel to flee the country.

*Known today as the **Moffatt-Ladd House**, the disastrous fire of 1802 spared the home John Moffat had built on Market Street by the slimmest of margins. The giant chestnut tree that still stands to the left of the house is said to have been planted in 1776.*

Moffat's daughter Catherine married signer of the Declaration of Independence William Whipple (see Whipple Street, page 122), who, like her father, was also a merchant. The couple moved into the mansion the same year as her father did. Whipple died in 1785; his father-in-law died the following year at the age of 92. Moffat's will was contested by Samuel's son, Robert C. Moffat, who prevailed, soon afterwards selling the Market Street property to Nathaniel A. Haven. Haven in turn left the property to his daughter, Maria Ladd, wife of Alexander Ladd, and so it came into the Ladd family.

But what of Whipple's widow, Catherine? With the contest and settlement of her father's estate, Madame Whipple found herself without a home. Removing herself far from the bustle of downtown Portsmouth, she settled into the gambrel-roofed house that still stands at the corner of the new Moffat Street. Referred to as the

'Secretary Waldron House,' it was built c. 1740, and lived in by Colonel Richard Waldron III (1694-1753), who had served as the secretary of the province in 1737. Here the Widow Whipple, née Moffat, lived out her days.

The Secretary Waldron House, lived in by Catherine Moffat Whipple, on the corner of Peverly Hill Road and the new Moffat Street. PA

THE NEW **HAWTHORNE ESTATES**, appended to the older Maple Haven Estates, consists of but one street, **NATHANIEL DRIVE**. Put the two together, and I believe we can assume the developer had that literary giant from Salem, Massachusetts, Nathaniel Hawthorne, in mind as he set to laying out his single street.

Hawthorne attended Bowdoin College in Brunswick, Maine. His roommate during his freshman and sophomore years was Alfred Mason, son of a prominent Portsmouth attorney Jeremiah Mason, mentor of Daniel Webster.

JOHN J. WHOLEY (1922-2001; pronounced 'Hooley') was elected mayor of Portsmouth three different times, in 1962-63, 1978-79, and again in 1980-81. A navy pilot in World War II and a lawyer by profession, Wholey sat on the Board of Education in 1956-57, helped oversee the building of Portsmouth High School and its two additions, the addition to Portsmouth Junior High, and the rebuilding of Dondero School, and served as city solicitor in 1958. He helped found the Portsmouth Economic Commission, the Portsmouth Housing Authority, and was once honored as

*Attorney and one-time mayor of Portsmouth **John J. Wholey** earned the honor of having a street named for him, the old fashioned way. PA*

man of the year by the NAACP. And he practiced law for over fifty years, eventually partnering with son-in-law Bernard Pelech as the firm of Wholey & Pelech.

"It was in the twilight of his legal career," Pelech told me, recounting the tale of how **WHOLEY WAY** got its name. Pelech, who does a great deal of real estate law, had been retained to represent this one-street development before the city's Planning Board. Winning approval, it turned out, had become an uphill battle – vociferous abutters were turning out in force. The project was due to go before the Board for a final vote, but Pelech had to be out of town. Wholey volunteered to step in, wholeheartedly. He turned the affair into a courtroom spectacle.

"My mother-in-law was on the phone to me. 'I'm watching it on T.V.,'" she told Pelech. "'He's going to have a heart attack!'" Wholey took on the Board and the neighbors like he was arguing the single most important court case of his career. He bellowed. He hollered. He pled his case. And he won.

The developer had never met Wholey before that evening, but when it came time to name his one street, he was adamant: it had to be Wholey Way. (The city makes exceptions to its usual requirement that any honoree be deceased for living mayors.) Wholey wasn't particularly comfortable with the idea – until he recalled how hard he'd fought for this street to exist. Then he demurred.

IN 2008, AS AMBITIOUS A PROJECT as downtown Portsmouth has ever seen began construction. According to an advertisement that year, **PORTWALK** was going to provide "a unique, branded, mixed-use lifestyle development including 175,000 square feet of

*The old **Parade Mall**, a relic of urban renewal and 1960s architecture.*

efficient first-class, projected LEED Silver Certified green office space; more than 75,000 square feet of premium retail space; 750+/- surface and garage parking spaces on-site; 28 luxury residential homes; and a 128-room extended-stay hotel..."

A completion date of 2010 was initially projected for the three square blocks of construction that will one day comprise the project in its entirety. Difficult economic times since ground was broken in 2008 have thrown a speed bump across the new street; One and Two Portwalk Place have yet to be built. But I was delighted the other day to notice a brand new street sign on the corner of Hanover Street: PORTWALK PLACE.

AFTERWORD

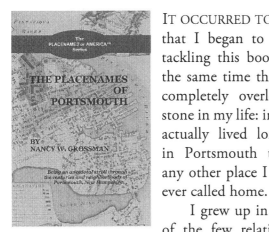

IT OCCURRED TO ME recently that I began to think about tackling this book just about the same time that I passed a completely overlooked milestone in my life: in 2002, I had actually lived longer in Portsmouth than any other place I had ever called home.

I grew up in one of the few relatively rooted families in a commuter suburb made up mostly of transients. The way I saw it, the transients had it right; the minute I finished high school, I was out of there, never to return. Since then, I have lived in six different states. *Very* different states. Most of the places I've landed I knew were temporary from the moment I finished unpacking. Only one has been hard to leave.

I have never consciously sought to sink roots, but apparently roots were sinking into Portsmouth's rich soil without my even noticing. One of the many nutrients of that soil, for me anyway, is Portsmouth's fertile history.

As I've said, I'm no historian. I just love the stuff of history. There's a big difference, and I'm the first to acknowledge it. I am in awe of academic historians. I have tried to emulate their rigor, but I'm a babe in the stacks when it comes to the hard work of mining history. I know I've only scratched the surface of Portsmouth's colorful story.

Some streets' stories I haven't found. This is where, you, gentle reader, come in. I am actively soliciting your

Do you live in a town or city whose streets also beg to have their stories told? Contact the author about how you can become a *Placenames of America* author yourself. Do you live in a town that's a mere two blocks wide and seven blocks long, but love the history of your area? Why not take on your county? Be in touch, and let's make history together!

ngstudio@comcast.net

input. If you have any information to contribute to the discussion, do please email me. I hope to learn as much from you as, hopefully, you have learned from me. I have intentionally kept printings of this book small; subsequent printings will incorporate any new information that comes my way in the meantime.

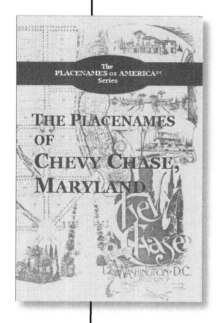

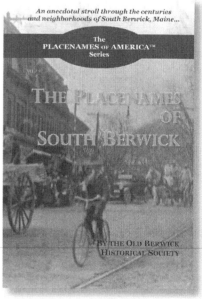

APPENDIX
THE MAYORS OF PORTSMOUTH
1850-2010

Those mayors listed in italics well may have had streets, buildings, schools, parks or playing fields named after themselves or their ancestors. Mayors were elected for a term of one year from 1850 to 1948. In 1948, mayors began serving terms of two years' duration.

Unless noted otherwise, all of the images in this section hang in the Council chambers at City Hall.

Adams, Edward H. Mayor, 1909, 1910. Attorney.

Adams, Joseph B. Mayor, 1870. Auctioneer and "commission" merchant.

Badger, Daniel W. Mayor, 1911, 1912, 1913. Founder of Badger Farms Creamery.

Bailey, John H. Mayor, 1864. Member of New Hampshire State Senate 1st District, 1869-70. Merchant of hardware.

Berry, Charles P. Mayor, 1893, 1894. Manager, close associate of Frank Jones.

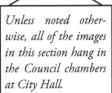

Charles P. Berry.

Brady, Arthur F. Mayor, 1972-73. Ford auto dealership. [See page 209.]

Broughton, John H. Mayor, 1876, 1877. Member of New Hampshire State Senate 24th District, 1879-80. Lumber merchant.

Arthur F. Brady. PA

John H. Broughton.

Butler, Theodore R. Mayor, 1952-53, 1954-55. Insurance and real estate.

Connors, Timothy J. Mayor, 1964-65, 1966-67. New England Telephone & Telegraph. [See page 76.]

Dale, Charles M. Mayor, 1926, '27, '43, '44. Member of NH State Senate 24th District, 1933-36, 1939-40. Delegate to Republican National Convention from NH, 1936, 1948. Member of NH Governor's Council, 1937-38. Governor of NH, 1945-49. Attorney.

Charles Dale.
Courtesy of the Governor's House Bed & Breakfast, Portsmouth, NH.

Dearborn, Jonathan. Mayor, 1862, 1867. [See page 96.] Hatter.

Dexter, Orel A. Mayor, 1924, 1925.

Dondero, Mary Carey. Mayor, 1945, 1946, 1947. Vice-chair of New Hampshire Democratic Party, 1945. Delegate from Portsmouth 1st Ward, 1948. Delegate to Democratic National Convention from New Hampshire, 1948. [See page 189.]

Mary Carey Dondero.

Eldredge, Marcellus. Mayor, 1885, 1886. Brewer.

Emery, John W. Mayor, 1897. Member of New Hampshire State Senate 24th District, 1897-98. Assistant secretary.

Faye, Edmund S. Mayor, 1889, 1890. Merchant of boots, shoes and clothing.

John W. Emery.

Thomas G. Ferrini.
Official photo from the city website.

Ferrini, Tomas G. Mayor, 2008-2012. Lawyer and mediator.

Foley, Eileen Dondero. Mayor, 1968-71, 1984-85, 1988-1997. Delegate to the Democratic National Convention from New Hampshire, 1972. [See page 127.]

Goldsmith, Kennard E. Mayor, 1937, 1938, 1939, 1940. Journalist.

Goodrich, Moses H. Mayor, 1874, 1875. Member of New Hampshire State Senate 24th District, 1885-86. Tanner and currier.

Eileen Dondero Foley.

Graves, Bruce R. Mayor, 1974-75, 1976-77. Iafolla Industries.

Greenleaf, Abner. Mayor, 1850. Member of New Hampshire State Senate 1st District, 1829-30. Started in life as a brass founder. [See page 153.]

Hackett, Wallace. Mayor, 1907, 1908. Attorney.

Hartford, Fernando W. Mayor, 1921, 1922, 1928-1932. Republican. Delegate to Republican National Convention from NH, 1912. Publisher. [See page 203.]

Abner Greenleaf.

Hislop, Albert. Mayor, 1919, 1920. Delegate to Republican National Convention from New Hampshire, 1924. Brewer. [See page 165.]

Hodgdon, George E. Mayor, 1887, 1888. Attorney.

Jarvis, Andrew. Mayor, 1958-59. Delegate to New Hampshire state constitutional convention from Portsmouth 2nd Ward, 1948. Alternate delegate to Republican National Convention from New Hampshire, 1960. Restaurateur. [See pages 208-9.]

Andrew Jarvis.

Jenness, Richard. Mayor 1856. Member of New Hampshire State Senate 1st District, 1849-51. Bank president and ship owner.

Jones, Frank (1832-1902). Mayor, 1868. U.S. Representative from NH 1st District, 1875-79. Delegate to Republican National Convention from NH, 1900. Brewer, primarily, with numerous other business interests. [See pages 137-8.]

Ale maker Frank Jones. PA

William O. Junkins.

Junkins, William O. Mayor, 1895, 1896. Physician. [See page 123.]

Keenan, Mary McEachern. Mayor, 1986-87. Real estate.

Ladd, Samuel T. Mayor, 1916, 1917, 1918, 1923. Delegate to Democratic National Convention from New Hampshire, 1916 (alternate), 1932 (alternate), 1936. Brewer. [See page 68.]

John J. Lasky.

Laighton, John. Mayor, 1851. Member of New Hampshire State Senate 24th District, 1883-84. Navy agent.

Laskey, John J. Mayor, 1891, 1892. Merchant of groceries, boots and shoes.

Leary, John J. Mayor, 1956-57. Grocer.

John J. Leary. From Charles Hazlett's History of Rockingham County.

Marchand, Steve. Mayor, 2006-08. Founder and former Managing Director of Pembroke Strategies, a public affairs management consulting firm.

Marcy, George D. Mayor, 1903, 1904. W. E. Peirce & Co., insurance. [See page 22.]

Margeson, Richman S. Mayor, 1950-51. Merchant of furniture. [See page 208.]

Marvin, Thomas E. O. Mayor, 1873. Manufacturer of cod liver oil.

Steve Marchand. Official photo from the city website.

Marvin, Robert E. Mayor, 1934, 1935, 1936. Attorney.

Marvin, William E. Mayor, 1905, 1906. Attorney.

McIntire, Edward E. Mayor, 1900, 1901. In charge of the coppersmith shop at the Portsmouth Naval Shipyard.

Miller, Frank W. Mayor, 1874. Journalist and developer. [See page 134.]

George D. Marcy.

Morrison, Robert. Mayor, 1857. School teacher.

Neal, Cecil M. Mayor, 1948-49. Proprietor, Penn-Hampshire Oil Company.

Page, Calvin. Mayor 1884, 1899. Member of New Hampshire State Senate 24th District, 1893-94, 1903-04. Attorney and president of New Hampshire Bank.

Pender, John. Mayor, 1902. Member of New Hampshire State Senate 24th District, 1911-12. Journalist.

Calvin Page.

Pickering, Sylvester F. A. Mayor, 1933. Dentist. [See pages 44-5.]

Reding, John Randall (1805-1892). Mayor, 1860. U.S. Representative from New Hampshire at-large, 1841-45. Member of New Hampshire State Legislature.

Evelyn Sirrell.
Official photo from the city
website.

John S. Tilton.

John J. Wholey. PA

Harry B. Yeaton.
From Charles Hazlett's
History of Rockingham
County.

Rowe, Steward E. Mayor, 1941, 1942. Attorney.

Shaines, Robert E. Mayor, 1960-61. Attorney.

Simes, William. Mayor, 1861. Ship owner.

Sirrell, Evelyn F. Mayor, 1998-99, 2000-02, 2002-03, 2004-05. Bank parking lot attendant.

Sise, William H. Mayor, 1878, 1879, 1880, 1881. Merchant.

Spear, Eric. Mayor, 1012- . Computer programmer.

Eric Spear

Tilton, John S. Mayor, 1898. News agent.

Toppan, Christopher S. Mayor, 1852. Merchant.

Treat, John S. Mayor, 1882, 1883. Member of New Hampshire State Senate 24th District, 1879-80. Operated a marble yard.

Walker, Horton D. Mayor, 1853, 1872. Member of New Hampshire Governor's Council, 1865-67. Merchant. [See pages 182-3.]

Weeks, Peter G. Mayor, 1982-83. Banker.

Wholey, John J. Mayor, 1962-63, 1978-79, 1980-81. Attorney. [See pages 221-2.]

Yeaton, Harry B. Mayor, 1914, 1915. H.A. Yeaton & Son, corn, flour, etc.

REFERENCES AND RESOURCES

Adams. *Annals of Portsmouth.* Portsmouth: Peter Randall, Publisher, 1971, a reprint of the 1824 edition.

Aldrich, Thomas Bailey. *Old Town by the Sea.* Boston and New York: Houghton Mifflin, 1893.

Barstow, George. *The History of New Hampshire: From its Discovery, in 1614, to the Passage of the Toleration Act, in 1819.* I.S. Boyd, 1842.

Belknap, Jeremy. *History of New Hampshire.* 2 volumes. New York, 1970.

Bell, Charles H. *History of the Town of Exeter, NH.* Boston: J.E. Farwell, 1888.

Brewster, Charles W. *Rambles About Portsmouth: Sketches of Persons, Localities, and Incidents of Two Centuries, Principally From Tradition and Unpublished Documents.* Portsmouth, NH: Lewis W. Brewster, 1859, 1869. [Text scanned courtesy of The Brewster Family Network as part of the History Hypertext project by SeacoastNH.com.]

Brighton, Ray. *They Came to Fish.* Portsmouth: Peter E. Randall Publisher, 1994. A second reprint of the original two-volume set published in 1973.

Candee, Richard M. *Atlantic Heights: A World War I Shipbuilder's Community.* Portsmouth: Peter E. Randell, c. 1985.

——. *Building Portsmouth: The Neighborhoods & Architecture of New Hampshire's Oldest City.* Portsmouth: Back Channel Press, 2006.

Clark, A. H. *The Clipper Ship Era.* New York, 1911.

Dinwoodie, Marrie J.P. *Pickering's Neck, 1633-1975, Portsmouth, New Hampshire: Piscataqua Marine Laboratory, Normandeau Associates, Inc.* Unpublished manuscript, 1975.

Dolph, James and Ronan Donohoe. *Around Portsmouth in the Victorian Era: The Photography of the Davis Brothers.* Dover: Arcadia, 1997.

Durel, John W. *From Strawbery Banke to Puddle Dock: The Evolution of a Neighborhood, 1630-1850.* Dissertation, University of New Hampshire, 1984.

Foss, Gerald. *Portsmouth: Images of America.* Dover: Arcadia, 1996.

Foster, Joseph. *The Portsmouth Guide Book.* 1884.

Foster, Sarah Haven. *The Portsmouth Guide Book.* Portsmouth: Portsmouth Journal Job Print, 1896.

Garvin, James. *Historic Portsmouth: Early Photographs from the Collections of Strawbery Banke, Inc.* Somersworth: New Hampshire Publishing Co., 1974.

"Genealogies of Connecticut Families, Vol. II, Record of the Marcy Family."

Giffen, Sarah L. and Murphy, Kevin D., eds. *"A Noble and Dignified Stream": The Piscataqua Region in the Colonial Revival, 1860-1930.* York, ME: Old York Historical Society, 1992.

Gilmore, Robert C. and Bruce Ingmire. *The Seacoast New Hampshire: Early Photographs from the Collections of Strawbery Banke,* second edition. Portsmouth: Strawbery Banke, 1995.

Gurney, Caleb Stevens. *Portsmouth, Historic and Picturesque.* Portsmouth: Strawbery Banke, 1980. (Reprint of a 1902 publication.)

Hazlett, Charles A. *History of Rockingham County, New Hampshire, and Representative Citizens.* Richmond-Arnold Publishing Co., 1915.

Historic District Survey, conducted by the Portsmouth Advocates, 1972.

Howells, John Mead. *The Architectural Heritage of the Piscataqua.* New York: Architectural Book Publishing Company, Inc., 1965.

Hurd, D. Hamilton. *History of Rockingham and Strafford Counties, New Hampshire, With Biographical Sketches of Many of its Pioneers and Prominent Men.* J. W. Lewis, 1882.

Kelly, Margaret Whyte. *Sarah – Her Story: The Life Story of Sarah Parker Rice Goodwin.* Portsmouth: Back Channel Press, 2006.

Ladd, Alexander H. *Alexander H. Ladd's Garden Book 1888-1895*. Rockport, ME: Penobscot Press, 1996.

Largee, Robert and Hames Mandelblatt. *USS* Albacore*: Forerunner of the Future*. Portsmouth: Peter E. Randall Publisher, 1999.

Lawson, Russell M. *Portsmouth: An Old Town by the Sea*. Portsmouth: Arcadia Publishing, 2003.

Morgan, Francis X. *Colonial Portsmouth in Pen and Ink*. Portsmouth: Peter E. Randall Publisher, 1989.

New Hampshire Almanac, www.nh.gov/nhinfo. Includes list of governors, likenesses, etc.

Openo, Woodard D. *The Sarah Mildred Long Bridge: A History of the Maine-New Hampshire Interstate Bridge from Portsmouth, New Hampshire, to Kittery, Maine*. Portsmouth: Portsmouth Marine Society, 1988.

Pearson, Helen and Harold Hotchkiss Bennett. *Vignettes of Portsmouth*. Portsmouth, 1913.

Pillsbury, Hobart. *New Hampshire: Resources, Attractions and Its People, a History*. Lewis Historical Publishing Co., 1928.

Randall, Peter. *Portsmouth and the Piscataqua*. Camden, ME: Down East Books, 1982.

——. "Framers of Freedom: Samuel Livermore." In *NH: Years of Revolution*, Profiles Publications and the NH Bicentennial Commission, 1976.

Robinson, J. Dennis. *A Brief History of Portsmouth, New Hampshire*. Portsmouth: The Portsmouth Historical Society, 1998.

——. *Strawbery Banke: A Seaport Museum 400 Years in the Making*. Portsmouth: Strawbery Banke Museum/Peter E. Randall Publisher, 2008.

——. www.SeacoastNH.com.

Rowe, John Frink. *Newington, New Hampshire: A Heritage of Independence Since 1630.* Canaan: Phoenix Pub., 1986.

Saltonstall, William G. *Ports of Piscataqua.* Boston: Harvard University Press, 1941.

Squires, James Duane. *Granite State of the United States.* 4 volumes. New York, 1956. Turner, Lynn Warren. *The Ninth State: New Hampshire's Formative Years.* Chapel Hill, NC: University of North Carolina Press, 1983.

Vaughan, Dorothy M., for the New Hampshire State Historical Commission. 1980 application to the NH State Historical Preservation concerning the Hunking Wentworth house at #6 Congress Street.

Warren, William T. and Constance S. *Then & Now: Portsmouth.* Charleston, SC: Arcadia Publishing, 2001.

Wiley, George F., ed. *State Builders: An illustrated Historical and Biographical Record of the State of New Hampshire at the Beginning of the 20th Century.* New Hampshire Publishing Co., 1943.

Winslow, Ola Elizabeth. *Portsmouth: The Life of a Town.* New York: The Macmillan Company, 1966.

Winslow, Richard E. III. *Wealth and Honour: Portsmouth During the Golden Age of Privateering, 1775-1815.* Portsmouth: Portsmouth Marine Society, 1988.

MAPS

1774 - *Plan of Portsmouth Harbor.* Surveyed and drawn by James Grant. Reproduced 1946 by the New Hampshire Historical Society.

1802 - *Map of the proposed subdivision of Trefethan property.* Portsmouth Athenaeum.

1813 - *Map of the Compact Park of the Town of Portsmouth in the State of New Hampshire.* Surveyed and drawn by J.G. Hales, engraved by T. Wrightman, Boston.

1839 - *Plan of Portsmouth, Lithographed for the Directory.* Surveyed and drawn by Benjamin Akerman. Bufford's Lith., 136 Nassau Street, New York.

1850 - *Map of the City of Portsmouth, N.H.* From the original surveys under the direction of H.F. Walling. C.W. Brewster, Publisher.

1866 - *Plan of Land Comprised Between Richards Avenue, South Road and Middle Street Showing the Location of Several Proposed New Streets.* H. Y. Hoyt, Surveyor.

1876 - *Plan of the City of Portsmouth.* Sold by Jos. H. Foster, Bookseller, No. 1 Congress Block.

1877 - *Bird's Eye View of Portsmouth, Rockingham Co., New Hampshire.* A. Ruger, Del.; D. Bremner & Co., Lith., Milwaukee, Wis. Published by J. J. Stoner.

c. 1900 - *Map of Portsmouth Harbor Including Historical Points and Landmarks.* Copyright, F. O. Ellery.

1903 - *Map of the City of Portsmouth.* Published by W.A. Greenough & Co., 92 Oliver St., Boston.

1925 - *Map of the City of Portsmouth, N.H.* Authorized and prepared under direction of the Portsmouth Chamber of Commerce in cooperation with W.A. Greenough Co., Publishers, Boston. Compiled by Dow, Harlow and Kimball, Boston - Portsmouth. Authorities: Stone & Webster, C.M. Rundlett, U.S. Coast Guard & Geodetic Survey.

1930 ~ *A Map of Portsmouth, N.H., An Old Town by the Sea.* By Dorothy Vaughan and Harold G. Rundlett.

1956 ~ *Map of Portsmouth, N.H.* Drawn for Beacon Pub. Co., Inc. by John W. Durgin III.

1972 ~ *Portsmouth, N.H. Street Map.* Portsmouth Planning Department.

1986 ~ *Seacoast New Hampshire: The Portsmouth Area.* Arrow Publishing, Taunton, MA.

1999 ~ *DeLorme Street Atlas, Seacoast Region.* Yarmouth, ME.

2003 ~ *DeLorme Street Atlas, Seacoast Region.* Yarmouth, ME.

2005 ~ *Portsmouth, New Hampshire.* Portsmouth Department of Public Works.

ACKNOWLEDGMENTS

W here to start? With thank-yous to:

~ First and foremost, to my husband the late John Grossman, who held my hand through – and brought me back from – computer crashes and worse, and who doctored every image in this book.

~ The prolific Dennis Robinson, and that bottomless rabbit hole of a website of his, SeacoastNH.com. Ask this man a question about Portsmouth history and you better have half an hour for the answer. Then he'll email you with more.

~ The staff at the Portsmouth Athenaeum: Tom Hardiman, Lynn Aber, Marsha Jebb, Susan Kindstedt, Robin Silva, and Ursula Wright, in particular, who fell most naturally into the roll of personal cheerleader from day one. And a special thank you to the late Robert Dunn, for poetic relief.

~ Likewise, the staff at the Portsmouth Public Library, in particular Michael Huxtable, who heads up the Research department, and our most excellent Special Collection librarian, Nicole Cloutier. Ah, that I could have finished this project in the new library.

~ Portsmouth's historical community, past and present. The contributors of the past are mentioned throughout the book. From the present: Richard Candee, Ronan Donohoe, Paige Roberts, Deb Child, Elizabeth Farish, Peter Randall, Joyce Volk, Zhana Morris and Dave Adams, to name just a few. The thought of any of you reading this book has made me dig all the deeper.

~ Valerie Cunningham and Mark Sammons for all their contributions to our knowledge of black history in Portsmouth.

~ Bob Gross of Drake Farm Books in North Hampton who presented me with my own set of *They Came to Fish* when he heard what I'd gotten myself into. How many trips to the library – and overdue fines – you saved me! And to Greta Kellenbeck, for the use of her 1860-61 City Directory.

~ Portsmouth City Hall and the Public Works Department, in particular City Clerk Kelli Barnaby, Planning Board member John Sullivan and Portsmouth's map guy, Jason Wise.

~ The many folks who's memories and photo collections I've tapped: Ted Connors, Joanne Grasso, Ted Gray, Mary Griffin, Ruth Griffin, Jeannette Hopkins, Tylene Jousse, Esther Kennedy, Holly Lasher, Evelyn Marconi, Jack McGee, Bernie Pelech, Judy Sabin, Bob Shaines, Sumner Weinbaum. And all the bemused or puzzled folks I checked in at the polls on election day, who, when they stated their address, I'd ask, "By the way – you wouldn't know how your street got its name, would you?"

~ Frank Roth, editor of the Friends of the South End newsletter, who encouraged me to try out some of my South End information publicly.

~ My readers and proofers, Barbara Hilton and Jim Fernald.

~ Indexing whiz, DJ and fairy goddaughter, Rebecca Pickett.

~ Dave Wright, who could find the promotional value in a grain of sand.

~ And a special thanks to the man who inspired this whole project, St. Louis postman William Magnan. He had close to a thousand streets to contend with. This undertaking was a cakewalk compared to what that man tackled.

NOTES CONCERNING THE INDEX

The use of italics for items listed in the index indicates the names or titles of ships, newspapers, books or works of art.

The use of italics among the page numbers indicates that an image of that item appears on that page.

NANCY W. GROSSMAN is a writer, editor, graphic designer, artist and amateur historian living and working in Portsmouth, New Hampshire. She has had four children's books published, and like anyone who has ever lived within fifty miles of Hollywood, has three or four unproduced film scripts in her bottom drawer. In 2004, she tried her hand at writing for the stage for the first time. Poetry provides comic relief.

Nancy has been hand painting tile and ceramics since the early 1980s. Her commissions can be found in baths and kitchens in homes on both the east and west coast. She also enjoys teaching her craft.

Nancy attended Converse College, the University of Dallas, University of Okahoma and is a graduate of California State University Dominguez Hills. Her residences of significance have been in Connecticut, New York, Texas, Oklahoma and California. She has been sinking serious roots in New Hampshire since 1991, when she and her husband John moved to Portsmouth to open the Governor's House Bed and Breakfast.

The publication of the original *Placenames of Portsmouth* in 2005 sent Nancy and John off in a new direction. Setting up shop as Back Channel Press, they offer a full menu of services to others who find the learning curve of self-publishing too steep or too time-consuming. To date, they have published in excess of seventy-five books.